THE DOUBLE AGENT

THE DOUBLE AGENT

Essays in Craft and Elucidation

BY

R. P. BLACKMUR

GLOUCESTER, MASS.

PETER SMITH

1962

Of the twelve essays in this book "The Method of Marianne Moore," "T. S. Eliot," and "A Critic's Job of Work" are published for the first time. The essays on D. H. Lawrence and Hart Crane appeared in *Direction*. The others appeared first in *Hound & Horn*. Special thanks are due to Charles Scribners' Sons for permission to reprint "The Critical Prefaces of Henry James" from *The Art of the Novel* by Henry James, to which it forms the introduction.

CONTENTS

		PAGE
I.	NOTES ON E. E. CUMMINGS' LANGUAGE	1
II.	MASKS OF EZRA POUND	30
III.	EXAMPLES OF WALLACE STEVENS	68
IV.	D. H. LAWRENCE AND EXPRESSIVE FORM	103
V.	NEW THRESHOLDS, NEW ANATOMIES. NOTES ON A TEXT BY HART CRANE	121
VI.	THE METHOD OF MARIANNE MOORE	141
VII.	THE DANGERS OF AUTHORSHIP	172
VIII.	T. S. ELIOT. FROM ASH WEDNESDAY TO MURDER IN THE CATHEDRAL	184
IX.	HERESY WITHIN HERESY	219
X.	SAMUEL BUTLER	226
XI.	THE CRITICAL PREFACES OF HENRY JAMES	234
XII.	A CRITIC'S JOB OF WORK	269

I

NOTES ON E. E. CUMMINGS' LANGUAGE

IN HIS four books of verse, his play, and the autobiographi-
cal *Enormous Room*,[1] Mr. Cummings has amassed a
special vocabulary and has developed from it a special use
of language which these notes are intended to analyse and
make explicit. Critics have commonly said, when they understood Mr. Cummings' vocabulary at all, that he has enriched
the language with a new idiom; had they been further interested in the uses of language, they would no doubt have said
that he had added to the general sensibility of his time.
Certainly his work has had many imitators. Young poets
have found it easy to adopt the attitudes from which Mr.
Cummings has written, just as they often adopt the superficial attitudes of Swinburne and Keats. The curious thing
about Mr. Cummings' influence is that his imitators have
been able to emulate as well as ape him; which is not so frequently the case with the influence of Swinburne and Keats.
Mr. Cummings is a school of writing in himself; so that it is
necessary to state the underlying assumptions of his mind,
and of the school which he teaches, before dealing with the
specific results in poetry of those assumptions.

It is possible to say that Mr. Cummings belongs to the anti-
culture group; what has been called at various times vorticism,
futurism, dadaism, surrealism, and so on.[2] Part of the gen-

---

[1] As of 1930. There would seem little modification of these notes necessary because of *Eimi* or the subsequent volumes of verse.

[2] The reader is referred to the late numbers *transition* for a serial and
collaborative expression of the latest form which this group has assumed:
the Battle of the Word. [As of 1930.]

eral dogma of this group is a sentimental denial of the intelligence and the deliberate assertion that the unintelligible is the only object of significant experience. These dogmas have been defended with considerable dialectical skill, on the very practical premise that only by presenting the unintelligible as viable and actual *per se* can the culture of the *dead intelligence* (Brattle Street, the Colleges, and the Reviews) be shocked into sentience. It is argued that only by denying to the intelligence its function of discerning quality and order, can the failures of the intelligence be overcome; that if we take things as they come without remembering what has gone before or guessing what may come next, and if we accept these things at their face value, we shall know life, at least in the arts, as it really is. Nothing could be more arrogant, and more deceptively persuasive to the childish spirit, than such an attitude when held as fundamental. It appeals to the intellect which wishes to work swiftly and is in love with immediate certainty. A mind based on it accepts every fragment of experience as final and every notion as definite, yet never suffers from the delusion that it has learned anything. By an astonishing accident, enough unanimity exists among these people to permit them to agree among themselves; to permit them, even, to seem spiritually indistinguishable as they appear in public.

The central attitude of this group has developed, in its sectaries, a logical and thoroughgoing set of principles and habits. In America, for example, the cause of the lively arts has been advanced against the ancient seven; because the lively arts are necessarily immediate in appeal and utterly transitory. Thus we find in Mr. Cummings' recent verse and in his play *Him* the side show and the cabaret set up as "inevitable" frames for experience. Jazz effects, tough dialects, tough guys, slim hot queens, barkers, fairies, and so on, are made into the media and symbols of poetry. Which is proper enough in Shakespeare where such effects are used ornamentally or for pure play. But in Cummings such effects are employed as substance, as the very mainstay of the poetry. There is a continuous effort to escape the realism of the intelligence in favour of the realism of the obvious. What might be stodgy or dull because not properly worked up into poetry is replaced by the tawdry and by the fiction of the immediate.

It is no great advantage to get rid of one set of flabby generalities if the result is merely the immersion of the sensibility in another set only superficially less flabby. The hardness of the tough guy is mostly in the novelty of the language. There is no hardness in the emotion. The poet is as far from the concrete as before. By denying the dead intelligence and putting on the heresy of unintelligence, the poet only succeeds in substituting one set of unnourished conventions for another. What survives, with a deceptive air of reality, is a surface. That the deception is often intentional hardly excuses it. The surface is meant to clothe and illuminate a real substance, but in fact it is impenetrable. We are left, after experiencing this sort of art, with the certainty that there was nothing to penetrate. The surface was perfect; the deceit was childish; and the conception was incorrigibly sentimental: all because of the dogma which made them possible.

If Mr. Cummings' tough-guy poems are excellent examples of this sentimentality, it is only natural that his other poems —those clothed in the more familiar language of the lyric— should betray even more obviously, even more perfectly, the same fault. There, in the lyric, there is no pretence at hardness of surface. We are admitted at once to the bare emotion. What is most striking, in every instance, about this emotion is the fact that, in so far as it exists at all, it is Mr. Cummings' emotion, so that our best knowledge of it must be, finally, our best guess. It is not an emotion resulting from the poem; it existed before the poem began and is a result of the poet's private life. Besides its inspiration, every element in the poem, and its final meaning as well, must be taken at face value or not at all. This is the extreme form, in poetry, of romantic egoism: whatever I experience is real and final, and whatever I say represents what I experience. Such a dogma is the natural counterpart of the denial of the intelligence.

Our interest is not in the abstract principle, but in the results of its application in poetry. Assuming that a poem should in some sense be understood, should have a meaning apart from the poet's private life, either one of two things will be true about any poem written from such an attitude as we have ascribed to Mr. Cummings. Either the poem will appear in terms so conventional that everybody will understand it—when it will be flat and no poem at all; or it will appear in language so far distorted from convention as to be inapprehensible except by lucky guess. In neither instance will the poem be genuinely complete. It will be the notes for a poem, from which might flow an infinite number of possible poems, but from which no particular poem can be certainly deduced. It is the purpose of this paper to examine a few of the more obvious types of distortion which Mr. Cummings has practiced upon language.

The question central to such a discussion will be what kind of meaning does Mr. Cummings' poetry have; what is the kind of equivalence between the language and its object. The pursuit of such a question involves us immediately in the relations between words and feelings, and the relations between the intelligence and its field in experience—all relations which are precise only in terms themselves essentially poetic—in the feeling for an image, the sense of an idiom. Such relations may only be asserted, may be judged only tentatively, only instinctively, by what seems to be the disciplined experience, but what amounts, perhaps, only to the formed taste. Here criticism is appreciation. But appreciation, even, can take measures to be certain of its grounds, and to be full should betray the constant apprehension of an end which is the necessary consequence, the proper rounding off, of just those grounds. In the examination of Mr. Cummings' writings the grounds will be the facts about the words he uses, and the end will be apprehended in the quality of the meaning his use of these words permits.

There is one attitude towards Mr. Cummings' language which has deceived those who hold it. The typographical peculiarities of his verse have caught and irritated public attention. Excessive hyphenation of single words, the use of lower case "i," the breaking of lines, the insertion of punctuation between the letters of a word, and so on, will have a possible critical importance to the textual scholarship of the future; but extensive consideration of these peculiarities to-day has very little importance, carries almost no reference to the *meaning* of the poems. Mr. Cummings' experiments in typography merely extend the theory of notation by adding to the number, *not* to the *kind,* of conventions the reader must bear in mind, and are dangerous only because since their uses cannot readily be defined, they often obscure rather than clarify the exact meaning. No doubt the continued practice of such notation would produce a set of well-ordered conventions susceptible of general use. At present the practice can only be "allowed for," recognised in the particular instance, felt, and forgotten: as the diacritical marks in the dictionary are forgotten once the sound of the word has been learned.

THE DOUBLE AGENT

The poem, after all, only takes wing on the page, it persists in the ear.[3]

Considering typographical peculiarities for our present purposes as either irrelevant or unaccountable, there remain the much more important peculiarities of Mr. Cummings' vocabulary itself; of the poem *after* it has been read, as it is in the mind's ear, as it is on the page only for reassurance and correction.

If a reader, sufficiently familiar with these poems not to be caught on the snag of novelty, inspects carefully any score of them, no matter how widely scattered, he will especially be struck by a sameness among them. This sameness will be in two sorts—a vagueness of image and a constant recurrence of words. Since the one depends considerably upon the other, a short list of some of Mr. Cummings' favourite words will be a good preliminary to the examination of his images. In *Tulips and Chimneys* words such as these occur frequently— thrilling, flowers, serious, absolute, sweet, unspeaking, utter, gradual, ultimate, final, serene, frail, grave, tremendous, slender, fragile, skilful, carefully, intent, young, gay, untimid, incorrigible, groping, dim, slow, certain, deliberate, strong, chiselled, subtle, tremulous, perpetual, crisp, perfect, sudden, faint, strenuous, minute, superlative, keen, ecstatic, actual, fleet, delicious, stars, enthusiastic, capable, dull, bright. In listing these as favourite words, it is meant that these words do the greater part of the work in the poems where they

[3] It is not meant to disparage Mr. Cummings' inventions, which are often excellent, but to minimize an exaggerated contemporary interest. A full discussion of the virtues of notation may be found in *A Survey of Modernist Poetry* by Laura Riding and Robert Graves (London, Heinemann, 1927), especially in Chapter III which is labelled: "William Shakespeare and E. E. Cummings: A study in original punctuation and spelling." Their point is made by printing sonnet 129 in its original notation beside a modern version; the point being that Shakespeare knew what he was doing and that his editors did not.

occur; these are the words which qualify the subject-matter of the poems, and are sometimes even the subjects themselves. Observe that none of them, taken alone, are very *concrete* words; and observe that many of them are the rather *abstract,* which is to say typical, *names* for precise qualities, but are not, and cannot be, as *originally important* words in a poem, very precise or very concrete or very abstract: they are middling words, not in themselves very much one thing or the other, and should be useful only with respect to something concrete in itself.

If we take Mr. Cummings' most favoured word "flower" and inspect the uses to which he puts it, we should have some sort of key to the kind of poetry he writes. In *Tulips and Chimneys* the word "flower" turns up, to a casual count, forty-eight times, and in *&,* a much smaller volume, twenty-one times. We have among others the following: smile like a flower; riverly as a flower; steeped in burning flowers; last flower; lipping flowers; more silently than a flower; snow flower; world flower; softer than flowers; forehead a flight of flowers; feet are flowers in vases; air is deep with flowers; slow supple flower of beauty; flower-terrible; flower of thy mouth; stars and flowers; mouth a new flower; flower of silence; god's flowers; flowers of reminding; dissonant flowers; flower-stricken air; Sunday flower; tremendous flower; speaking flower; flowers of kiss; futile flowers, etc., etc. Besides the general term there is a quantity of lilies and roses, and a good assortment of daisies, pansies, buttercups, violets and chrysanthemums. There are also many examples of such associated words as "petals" and "blooms" and "blossoms," which, since they are similarly used, may be taken as alternative to flowers.

Now it is evident that this word must attract Mr. Cummings' mind very much; it must contain for him an almost

[7]

unlimited variety and extent of meaning; as the mystic says god, or at least as the incomplete mystic repeats the name of god to every occasion of his soul, Mr. Cummings in some of his poems says flower. The question is, whether or not the reader can possibly have shared the experience which Mr. Cummings has had of the word; whether or not it is possible to discern, after any amount of effort, the precise impact which Mr. Cummings undoubtedly feels upon his whole experience when he uses the word. "Flower" like every other word not specifically the expression of a logical relation, began life as a metaphor, as a leap from feeling to feeling, as a bridge in the imagination to give meaning to both those feelings. Presumably, the amount of meaning possible to the word is increased with each use, but only the meaning *possible*. Actually, in practice, a very different process goes on. Since people are occupied mostly with communication and argument and conversation, with the erection of discursive relationships, words are commonly spoken and written with the *least* possible meaning preserved, instead of the most. History is taken for granted, ignored, or denied. Only the outsides of words, so to speak, are used; and doubtless the outsides of words are all that the discursive intellect needs. But when a word is used in a poem it should be the sum of all its appropriate history made concrete and particular in the individual context; and in poetry all words act *as if* they were so used, because the only kind of meaning poetry can have requires that all its words resume their full life: the full life being modified and made unique by the *qualifications* the words perform one upon the other in the poem. Thus even a very bad poem may seem good to its author, when the author is not an acute critic and believes that there is life in his words merely because there was life (and a very different sort of life, truly) in the feelings which they represent. An

author should remember, with the Indians, that the reality of
a word is anterior to, and greater than, his use of it can ever
be; that there is a perfection to the feelings in words to which
his mind cannot hope to attain, but that his chief labour will
be toward the approximation of that perfection.

We sometimes speak of a poet as a master of his words, and
we sometimes say that a man's poetry has been run away with
by words—meaning that he has not mastered his words but
has been overpowered by his peculiar experience of certain
among them. Both these notions are commonly improper,
because they represent misconceptions of the nature of poetry
in so far as they lay any stress upon originality, or the lack of
it, in the poet's use of words. The only mastery possible to the
poet consists in that entire submission to his words which is
perfect knowledge. The only originality of which the poet is
properly capable will be in the choice of order, and even this
choice is largely a process of discovery rather than of origina-
tion. As for words running away with a poet or a poem, it
would be more accurate to say that the poet's *ideas* had run
away with him than his words.

This is precisely what has occurred to Mr. Cummings in
his use of the word "flower" as a maid of all work. The word
has become an idea, and in the process has been deprived of
its history, its qualities, and its meaning. An idea, the intellectual pin upon which a thought is hung, is not transmissible
in poetry as an important element in the poem and ought only
to be employed to pass over, with the greatest possible
velocity, the area of the uninteresting (what the poet was not
interested in). That is, in a poem whose chief intent was the
notation of character and yet required a descriptive setting
might well use for the description such vague words as space
and time, but could not use such words as goodness or
nobleness without the risk of flatness. In Mr. Cummings'

poetry we find the contrary; the word "flower," because of the originality with which he conceives it, becomes an idea and is used to represent the most interesting and most important aspect of his poem. Hence the centre of the poem is permanently abstract and unknowable for the reader, and remains altogether without qualifications and concreteness. It is not the mere frequency of use that deadens the word flower into an idea; it is the kind of thought which each use illustrates in common. By seldom saying *what* flower, by seldom relating immitigably the abstract word to a specific experience, the content of the word vanishes; it has no inner mystery, only an impenetrable surface.

This is the defect, the essential deceit, we were trying to define. Without questioning Mr. Cummings, or any poet, as to sincerity (which is a personal attitude, irrelevant to the poetry considered) it is possible to say that when in any poem the important words are forced by their use to remain impenetrable, when they can be made to surrender nothing actually to the senses—then the poem is defective and the poet's words have so far deceived him as to become ideas merely.[4] Mr. Cummings is not so much writing poetry, as he is dreaming, idly ringing the changes of his reveries.

Perhaps a small divagation may make clearer the relation of these remarks to Mr. Cummings' poems. Any poetry which does not consider itself as much of an art and having the same responsibilities to the consumer as the arts of silver-

[4] It should be confessed that for all those persons who regard poetry only as a medium of communication, these remarks are quite vitiated. What is communicated had best remain as abstract as possible, dealing with the concrete as typical only; then "meaning" will be found to reside most clearly in the realm of ideas, and everything will be given as of equal import. But here poetry is regarded not at all as communication but as expression, as statement, as presentation of experience, and the emphasis will be on what is made known concretely. The question is not what one shares with the poet, but what one knows in the poem.

smithing or cobbling shoes—any such poetry is likely to do little more than rehearse a waking dream. Dreams are everywhere ominous and full of meaning; and why should they not be? They hold the images of the secret self, and to the initiate dreamer betray the nerve of life at every turn, not through any effort to do so, or because of any inherited regimen, but simply because they cannot help it. Dreams are like that—to the dreamer the maximal limit of experience. As it happens, dreams employ words and pictorial images to fill out their flux with a veil of substance. Pictures are natural to everyone, and words, because they are prevalent, seem common and inherently sensible. Hence, both picture and word, and then with a little stretching of the fancy the substance of the dream itself, seem expressible just as they occur— as things created, as the very flux of life. Mr. Cummings' poems are often nothing more than the report of just such dreams. He believes he knows what he knows, and no doubt he does. But he also believes, apparently, that the words which he encourages most vividly to mind are those most precisely fitted to put his poem on paper. He transfers the indubitable magic of his private musings from the cell of his mind, where it is honest incantation, to the realm of poetry. Here he forgets that poetry, so far as it takes a permanent form, is written and is meant to be read, and that it cannot be a mere private musing. Merely because his private fancy furnishes his liveliest images, is the worst reason for assuming that this private fancy will be approximately experienced by the reader or even indicated on the printed page.

But it is unfair to limit this description to Mr. Cummings; indeed, so limited, it is not even a description of Mr. Cummings. Take the Oxford Book of English Verse, or any anthology of poems equally well known, and turn from the poems printed therein of such widely separated poets as

Surrey, Crashaw, Marvell, Burns, Wordsworth, Shelley, and Swinburne, to the collected works of these poets respectively. Does not the description of Mr. Cummings' mind at work given above apply nearly as well to the bulk of this poetry as to that of Mr. Cummings, at least on the senses' first immersion? The anthology poems being well known are conceived to be understood, to be definitely intelligible, and to have, without inspection, a precise meaning. The descent upon the collected poems of all or of any one of these authors is by and large a descent into tenuity. Most of their work, most of any poet's work, with half a dozen exceptions, is tenuous and vague, private exercises or public playthings of a soul in verse. So far as he is able, the reader struggles to reach the concrete, the solid, the definite; he must have these qualities, or their counterparts among the realm of the spirit, before he can understand what he reads. To translate such qualities from the realm of his private experience to the conventional forms of poetry is the problem of the poet; and the problem of the reader, likewise, is to come well equipped with the talent and the taste for discerning the meaning of those conventions as they particularly occur. Neither the poet's casual language nor the reader's casual interlocution is likely to be much help. There must be a ground common but exterior to each: that is the poem. The best poems take the best but not always the hardest reading; and no doubt it is so with the writing. Certainly, in neither case are dreams or simple reveries enough. Dreams are natural and are minatory or portentous; but except when by accident they fall into forms that fit the intelligence, they never negotiate the miracle of meaning between the poet and the poem, the poem and the reader.

Most poetry fails of this negotiation, and it is sometimes assumed that the negotiation was never meant, by the poet, to be made. For the poet, private expression is said to be enough; for the reader, the agitation of the senses, the perception of verbal beauty, the mere sense of stirring life in the words, are supposed sufficient. If this defence had a true premise—if the poet did express himself to his private satisfaction—it would be unanswerable; and to many it is so. But I think the case is different, and this is the real charge against Mr. Cummings, the poet does not ever express himself privately. The mind cannot understand, cannot properly know its own musings until those musings take some sort of conventional form. Properly speaking a poet, or any man, cannot be adequate to himself in terms of himself. True consciousness and true expression of consciousness must be external to the blind seat of consciousness—man as a sensorium. Even a simple image must be fitted among other images, and conned with them, before it is understood. That is, it must take a form in language which is highly traditional and conventional. The genius of the poet is to make the convention apparently disappear into the use to which he puts it.

Mr. Cummings and the group with which he is here roughly associated, the anti-culture or anti-intelligence group, persists to the contrary. Because experience is fragmentary as it strikes the consciousness it is thought to be essentially discontinuous and therefore essentially unintelligible except in the fragmentary form in which it occurred. They credit the words they use with immaculate conception and there hold them unquestionable. A poem, because it happens, must mean something and mean it without relation to anything but the private experience which inspired it. Certainly it means something, but not a poem; it means that something exciting happened to the writer and that a mystery is happening to the reader. The fallacy is double: they believe in the inexorable significance of the unique experience; and they have discarded the only method of making the unique experience into a poem—the conventions of the intelligence. As a matter of fact they do not write without conventions, but being ignorant of what they use, they resort most commonly to their own inefficient or superficial conventions— such as Mr. Cummings' flower and doll. The effect is convention without substance; the unique experience becomes a rhetorical assurance.

If we examine next, for the sake of the greatest possible contrast, one of the "tough" poems in *Is 5,* we will find a similar breach with the concrete. The use of vague words like "flower" in the lyrical poems as unexpanded similes, is no more an example of sentimental egoism than the use of vague conventions about villains. The distortion differs in terms but is essentially identical.

Sometimes the surface of the poem is so well constructed that the distortion is hard to discover. Intensity of process occasionally triumphs over the subject. Less frequently the subject itself is conceived directly and takes naturally the terms which the language supplies. The poem numbered One-XII in *Is 5* is an example in so far as the sentimental frame does not obscure the process.

> now dis "daughter" uv eve (who aint precisely slim) sim
> ply don't know duh meanin uv duh woid sin in
> not disagreeable contras tuh dat not exactly fat
> "father" (adjustin his robe) who now puts on his flat hat.

It is to be noted in this epigram, that there is no inexorable reason for either the dialect or the lapses from it into straight English. No one in particular is speaking, unless it be Mr. Cummings slumming in morals along with he-men and lady social workers, and taking it for granted that the dialect and the really refined language which the dialect exercises together give a setting. There are many other poems in *Is 5*, more sentimental and less successful, where the realism is of a more obvious sort; not having reference to an ideal so much as to a kind of scientific reality. That is, there is an effort to ground an emotion, or the facts which make the emotion, in the style of the character to whom the emotion happens. It is the reporter, the man with the good ear for spoken rhythms, who writes out of memory. The war poems and the poem about Bill and his chip (One XVI) are examples. Style in this sense (something laid on) is only an attribute; is not the man; is not the character. And when it is substituted for character, it is likely to be sentimental and melodramatic. That is, the emotion which is named in the poem (by one of its attributes) is in excess of its established source (that same attribute). There is a certain immediate protection afforded to this insufficiency by the surface toughness, by the convention of burlesque; as if by mocking oneself one made sure there was something to mock. It is a kind of trickery resulting from eager but lazy senses; where the sensation itself is an excess, and appears to have done all the work of intuition and intelligence; where sensation seems expert without incorporation into experience. As if sensation could be anything more than the idea of sensation, so far as poetry goes, without being attached to some central body of experience, genuinely understood and *formed* in the mind.

The intrusion of science into art always results in a sentimental realism and always obfuscates form when that science is not kept subordinate to the qualitative experience of the senses—as witness the run of sociological novels. The analogues of science, where conventions are made to do the work of feeling instead of crowning it, are even more dangerous. Mr. Cummings' tough guy and his hard-boiled dialects are such analogues.

Mr. Cummings has a fine talent for using familiar, even almost dead words, in such a context as to make them suddenly impervious to every ordinary sense; they become unable to speak, but with a great air of being bursting with something very important and precise to say. "The bigness of cannon is *skilful* . . . enormous rhythm of *absurdity* . . . *slimness* of *evenslicing* eyes are chisels . . . electric Distinct face haughtily vital *clinched* in a swoon of *synopsis* . . . my friend's being continually whittles *keen* careful futile *flowers*," etc. With the possible exception of the compound *evenslicing* the italicized words are all ordinary words; all in normal contexts have a variety of meanings both connotative and denotative; the particular context being such as to indicate a particular meaning, to establish precisely a feeling, a sensation or a relation.

Mr. Cummings' contexts are employed to an opposite purpose in so far as they wipe out altogether the history of the word, its past associations and general character. To seize Mr. Cummings' meaning there is only the free and *uninstructed* intuition. Something precise is no doubt intended; the warrant for the belief is in the almost violent isolation into which the words are thrown; but that precision can seldom, by this method, become any more than just that "something precise." The reality, the event, the feeling, which we will allow Mr. Cummings has in mind, is not sensibly in the word. It is one thing for meaning to be difficult, or abstruse—hidden in its heart, that is. "Absent thee from *felicity* a while," Blake's "Time is the *mercy* of eternity" are reasonable examples; there the mystery is inside the words. In Mr. Cummings' words the mystery flies in the face, is on the surface; because there is no inside, no realm of possibility, of essence.

The general movement of Mr. Cummings' language is

away from communicable precision. If it be argued that the particular use of one of the italicized words above merely makes that word unique, the retort is that such uniqueness is too perfect, is sterile. If by removing the general sense of a word the special sense is apotheosized, it is only so at the expense of the general sense itself. The destruction of the general sense of a word results in the loss of that word's individuality; for in practice the character of a word (which is its sense) is manifest only in good society, and meaning is distinguished only by conventional association. Mr. Cummings' use of words results in a large number of conventions, but these conventions do not permeate the words themselves, do not modify their souls or change their fates; they cannot be adopted by the reader because they cannot be essentially understood. They should rather be called inventions.

If we take a paragraph from the poem beginning on page thirty in *Is 5*, we will discover another terminus of the emotional habit of mind which produced the emphasis on the word "flower" in *Tulips and Chimneys.*

the Bar. tinking luscious jugs dint of ripe silver with warmly-ish wetflat splurging smells waltz the glush of squirting taps plus slush of foam knocked off and a faint piddle-of-drops she says I ploc spittle what the lands thaz me kin in no sir hopping sawdust you kiddo he's a palping wreaths of badly Yep cigars who jim him why gluey grins topple together eyes pout gestures stickily point made glints squinting who's a wink bum-nothing and money fuzzily mouths take big wobbly foot-steps every goggle cent of it get out ears dribbles sofe right old feller belch the chap hic summore eh chuckles skulch.

Now the point is that the effect of this whole paragraph has much in common with the effect of the word "flower." It is a flower disintegrated, and the parts are not component;

so that by presenting an analysis of his image Mr. Cummings has not let us into its secret: the analysis is not a true analysis, because it exhibits, finally, what are still only the results, not the grounds, of his private conventions, his personal emotions. It is indubitable that the words are alive; they jostle, even overturn, the reader in the assurance of their vitality; but the notion of what their true vitality is remains Mr. Cummings' very own. The words remain emotive. They have a gusty air of being something, but they defeat themselves in the effort to say what, and come at last to a bad end, all fallen in a heap.

The easiest *explanation* of the passage would be to say that each separate little collection of words in it is a note for an image; an abstraction, very keen and lively in Mr. Cummings' mind, of something very precise and concrete. Some of the words seem like a painter's notes, some a philologist's. But they are all, as they are presented, notes, abstractions, ideas—with their concrete objects unknown—except to the most arbitrary guess. The guess must be arbitrary because of the quantity, not the quality, of the words employed. Mr. Cummings is not here overworking the individual words, but by heaping so many of them together he destroys their individuality. Meaning really residual in the word is not exhausted, is not even touched; it must remain abstract and only an emotional substitute for it can be caught. The interesting fact about emotional substitutes in poetry, as elsewhere, is their thinness, and the inadequacy resulting from the thinness. The thinness is compulsory because they can, so far as the poem is concerned, exist only as a surface; they cannot possess tentacular roots reaching into, and feeding on, feelings, because the feelings do not exist, are only present by legerdemain. Genuine emotion in poetry perhaps does not *exist* at all; though it is none the less real for that, because a genuine emotion does not need the warrant of existence: it is the necessary result, in the mind, of a convention of feelings: like the notion of divine grace.

In *Tulips and Chimneys* (p. 109) there is a poem whose first and last lines supply an excellent opposition of proper and improper distortion of language.

> the Cambridge ladies who live in furnished souls . . .
>
>   the
> moon rattles like a fragment of angry candy.

In the context the word "soul" has the element of surprise which is surprise at *justness;* at *aptness;* it fits in and finishes off the notion of the line. "Furnished souls" is a good, if slight, conceit; and there is no trouble for the reader who wishes to know what the line means: he has merely to *extend* his knowledge slightly, just as Mr. Cummings merely extended the sense of his language slightly by releasing his particular words in this particular order. The whole work that the poet here demands of his reader is pretty well defined. The reader does not have to *guess;* he is enabled to *know.* The reader is not collecting data, he is aware of a meaning.

It would be unfair not to quote the context of the second line.

> . . . the Cambridge ladies do not care, above
> Cambridge if sometimes in its box of
> sky lavender and cornerless, the
> moon rattles like a fragment of angry candy.

We can say that Mr. Cummings is putting beauty next to the tawdry; juxtaposing the dead with the live; or that he is being sentimentally philosophical in verse—that is, releasing from inadequate sources something intended to be an emotion.[5]

We can go on illustrating Mr. Cummings' probable intentions almost infinitely. What Mr. Cummings likes or admires, what he holds dear in life, he very commonly calls flowers, or dolls, or candy—terms with which he is astonishingly generous; as if he thought by making his terms general enough their vagueness could not matter, and never noticed that the words so used enervate themselves in a kind of hardened instinct. We can understand what Mr. Cummings intended by "moon" and "candy" but in the process of understanding, the meaning of the words themselves disappears. The thrill of the association of "rattles" with "moon" and "angry" with "candy" becomes useless as a guide. "Rattles" and "angry" can only be continued in the meaning of the line if the reader supplies them with a force, a definiteness of suggestion, with which Mr. Cummings has not endowed them.

The distortion is here not a release of observation so keen that commonplace language would not hold it; it is not the presentation of a vision so complete that words must lose their normal meanings in order to suggest it. It is, on the contrary, the distortion of the commonplace itself; and the difficulty about a commonplace is that it cannot be known, it has no character, no fate, and no essence. It is a substitute for these.

True meaning (which is here to say knowledge) can only exist where some contact, however remote, is preserved between the language, forms, or symbols in which it is given

[5] That is, as the most common form of sentimentality is the use of emotion in *excess* of its impetus in the feelings, here we have an example of emotion which fails by a great deal to *come up* to its impetus. It is a very different thing from understatement, where the implications are always definite and where successful disarming.

and something concrete, individual, or sensual which inspired it; and the degree in which the meaning is seized will depend on the degree in which the particular concreteness is realised. Thus the technique of "meaning" will employ distortion only in so far as the sense of this concreteness is promoted by it. When contrast and contradiction disturb the ultimate precision of the senses the distortion involved is inappropriate and destructive. Mr. Cummings' line about the moon and candy does not weld a contradiction, does not identify a substance by a thrill of novel association. It leaves the reader at a loss; where it is impossible to *know,* after any amount of effort and good will, what the words mean. If it be argued that Mr. Cummings was not interested in meaning then Mr. Cummings is not a serious poet, is a mere collector of sensations, and can be of very little value to us. And to defend Mr. Cummings on the ground that he is in the pretty good company of Swinburne, Crashaw, and Victor Hugo, is partly to ignore the fact that by the same argument all four also enjoy the companionship of Mr. Guest. Such defence would show a very poor knowledge of the verses of Mr. Cummings, who is nothing if not serious in the attempt to exhibit precise knowledge. His interest in words and in their real meaning is probably greater than that of most poets of similar dimensions. He has consciously stretched syntax, word order, and meaning in just the effort to expand knowledge in poetry; and his failure is because he has gone too far, has lost sight of meaning altogether—and because, perhaps, the experience which he attempts to translate into poetry remained always personal to him and was never known objectively as itself. By his eagerness Mr. Cummings' relation to language has become confused; he has put down what has meant much to him and can mean little to us, because for us it is not put down—is only indicated, only possibly there. The freshness and depth of his private experience is not denied; but it is certain that, so far as its meaning goes, in the poetry into which he translated it, sentimentality, empty convention, and commonplace rule. In short, Mr. Cummings' poetry ends in ideas *about* things.

When Mr. Cummings resorts to language for the *thrill* that words may be made to give, when he allows his thrill to appear as an equivalent for concrete meaning, he is often more successful than when he is engaged more ambitiously. This is true of poets like Swinburne and Poe, Shelley and the early Marlowe: where the first pair depended almost as much upon *thrill* as Mr. Cummings in those poems where they made use of it at all, and where the second pair, particularly Marlowe, used their thrills more appropriately as ornament: where all four were most successful in their less ambitious works, though perhaps not as interesting. Likewise, to-day, there is the example of Archibald MacLeish, whose best lines are those that thrill and do nothing more. So that at least in general opinion Mr. Cummings is in this respect not in bad company. But if an examination of thrill be made, whether in Mr. Cummings' verse or in that of others, it will be shown that the use of thrill has at heart the same sentimental impenetrability that defeats the possibility of meaning elsewhere. Only here, in the realm of thrill, the practice is comparatively less illegitimate. Thrill, by itself, or in its proper place, is an exceedingly important element in any poem: it is the circulation of its blood, the *quickness* of life, by which we know it, when there is anything in it to know, most intimately. To use a word for its thrill, is to resurrect it from the dead; it is the incarnation of life in consciousness; it is movement.

<hr/>

[6] Cf. Owen Barfield's *Poetic Diction* (London, Faber and Gwyer, 1928), page 202. "For what is absolutely necessary to the present existence of poetry? Movement. The wisdom which she has imparted may remain for a time at

But what Mr. Cummings does, when he is using language as thrill, is not to resurrect a word from the dead: he more often produces an apparition, in itself startling and even ominous, but still only a ghost: it is all a thrill, and what it is that thrilled us cannot be determined. For example in *XLI Poems,* the following phrases depend considerably for their effect upon the thrill that is in them: "Prisms of sharp *mind;* where strange birds *purr;* into the *smiling* sky *tense* with *blending;* ways cloaked with *renewal;* sinuous riot; *steeped* with burning flowers; little kittens who are called *spring;* electric Distinct face haughtily vital clinched in a *swoon* of synopsis; unreal *precise* intrinsic fragment of actuality; an orchid whose *velocity* is *sculptural;* scythe takes *crisply* the *whim* of thy *smoothness;* perpendicular *taste;* wet stars, etc., etc. (The italics are mine.)

Take especially the phrase, "scythe takes *crisply* the *whim* of thy *smoothness.*" We know in the poem that it is the scythe of death and that it is youth and beauty (in connection with love) that is to be cut off. So much is familiar, is very conventional; and so the conventional or dead emotion is placed before us; the educated reader receives it and reacts to it without a whimper. But Mr. Cummings must not have been content with presenting the conventional emotion in its conventional form; he felt bound to enliven it with metaphor, with overtones of the senses and the spirit: so that he substituted for the direct statement a rather indirect image

---

rest, but she herself will always be found to have gone forward to where there is life, and therefore movement, *now.* And we have seen that the experience of aesthetic pleasure betrays the real presence of movement. . . . But without the continued existence of poetry, without a steady influx of new meaning into language, even the knowledge and wisdom which poetry herself has given in the past must wither away into a species of mechanical calculation. Great poetry is the progressive incarnation of life in consciousness." That is we must know what thrills us; else being merely thrilled we are left gasping and aghast, like the little girl on the roller-coaster.

THE DOUBLE AGENT

combining three unusually sensed words for the sake of the *thrill* the special combination might afford. As the phrase stands there is no precision in it. There is a great suggestion of precision about it—like men going off to war; but precisely *what* is left for the reader to guess, to supply from his own heart. By themselves *whim* and *smoothness* are abstract quality words; and in order for them to escape the tensity, the dislocated strain, of abstractness and gain the intensity, the firm disposition, of concrete meaning, they should demand a particular reference.

Smoothness is probably the smoothness of the body and is used here as a kind of metonomy; but it may be pure metaphor and represent what is really to die—the spirit—taken in its physical terms; or it may be that all that is to be understood is a pure tautology. And so on. Even with this possible variety of reference, *smoothness* would not be very objectionable, were it the only word in the phrase used in this way, or were the other words used to clarify the *smoothness*. But we have also the noun *whim* bearing directly on *smoothness* and the adverb *crisply* which while it directly modifies *takes,* really controls the entire phrase. Taken seriously *whim*, with reference to the smoothness of either the body or the spirit or the love it inspires, is to say the least a light word; one might almost say a "metrical" word, introduced to stretch the measure, or because the author liked the sound of it, or enjoyed whimsy. It diminishes without limiting the possibilities of *smoothness*. Because it is here, in the phrase, it is inseparable from the phrase's notion of smoothness; yet instead of assisting, tends to prevent what that notion of smoothness is from being divulged.

Crisply is even more difficult to account for; associated with a scythe it perhaps brings to mind the sound of a scythe in a hayfield, which is surely not the reference here intended;

it would be very difficult for such a crispness to associate itself with death, which the scythe represents, or *whim,* or *smoothness* in either the spiritual or fleshly sense. If it implies merely a cleanness, a swiftness of motion in the apparition of death, some other word would have seemed better chosen. If this analysis be correct, the three words are unalterably combined by the force of *crisply* in such a way as to defeat the only possible sense their *thrilling* use would have had. They are, so to speak, only the notions of themselves and those selves must remain forever unknown. All we are left with in such a phrase as this is the strangeness which struck us on our first encounter; and the only difference is that the strangeness is the more intensified the more we prolong the examination. This is another test of poetry: whether we understand the *strangeness* of a poem or not.[7]

As it happens there is an exquisite example of the proper use of this strangeness, this thrill, in another poem of Mr. Cummings: where he speaks of a cathedral before whose face "the streets turn *young* with rain." While there might be some question as to whether the use of *young* presents the only adequate image, there is certainly no question at all that the phrase is entirely successful: that is, the suggestive feeling in *young* makes the juncture, the emotional conjugation, of streets and rain transparent and perfect. This may be so because there is no element of essential contradiction, in the terms of feeling, between the emotional word *young* and the factual word *streets* and *rain;* or because, positively, what

---

[7] *Poetic Diction, op. cit.,* pp. 197-8: "It (strangeness) is not synonymous with wonder; for wonder is our reaction to things which we are conscious of not quite understanding, or at any rate of understanding less than we had thought. The element of strangeness in beauty has the contrary effect. It arises from contact with a different kind of *consciousness* from our own, different, yet not so remote that we cannot partly share it, as indeed, in such a connexion, the mere word 'contact' implies. Strangeness, in fact, arouses wonder when we do not understand; aesthetic imagination when we do."

happens to the context by the insertion of *young* is, by a necessary leap of the imagination, something qualified. *Young* may be as abstract a word by itself, as purely relative and notional a word, as any other; but here it is brought into the concrete, is fixed there in a proper habitation. Just because reference is not commonly made either to young streets or young rain, the combination here effected is the more appropriate. The surprise, the contrast, which lend force to the phrase, do not exist in the poem; but exist, if at all, rather in the mind of the reader who did not forsee the slight stretch of his sensibility that the phrase requires—which the phrase not only requires, but necessitates. This, then, is a *strangeness* understood by its own viableness. No preliminary agreement of taste, or contract of symbols, was necessary.

The point is that Mr. Cummings did not here attempt the impossible, he merely stretched the probable. The business of the poet who deals largely with tactual and visual images, as Mr. Cummings does, for the meat of his work, is to escape the prison of his private mind; to use in his poem as little as possible of the experience that happened to him personally, and on the other hand to employ as much as possible of that experience as it is data.

It is idle for a critic to make the familiar statement that the mind of the writer is his work, or that "the style is the man," when by mind and man is meant the private experience of the author. So far as, in this sense, the mind *is* the work, or the style *is* the man, we can understand the work or the style only through an accidental unanimity; and what we understand is likely to be very thin—perhaps only the terms of understanding. For the author himself, in such circumstances, can have understood very little more. He has been pursuing the impossible, when the probable was right at hand; he has been transcending his experience instead of submitting to it. And this is just what Mr. Cummings does in the phrases quoted above.

It would be ungracious to suppose that as a poet "a swoon of synopsis" did not represent to Mr. Cummings a very definite and very suggestive image. But to assent to that image would be a kind of *tour de force;* the application of such assent would imply that because the words appear, and being words contain notions, they must in this particular instance exhibit the undeniable sign of interior feeling. The proper process of poetry designs exactly what the reader will perceive; that is what is meant when a word is said to be inevitable or *juste.* But this exactness of perception can only come about when there is an extreme fidelity on the part of the poet to his words as living things; which he can discover and control— which he must learn, and nourish, and stretch; but which he cannot invent. This unanimity in our possible experience of words implies that the only unanimity which the reader can feel in what the poet represents must be likewise exterior to the poet; must be somehow both anterior and posterior to the poet's own experience. The poet's mind, perhaps, is what he is outside himself with; is what he has learned; is what he knows: it is also what the reader knows. So long as he is content to remain in his private mind, he is unknowable, impenetrable, and sentimental. All his words perhaps must thrill us, because we cannot know them in the very degree that we sympathise with them. But the best thrills are those we have without knowing it.

This essay has proceeded so far on the explicit assumption that the poems of Mr. Cummings are unintelligible, and that no amount of effort on the part of the reader can make them less so. We began by connecting Mr. Cummings to two schools, or groups, which are much the same essentially—

the anti-culture group which denies the intelligence, and the group, not limited to writers, of which the essential attitude is most easily defined as sentimental egoism or romantic idealism. Where these schools are most obviously identical is in the poetry they nourish: the avowed interest is the relentless pursuit of the actual in terms of the immediate as the immediate is given, without overt criticism, to the ego. Unintelligibility is a necessary consequence of such a pursuit, if by the intelligible we mean something concrete, qualified, permanent, and public. Poetry, if we understand it, is not in immediacy at all. It is not given to the senses or to the free intuition. Thus, when poetry is written as if its substance were immediate and given, we have as a result a distorted sensibility and a violent inner confusion. We have, if the poet follows his principles, something abstract, vague, impermanent, and essentially private. When every sensation and every word is taken as final and perfect, the substance which sensations report and for which words must stand remain inexplicable. We can understand only by accident.

Of course there is another side to the matter. In a sense anyone can understand Mr. Cummings and his kind by the mere assertion that he does understand. Nothing else is needed but a little natural sympathy and a certain aptness for the resumption of a childish sensibility. In much the same way we understand a stranger's grief—by setting up a private and less painful simulacrum. If we take the most sentimental and romantic writers as they come, there will be always about their works an excited freshness, the rush of sensation and intuition, all the ominous glow of immediacy. They will be eagerly at home in the mystery of life. Adroitness, expertness, readiness for any experience, will enlighten their activities even where they most miserably fail. They are all actors, ready to take any part, for they put themselves, and nothing else, into every part they play. Commonly their real success will depend on the familiarity of the moments into which they sink themselves; they will depend on convention more than others, because they have nothing else to depend on.

So with the poetry of Mr. Cummings we might be altogether contented and pleased, were he himself content with the measure of his actual performance. But no poetry is so pretentious. No poetry ever claimed to mean more; and in making this claim it cannot avoid submitting itself, disastrously, to the criticism of the intelligence. So soon as we take it seriously, trying to discover what it really says about human destiny and the terms of love and death, we see how little material there is in this poetry except the assurance, made with continuous gusto, that the material exists. We look at the poetry. Sometimes one word, in itself vague and cloudy, is made to take on the work of an entire philosophy—like flower. Sometimes words pile themselves up blindly, each defeating the purport of the others. No feeling is ever defined. No emotion betrays a structure. Experience is its own phantoms, and flows willy-nilly. With the reality of experience the reality of language is lost. No metaphor crosses the bridge of tautology, and every simile is unexpanded. All the "thought" is metonomy, yet the substance is never assigned; so in the end we have only the thrill of substance.

Such an art when it pretends to measure life is essentially vicarious; it is a substitute for something that never was—like a tin soldier, or Peter Pan. It has all the flourish of life and every sentimental sincerity. Taken for what it is, it is charming and even instructive. Taken solemnly, as it is meant to be, the distortion by which it exists is too much for it, and it seems a kind of baby-talk.

1930

II

MASKS OF EZRA POUND

THE work of Ezra Pound has been for most people almost as difficult to understand as Soviet Russia. Ignorance, distance, and propaganda have about equally brought reaction to violent terms—either of idolatry or frightened antipathy. Enthusiasm and hatred, in matters of literature, are even more injurious than in economy; the chosen emotions seem entirely to obviate the need for a reasoned attitude. Enthusiasm is whole-hearted and hatred instinctive, and their satisfactions, to those who experience them, seem acts of sufficient piety. But what is obviated is only suppressed, never destroyed; and the more work—especially the more Cantos [1]— Mr. Pound publishes the more need there is for an attitude, both less whole-hearted and less instinctive, from which the work can be appreciated.

First statements had better be negative and dogmatic. Mr. Pound is neither a great poet nor a great thinker. Those of his followers who declare him the one only belittle him, and when he writes as the other, he belittles himself. Except where in his belittled forms he has done or received wrong to his verse, this essay is not concerned either with his influence upon others or with the misinterpretations of which he has been the victim. For Mr. Pound is at his best a maker of great verse rather than a great poet. When you look into him, deeply as you can, you will not find any extraordinary rev-

[1] Perhaps it should be said the more available the Cantos become. After years of scarcity and costliness, Farrar and Rinehart of New York published *A Draft of Thirty Cantos* at $2.50, followed by Cantos XXXI-XL. The text for this essay is that of the earlier volume.

elation of life, nor any bottomless fund of feeling; nor will you find any mode of life already formulated, any collection of established feelings, composed or mastered in new form. The content of his work does not submit to analysis; it is not the kind of content that can be analysed—because, separated, its components retain no being. It cannot be talked about like the doctrines of Dante or the mental machinery of Blake. It cannot be deduced from any current of ideas. It is not to be found in any book or set of books. Only in a very limited way can Mr. Pound be discussed as it is necessary to discuss, say, Yeats: with reference to what is implicit and still to be said under the surface of what has already been said.

Mr. Pound is explicit; he is all surface and articulation. For us, everything is on the outsides of his words—of which there is excellent testimony in the fact that his best work is his best translation. In reading even his most difficult verse, such as the Cantos, there should never be any intellectual problem of interpretation. It is unnecessary to pierce the verse to understand it, and if by chance the verse is punctured and the substance seems obscure or esoteric it will be because contact has been lost with the verse itself. The difficulties of the Cantos are superficial and their valuable qualities are all qualities or virtues of a well-managed verbal surface; which is far from saying that the virtues are superficial or slight.

On the contrary, the kind of surface which Mr. Pound makes—the type of poetry into which the best parts of his Cantos fall—is a very important kind of surface and reflects a great deal of critical labour. His surface is a mask through which many voices are heard. Ever since he began printing his poems, Mr. Pound has played with the latin word *persona*. *Persona,* etymologically, was something through which sounds were heard, and thus a mask. Actors used masks through which great thoughts and actions acquired voice.

[31]

Mr. Pound's work has been to make *personae,* to become himself, as a poet, in this special sense a person through which what has most interested him in life and letters might be given voice.

Such a surface, such a mask, consumes more critical than naively "original" talent; as may be seen when in the Cantos Mr. Pound demonstrates his greatest failures where he is most "original," where he has not remembered to be a mask. That is, the verse which is left after he has selected and compressed what voices he wants to be heard, will be both a result of criticism and a species of criticism itself, and the better the criticism the better the verse. Where the critical labour has been forgone and the other, commonplace kind of personality has been brought in as a substitute, the dull reading of duller gossip in bad verse is the result.[2]

We may accept, then, the thirty-odd published Cantos of Mr. Pound's long poem as a mask which is also a criticism of the men and books and gods whose voices he wishes us to hear. We cannot quarrel with what he chooses to personify any more than we quarrel with Shakespeare for writing about Caesar rather than Socrates—although if it pleases us we may be puzzled and regret missed opportunities. Here, however it may be in writers whose work is differently weighted, we are concerned with a poetry of which the finished surface is to the maximum degree its subject, and the object of criticism will be to see whether it enforces the terms itself exacts.

Before examining the large, unfinished mask of the Cantos, Mr. Pound's two principal finished works—"Hugh Selwyn

[2] The doctrinaire and hortatory sections of Mr. Pound's prose criticism are but the apotheosis of the bad parts of the Cantos. The further he gets from the centre of his verse the greater his self-indulgence. In verse and when directly handling the fabric of verse perhaps our most acute critic, he is in his general prose our least responsible.

Mauberley" and "Homage to Sextus Propertius"—may first be considered. The first is Mr. Pound's most nearly, in the ordinary sense, "original" work, and the second, as a translation, the least. The reverse ascriptions are in fact more accurate; and the paradox is verbal not substantial. The substance of "Mauberley," what it is about, is commonplace, but what the translator has contributed to "Propertius" is his finest personal work. In both poems a medium is set up and managed as near perfectly as may be in such qualities as phrasing, rhyme (in "Mauberley"), cadence and echo. One indication of the perfection of the medium is that, almost without regard to content, both poems are excessively quotable. With no compunction as to substantial relevance phrase after phrase comes to mind in a kind of willy-nilly elegance.

"Mauberley" as a whole combines homage to a poet half contemporary and half ninetyish with an attack on the circumstances which make the success of such a poet difficult, and possible. It is the cry of the romantic poet against the world which surrounds him and the cry of a poet choosing a different world in his mind; but the romantic cries are uttered with a worldly, even a tough elegance. As a whole, "Mauberley" must be either swallowed or rejected; that is, after reading, one operation or the other will be found to have been made. There is no logic, no argument, in the poem, to compel the reader's mind to adherence; it is a matter for assimilation.[3]

[3] T. S. Eliot in his Introduction to Pound's *Selected Poems* (London: Faber & Gwyer, 1928) expresses very firmly a larger belief. "It is compact of the experience of a certain man in a certain place at a certain time; and it is also a document of an epoch; it is genuine tragedy and comedy; and it is in the best sense of Arnold's worn phrase, a 'criticism of life'." More recently, in a group of fifteen Testimonies put out by Farrar and Rinehart to accompany the Cantos, Mr. Eliot goes even further. "I find that, with the exception of MAUBERLEY, there is no other contemporary—with disrespect for none, for I include myself—whom I ever want to re-read for pleasure." Against

However, "Mauberley" need not be taken as a whole; wholeness, preconceived, is a prison into which the mind is not compelled to thrust itself; the parts, taken seriatim, establish parallels, sequences, connections, and conspire, in spite of the prejudiced mind, to produce an aggregate better, that is more useful than the prison. It is a matter of adding. Here the addition will not be exhaustive, because the task is preliminary, to come at the addition of the Cantos.

The first stanza of the first poem ("Ode pour L'Election de Son Sepulchre") sets the subject of which the remaining seventeen poems are variations.

> For three years, out of key with his time,
> He strove to resuscitate the dead art
> Of poetry; to maintain "the sublime"
> In the old sense. Wrong from the start—

"No, hardly," the poem goes on—the rest of "Mauberley" goes on—listing contrasts between the present time and the sublime in the old sense. The next four stanzas contain references to Capaneus, the gods lawful in Troy, Penelope, Flaubert, Circe, The Grand Testament of Villon, and the Muses' diadem. The only difficulties are Capaneus, who appears between semicolons unadorned, and the fact that the Trojan gods are given in Greek; and these difficulties—as will be illustrated later—are typical of all the difficulties in Mr. Pound's work. They are not difficulties in the substance

---

these periods it may not be unilluminating to expose another, equally rigid point of view. Mr. Yvor Winters (Hound & Horn, April—June, 1933, p. 538) has this to say of "Mauberley" (he has been speaking of the defect of Romantic irony in the Middle Generation of American writers): "Pound writes a lugubrious lament for the passing of Pre-Raphaelitism, yet deliberately makes Pre-Raphaelitism (and himself) appear ludicrous. The result is a kind of slipshod elegance: the firmness of the secure ironist . . . is impossible." Mr. Eliot presses his acceptance, and Mr. Winters his rejection, too hard; both for reasons outside the poem, so that both end in misconstruction. As the dilemma is false the poem refuses to be impaled.

of the poem, but superficial, in the reader's mind. This poet expects the reader to know, or to find out, that Capaneus was one of the seven against Thebes, that he was presumptuous enough to say that Zeus himself could not destroy him, that Zeus did destroy him with appropriate lightning; that, finally, the poet like Capaneus is full of *hubris* and is likely to be himself similarly destroyed. The line about the gods is in Greek script because the syntax of the poem demands it; the substance, perhaps, is in the fact that it is in Greek. In English the lovely rhyme of Τροίη and *leeway* would have been impossible; but that is not the only loss that would have been incurred. In English, "Be the gods known to thee which are lawful in Troy," could never have been "caught in the unstopped ear" (the next line), at least not without considerable circumlocution. The ear would have been stopped, and the Sirens do not sing in English. If the reader protests that he cannot be expected to know Capaneus at first sight and that his knowledge of Greek characters is visual at best, Mr. Pound's retort might well be that the reasons for that protest made the subject of his poem; that anyway, the poem is there and the reader can come at it if he wants to, and that, besides, the reader's ignorance, if he have wit, is likely to be as illuminating as any instruction he can come by.

Without pre-judging either protest or retort, the point here to be emphasized is this: this is the sort of poem Mr. Pound writes when he writes most personally. Nothing is based on sensation, very little on direct feeling or vision, and the emotion is conventional, agreed upon, or given, beforehand. What Mr. Pound does is to support his theme with the buttresses of allusion. This is as true of poems numbered IV and V, which deal with the war and contain only one literary tag ("Died some pro patria non dulce non et decor") as it is true of "Medallion," the last of the group, which is perhaps the most literary. The object is to give conventional, mask-like form, in the best possible verse, to the given attitude or emotion.

> Charm, smiling at the good mouth,
> Quick eyes gone under earth's lid,
>
> For two gross of broken statues,
> For a few thousand battered books

is no better verse and no less conventional than

> The sleek head emerges
> From the gold-yellow frock
> As Anadyomene in the opening
> Pages of Reinach.

What we see is Mr. Pound fitting his substance with a surface; he is a craftsman, and we are meant to appreciate his workmanship. When we try to discern the substance, we find that the emphasis on craft has produced a curious result. Instead of the poem being, as with most poets of similar dimensions, a particularised instance of a plot, myth, attitude, or convention, with Mr. Pound movement is in the opposite direction; the poem flows into the medium and is lost in it, like water in sand. Shakespeare used what are called the sources of *King Lear* to encompass and order a vast quantity of his own experience, and as the play is digested we are left, finally, with Shakespeare's material rather than the source-material. With Mr. Pound, we begin with his own experience and end up with the source. The Pound-material has been lost sight of; it is no longer necessary or relevant, because it has been generalised into the surface of the poem, and has thus lost its character in the character of the mask.[4]

---

[4] There may be some connection between this procedure in poetry and Mr. Pound's recent declaration that he is giving up letters and will devote his mind to economics.

In other words, with a little exaggeration, Mr. Pound behaves as if he were translating; as if there were, somewhere, an original to which "Mauberley" must conform. He is not looking for an objective form to express or communicate what he knows; the objective form is in his mind, in the original, which requires of him that he find and polish only a verbal surface. It is therefore not unnatural that where there is actually an original to control him, he will do his freest, best, and also his most personal work. The "Homage to Sextus Propertius," if only because it is longer, more complex, and has a more available original, is a better example of his success than "The Seafarer" or "Cathay."

"Propertius" is made up of passages, some as short as three or four lines, one as long as ninety-four, taken from Books II and III of the Elegies. The selections are neither consecutive in the Latin nor complete in themselves; nor does Mr. Pound always give all of the passage chosen. He arranges, omits, condenses, and occasionally adds to, the Latin for his own purposes: of homage, of new rendering, and of criticism.[5]

What is characteristic of this poem more than its attitudes towards love and towards the poet's profession, is the elegance of the language in which these attitudes are expressed. By elegance is meant—and the meaning may be recovered in the term itself—a consistent choice of words and their arrangement such as to exemplify a single taste; a quality, like Mr. Pound's other qualities, which may be associated with craftsmanship; a quality which can be acquired, and may be retained only with practice. Usually associated with poets of the lesser talent, or with the lesser works of greater talent,

[5] It may save the interested reader trouble and will certainly clarify Mr. Pound's structural method to list the passages rendered, in the order in which Mr. Pound presents them. III i; II ii; III iii; III xvi; III vi; II x; II i; II xiii; III v; III iv; II xv; II xxviii; II xxix; II xxx; II xxxii; II xxxiv. Omissions, inventions and the minutiae of rearrangement are not given.

elegance is commonly taken as an end in itself. Its sustaining, its transforming powers are not seen or are underestimated. Dryden and Pope are sometimes reduced to the level of Gray and Collins for reasons which come very nearly to this: that the elegance of all four poets is taken as equally ornamental and, once appreciated, equally for granted. The truth is that in relation to the subject or inspiration of verse there are contrary sorts of elegance, the sort which enriches because it transforms and the sort which impoverishes because it merely clothes. Gray and Collins, aside from their single successes, exhibit the impoverishing elegance to which an insufficiently mastered taste can lead: too much of their work reads like water and leaves no trace. Dryden and Pope, in their mature work, are always strong, the elegance of their language is powerful enough to sustain and transform any subject however commonplace or weak its surd may be. Mr. Pound's "Propertius" has this quality of tough elegance, and to a degree great enough to surpass what might have been the insuperable difficulties of a loose metrical form and a highly conventional subject-matter.[6] What and how Mr. Pound transforms in his English Propertius' Latin can only be illustrated by quotation and comparison—from Mr. Pound, from the Latin, and from the prose version of H. E. Butler in the Loeb Library.

Callimachi Manes et Coi sacra Philetae,
   in vestrum, quaeso, me sinite ire nemus.
primus ego ingredior puro de fonte sacerdos
   Itala per Graios orgia ferre choros.

[6] Readers who have consulted the classics only in metrical translation, must often have been struck with the commonplaceness of great poets. Most poetry is on commonplace themes, and the freshness, what the poet supplies, is in the language. There are other matters of importance in original poetry, but it is the freshness of Mr. Pound's language, not the power of his mind or of a sounder interpretation, that makes his translations excellent poetry.

dicite, quo pariter carmen tenuastis in antro?
 quove pede ingressi? quamve bibistis aquam?
a valeat, Phoebum quicumque moratur in armis!
 exactis tenui pumice versus eat,—
quo me Fama levat terra sublimis, et a me
 nata coronatis Musa triumphat equis,
et mecum curru parvi vectantur Amores,
 scriptorumque meas turba secuta rotas.
quid frustra missis in me certatis habenis?
 non data ad Musas currere lata via.
multi, Roma, tuas laudes annalibus addent,
 qui finem imperii Bactra futura canent;
sed, quod pace legas, opus hoc de monte Sororum
 detulit intacta pagina nostra via.
mollia, Pegasides, date vestro serta poetae:
 non faciet capiti dura corona meo
at mihi quod vivo detraxerit invida turba,
 post obitum duplici faenere reddet Honos;
omnia post obitum fingit maiora vetustas:
 maius ab exsequiis nomen in ora venit.

(Elegies III,i,1-24.)

Shades of Callimachus, Coan ghosts of Philetas
It is in your grove I would walk,
I who come first from the clear font
Bringing the Grecian orgies into Italy,
                              and the dance into Italy.
Who hath taught you so subtle a measure,
                    in what hall have you heard it;
What foot beat out your time-bar,
               what water has mellowed your whistles?

Out-weariers of Apollo will, as we know, continue their
    Martian generalities.
          We have kept our erasers in order,
A new-fangled chariot follows the flower-hung horses;
A young Muse with young loves clustered about her
                    ascends with me into the ether, . . .
And there is no high-road to the Muses.

[39]

Annalists will continue to record Roman reputations,
Celebrities from the Trans-Caucasus will belaud Roman
      celebrities
And expound the distentions of Empire,

But for something to read in normal circumstances?
For a few pages brought down from the forked hill
      unsullied?
               I ask a wreath which will not crush my head.
                   And there is no hurry about it;
I shall have, doubtless, a boom after my funeral,
Seeing that long standing increases all things,
                       regardless of quality.
          ("Homage to Sextus Propertius" I.)

"Shade of Callimachus and sacred rites of Philetas, suffer
me, I pray, to enter your grove. I am the first with priestly
service from an unsullied spring to carry the Italian mysteries among the dances of Greece. Tell me, in what grotto
did ye weave your songs together? With what step did ye
enter? What sacred fountain did ye drink?

"Away with the man who keeps Phoebus tarrying among
the weapons of war! Let verse run smoothly, polished with
fine pumice. 'Tis by such verse as this that fame lifts me
aloft from earth, and the Muse, my daughter, triumphs with
garlanded steeds, and tiny Loves ride with me in my chariot,
and a throng of writers follows my wheels. Why strive ye
against me vainly with loosened reins? Narrow is the path
that leadeth to the Muses. Many, O Rome, shall add fresh
glories to thine annals, singing that Bactra shall be thine
empire's bound; but this work of mine my pages have
brought down from the Muses' mount by an untrodden way,
that thou mayest read it in the midst of peace.

"Pegasid Muses, give soft garlands to your poet: no hard
crown will suit my brow. But that whereof the envious
throng have robbed me in life, Glory after death shall repay
with double interest. After death lapse of years makes all
things seem greater; after the rites of burial a name rings
greater on the lips of men."   (Butler, *Propertius*, III, i.)

If the differences rather than the similarities of the three versions are sufficiently emphasised the connections between them become slight. The "original," whatever it was, perhaps equally inspired all three; that is, the Latin itself seems as much a version as either translation. Not only the tone and texture vary, but the intent, the inner burden, of any one is incompatible with either of the others. The prose version is the most poetical, the Latin less, and Mr. Pound's, while the least, is to-day, whatever it might have been in the first century, the best verse—because its intent is suitable to our own times, and because Mr. Pound carries only the baggage to hold down and firm that intent.

Such general statements require no insight to make and emerge from general reading alone. But support is available and at least a sort of definition possible in an examination of specific words and phrases. "Coan ghosts . . . Grecian orgies . . . mellowed your whistles . . . Martian generalities . . . something to read in normal circumstances . . . expound the distentions of empire . . . a boom after my funeral"—these phrases spring from the same source as Propertius' Latin and Butler's prose; but they have an element common to neither, or at any rate not found in either to the same degree, the element of conversational, colloquial ease used formally, almost rhetorically, to heighten the seriousness of the verse. The words "ghosts, orgies, whistles, normal, distentions, generalities, boom" do not appear either in the Latin or in Butler's English. They make Butler superfluous, for this purpose, and transform Propertius; and they are the result of the operation of a very definite taste.

The matter may become clearer if two lines are taken where the verbal transformations are less obvious and what is called fidelity to the original is greater. "Exactus tenui pumice versus eat" becomes with Butler "Let verse run

smoothly, polished with fine pumice" and with Mr. Pound
"We have kept our erasers in order." So far as facts go, the
words come to the same thing in all three, but the tones are
utterly different. Even closer to the Latin "non data ad Musas
currere lata via" is Mr. Pound's "And there is no high-road
to the Muses." Butler's "Narrow is the path that leads to the
Muses" illustrates the difference between Mr. Pound and
Propertius, and points the value of it: the value, that is, in
translation, of making a critical equivalent, rather than a
duplicate, of the original.

Forgetting now the differences between Propertius and
Mr. Pound—forgetting them because once apprehended they
no longer matter—it is possible to judge better the likeness.
We know better what sort of likeness to look for. We know
that this Homage is a portrait not a photograph, the voice a
new recital not a dictaphone record. We know, in short, that
Mr. Pound begins his work where ordinary translations leave
off—with a reduction of English and Latin fractions to a
common denominator; he proceeds to a new work built up
from that denominator. The denominator was that quality,
really, of which examples were given above. The dissimi-
larity is superficial, in the form of expression, and only by
exaggerating the surface difference could the quality be given
in English at all. Mr. Pound felt the quality in the Latin, and
determined that it was what made Propertius valuable; he
therefore concentrated upon rendering that quality very
nearly to the exclusion of Propertius' other qualities. Where
the quality was lacking, he either omitted the text, condensed,
or supplied it himself in his English. Thus he performed both
a general and a minutely specific criticism upon Propertius.
If the result is not Propertius to the classicist, or only a little
of him, it is for the English reader better than Propertius,

how much better the reader cannot appreciate unless he compares the passages he likes best with the Latin.

With reference to the Cantos and in comparison to "Mauberley" there are three points of importance about the "Propertius": that it is, although a translation, an original poem; that it is a criticism as well as a poem; and that it is exactly as much a mask, a *persona,* as "Mauberley," though constructed in the opposite direction. The structure, which is to say the secret, if there is one, of the Cantos, is a combination, with variations, of the structure of these two poems. The Cantos ought not to be read without them, and both of them may be considered—and especially the "Propertius" of which even the metre is similar—as themselves part of the Cantos.

Of the three points mentioned, two have already been dealt with: that translation of this order makes new English poetry; and that the critical element—what the translation emphasizes, what it excludes, and in what it differs with relation to the Latin—is as necessary to appreciate as the craftsmanship. The third point needs only to be made explicit to be seized, when it is seen to have a definite connection with the other two points. In "Mauberley," if the account was correct, all the work flowed into and ended in a convention; the intellectual intent, so far as there was one, was the declaration of a conventional attitude about the poet and his profession. In "Propertius" the convention, and very nearly the same one, was given beforehand, and the work flowed away from it, to illustrate and particularise it. Hence, having a centre rather than a terminal, the "Propertius" is a sturdier, more sustained, and more independent poem than "Mauberley." Craftsmanship may be equally found in both poems; but Mr. Pound has contributed more of his own individual sensibility, more genuine personal voice, in the "Propertius" where he had something to proceed from, than in "Mauberley" where he was on his own and had, so to speak, only an end in view. This fact, which perhaps cannot be demonstrated but which can be felt when the reader is familiar enough with the poems, is the key-fact of serious judgment upon Mr. Pound. It establishes his principal limitation and measures his freedom. But the quality of judgment need no more be harsh than humane; it will be judgment of kind and degree; it will help acceptance and rejection. By emphasising the talents Mr. Pound possesses, it will perhaps enlighten his defects, and explain his failures as well as his successes; but that is a critical gain more than a loss. It amounts to saying that Mr. Pound is equipped to write one kind of poetry and that when he attempts with the same equipment to write other sorts of poetry, he fails, or, at most, does not write as well.

The superiority of "Propertius" over "Mauberley," where the craftsmanship is equally skilled, may be seen analogously in Mr. Pound's earlier work. The translations are in every case more mature and more original. "The Seafarer" is better than "N.Y."; and "Cathay" is better than the epigrams in *"Lustra,"* and so on. That is, and this is the severest form in which the judgment can be framed,—lacking sufficient substance of his own to maintain an intellectual discipline, Mr. Pound is always better where the discipline of craftsmanship is enough. And this is especially true of the Cantos.

II

In the Cantos the reader who is not, at least at first, selective, will be lost, and will mistake, in this packed archipelago, every backwash for a thoroughfare, each turn of the tide for the set of an ocean current. It is the mistake of assuming that the Cantos make a good part of an ordinary, complex, logically and emotionally arrayed long poem, having as a purpose the increasing realisation of a theme. The Cantos are not complex, they are complicated; they are not arrayed by logic or driven by pursuing emotion, they are connected because they follow one another, are set side by side, and because an anecdote, an allusion, or a sentence, begun in one Canto may be continued in another and may never be completed at all; and as for a theme to be realised, they seem to have only, like "Mauberley," the general sense of continuity—not unity —which may arise in the mind when read seriatim. The Cantos are what Mr. Pound himself called them in a passage now excised from the canon, a rag-bag.

Hang it all, there can be but the one "Sordello,"
But say I want to, say I take your whole bag of tricks
Let in your quirks and tweeks, and say the thing's an art-form,
Your "Sordello," and that the "modern world"
Needs such a rag-bag to stuff all its thought in . . .
                    (*Lustra*. New York, 1917, p. 181.)

These and the following lines from Canto XI together make an adequate account of the content and one view of the method of the poem as it has so far appeared.

And they want to know what we talked about?
    "de litteris et de armis, praestantibusque ingeniis,
Both of ancient times and our own; books, arms,
And of men of unusual genius,
Both of ancient times and our own, in short, the usual subjects
Of conversation between intelligent men."

That is, we have a rag-bag of what Mr. Pound thinks is intelligent conversation about literature and history. As you pull out one rag, naturally, so well stuffed is the bag, you find it entangled with half the others. Since it is a poetical bag the entanglements are not as fortuitous as they at first seem, the connections may be examined, and some single pieces are large and handsome enough to be displayed alone.

An exhibition of the principal subject-matters in summary form should give at least the directions the poem takes. Most of the first Canto is translation from the eleventh book of the *Odyssey* where Odysseus visits hell, followed by a few lines, used as an invocation, from the second hymn to Aphrodite. The translation is not from the Greek but from a Latin version. The second Canto, after half a page of allusions to Browning, Sordello, Aeschylus, the *Iliad* and the *Odyssey,* proceeds with a translation from the third book of Ovid's *Metamorphoses* of how Acoetes found Bacchus. Then, with mixed allusions, the Tyro episode from the *Odyssey* is taken up again. The third Canto is mixed: dealing briefly with Venice, the gods, the Cid, and Ignez da Castro. The fourth Canto is a deliberate combination, rather than a mixture, of Provençal, Latin, and Japanese mythology. The fifth Canto sets Iamblichus, Catullus, the Provençal Poets, the Borgias, and the Medici side by side. The sixth Canto is twelfth century French history, Provençal poetry and Sordello, with Greek tags. The seventh Canto ties up Eleanor of Acquitaine with Helen of Troy, adds Diocletian's Arena, Ovid, a tournament, Dante, and proceeds with Flaubert and Henry James, and ends with an allusive apostrophe to the murder of Alessandro de' Medici by his cousin Lorenzino. Cantos eight through eleven concern the fifteenth century Italian despot Sigismondo Malatesta, his friends, loves, learning, and wars. The twelfth Canto is about Baldy Bacon and Jim X, two modern adventurers and is mostly anecdotal in character. By contrast, the thirteenth Canto is Chinese Philosophy in conversational form. The next three Cantos present an obscene inferno of British money, press, and war Lords, with alleviations in the form of war anecdotes. Canto seventeen returns to the classics with interspersed allusions to the Italian Renaissance. A quotation from Marco Polo begins the eighteenth Canto; modern analogues of Marco Polo fill the remainder of this and all the next Canto. The twentieth Canto mixes Provençal, fifteenth century Italian, philology, a partial resume of the *Odyssey,* and returns to the Malatesti. The Medici occupy the first part of the twenty-first Canto, classical mythology ends it. Canto twenty-two begins with economics, Indian wars, adventure in the near east, and ends with an anecdote about Florentine sumptuary legislation *circa* 1500. In Canto twenty-three appear the Platonists, modern science, the Malatesti, a poem by Stesichoros in the Greek, Provençal Troubadors, and concealed references to the first Hymn to Aphrodite. The twenty-fourth Canto is Italian scraps about the Este and Malatesti dating from 1422 to 1432. Canto twenty-five is mostly Venetian, quotes documents of the fourteenth century, letters by and about Titian of the sixteenth century, with quotations from Tibullus and Homer interlarded. Canto twenty-six centres on the Council of Florence, 1438, adds further material on the Malatesti, Medici, and Este families, quotes letters by Pisanello and Carpaccio and one about the murder of Alessandro de' Medici. Canto twenty-seven skips over several centuries and tongues and ends with a rather lovely tale about tovarisch, Xarites, and Cadmus. Canto twenty-eight is modern science, business, small wars, and adventure. Canto twenty-nine mixes the contemporary with fourteenth and fifteenth century Italian. Canto thirty begins with Artemis and Mars, touches on Ignez da Castro, and ends with the death of Pope Alessandro Borgia in 1503. Subsequent Cantos deal with American statesmen in the first quarter of the nineteenth century, particularly with Jefferson and John and John Quincy Adams.

It ought perhaps to be recalled that the full title of Mr.

Pound's poem is *A Draft of XXX Cantos*. That which is a draft is unfinished and may be altered, may gain proportion and assume order; and so sets up a *prima facie* defence against criticism on those scores. But what is deliberately not final, avowedly inchoate, lays itself open, as nothing else, to the kind of criticism in which Henry James—another craftsman—deeply and habitually delighted. James somewhere says that when he read a novel, he began immediately to rework it as he would have written it himself, had the *donnée* been presented to him. Under such an eager light all that is unfeasible in the Cantos luminously declares itself.

Most poets read a good deal and some are immoderately talkative. A draft of a poem of some length might well be written by a poet whose reading was in the sources of Anglo-Saxon law and the marriage-customs of the Aleutian Indians, subjects which to the adept may be as exciting as Ovid or the Italian condottieri—and no further from the modern reader's experience. The point is an advocate's, forensical, and had better be left in the air.

We had better deal with the Cantos as if they were finished, as if they made samples of the poem to be finished, and hence select from these samples items typical of the whole.

The first thing to notice is that the classical material is literary—translation and paraphrase; the renaissance material is almost wholly historical; and the modern material is a composition of the pseudo-autobiographical, the journalistic, and the anecdotal. Excepting the two Cantos—the first and third—which are longish translations, the narrative structure is everywhere anecdotal—and the special technique within the anecdote is that of the anecdote begun in one place, taken up in one or more other places, and finished, if at all, in still another. This deliberate disconnectedness, this art of a thing continually alluding to itself, continually breaking off short, is the method by which the Cantos tie themselves together. So soon as the reader's mind is concerted with the material of the poem, Mr. Pound deliberately disconcerts it, either by introducing fresh and disjunct material or by reverting to old and, apparently, equally disjunct material. Success comes when the reader is forced by Mr. Pound's verbal skill to take the materials together; failure, when it occurs, is when Mr. Pound's words are not skilful enough and the internal dissensions are all that can be seen, or when the reader, as often, is simply ignorant of what is being talked about.

These effects, which may seem wilful in the bad sense, are really necessary results of the anecdotal method as used by Mr. Pound. The presumption must always be, in an anecdote, that the subject and its import are known before the story is begun; they cannot be given in the anecdote itself. An anecdote illustrates, it does not present its subject; its purpose is always ulterior or secondary. Thus Mr. Pound's treatment of the *Odyssey* in the first and twentieth Cantos and *passim.,* requires, to be understood, that the reader be previously well acquainted with it. The point of the paraphrase from the Eleventh Book in the first Canto is beyond mere sound acquaintance; is perhaps that a better translation can be made through the old Latin translations than direct from the Greek: the actual subject-matter translated has no substantial bearing upon the rest of the Cantos—except in so far as it deals with a divination of the dead and serves as a general invocation. Likewise the invocation to Aphrodite which follows the passage from the *Odyssey* is, very likely, not the succour of the goddess herself, but the fact that Mr. Pound used the

[49]

same text for both paraphrases: thus that Latin is also a good medium for *The Hymns to the Gods.*[7]

The Malatesta Cantos (VIII-XI) make a different illustration of the same method. As a unit they have only the most general relation to the other Cantos. As the Cantos about Jefferson and Adams are representative of the early American Republic, these Cantos are representative of the Italian Renaissance, and the reader is at liberty to compare the two sets. It is their character within themselves that is interesting, however, rather than the external relations in which they may be enfolded. By far the longest and most detailed in treatment of a single figure, this section of the Cantos turns out to require more rather than less anterior knowledge than some of the frankly mixed Cantos (II, IV, or XXIII). The reason for the additional requirement is external to the content of the Cantos and rises from the method used by Mr. Pound in handling that content. This is that allusive method which *must* take it for granted that the object of allusion is known, and is characteristically unable to explain it: a method that cannot take account of the reader's probable state of knowledge. Americans may be expected to know something about Jefferson and the Adamses; that Jefferson and John Adams dissolved their enmity in years of correspondence, that John Quincy Adams kept a monumental diary; at least enough to make any material used by Mr. Pound relevant to the reader's existing knowledge. That is not the state of the American mind with regard to the minor history of fifteenth century Italy. Yet Mr. Pound writes as if conditions were identical; he writes as if Monticello and the Temple of Isotta were equally present and significant in the reader's mind,

---

[7] Documentary evidence for this emphasis may be found in Mr. Pound's *Instigations* (New York, 1920. pp. 334-345) where the texts in question are printed and commented upon.

and, for example, he refers to the most astonishing and bloody of the legends about Sigismondo as casually and indirectly as he might refer to the Louisiana Purchase: as if a hint and a pun would awaken complete memory. The reference is brief and will prove the point in question.

And there was the row about that German-Burgundian
     female
And it was his messianic year, Poliorcetes, but he was being a
     bit too POLUMETIS.
                        (Canto IX)

Poliorcetes was a Macedonian king and his name meant besieger of cities, and thus might fit Sigismondo who spent his life besieging cities. POLUMETIS means in the Greek, possessed of much wisdom and sagacity. The year was 1450, the year of the Jubilee at Rome. The row was because Sigismondo, finding persuasion ineffectual, stripped, murdered, and raped a Burgundian noblewoman returning from the Jubilee.

This may be taken as the extreme type of anecdotal allusion: where the meaning is ineluctable without the gloss. Other examples could be given where the difficulty is of a contrary character, where, that is, a long catalogue of names and items appears without any statement being made of the general event they catalogue. A third type may be illustrated as follows:

> Ye spirits who of old were in this land
> Each under Love, and shaken,
> Go with your lutes, awaken
> The summer within her mind,
> Who hath not Helen for peer
>   Yseut nor Batsabe.
>   (Canto VIII)

This is partly translation, partly modification, of a passage beginning *O Spreti che gia fusti in questi regny,* from a long poem written by Sigismondo in honour of Isotta degli Atti, later his third wife. The loveliness of the verse gains nothing by recovery of the origin, but the structure and sense of the Canto gain considerably.

Other parts of this section of the Cantos present none of these difficulties, and despite inversions of chronology and telescoped detail read swiftly and straightforwardly, as for example the first page and a half of Canto IX. The reader has the choice either of reading all the Cantos as if they were similarly straightforward and self-explanatory, or of going behind the verses to the same material, or as much as he can discover of it, that Mr. Pound himself used.[8] The poem the reader seizes will be very different depending on the choice he makes. In the one case, unglossed reading will give him, with many fine lines and lucid passages, the feeling that he has traversed a great deal of material, without having at any time been quite certain what the material was about,— and without, perhaps, distinguishing any need to find out. Each person was someone, each letter written, each voice spoken, each deed historical—or each invented; collected, the parts attract each other, and without the cohesive power of obvious design or continuing emotion, cling together, a quilt in the patch work, a string of rags from the inexhaustible bag. To such phrasing might appreciation run.

But an active mind will not always stop short at the uncertain, however persuasive, when the ascertainable is at hand. Then, in the second case, glossed not unreasonably with a little history, these Malatesta Cantos exhibit not greater light but more difficulty. The sum of what is discov-

[8] The principal sources of the Malatesta Cantos are an unpublished life of Sigismondo by Gaspare Broglio; Clementini, *Raccolto Istorico della Fondatione di Rimini e dell' origine e vite dei Malatesti;* and Yriarte, *Un Condottiere de XVme Siècle.* More available in English is Hutton's *Sigismondo Malatesta.*

ered as this or that, as fitting here and there, is only surpassed by what is undiscoverable. Not every word, but every
paragraph at least, requires to be situated, expanded, dated,
restored or brought up to the plain sense of history.

Not only must the reader know exactly what books Mr.
Pound used but must himself use them in the way Mr. Pound
used them. When he discovers that "But dey got de mos'
bloody rottenes' peace on us" is Mr. Pound's equivalent for
Broglio's statement that the Pope imposed a bad peace, he
will not be so much pleased with his acumen as irritated by
the probability that many other lines are equally, but undis-
coverably, quirky. In short, at the maximum vantage of half-
instructed guessing, he will be convinced he was much better
off, and the Cantos were better poetry, when he was ignorant
of the intricacy of their character; and the conviction will
be supported by the reflection that though the Cantos led him
to history, the history did not lead him back to the Cantos.

Instruction, instead of diminishing, emphasised the anecdotal character of the poetry. Mr. Pound put together the
materials and roused the interest appropriate to a narrative,
and then deliberately refused the materials a narrative form,
without, however, destroying the interests that expected it.
Whether intentionally or not, it is the presence of this defeated
expectation which holds these Cantos together. That is the
attraction which the parts exert over each other; an attraction
which constantly makes the Cantos seem on the point of
re-arranging themselves in an order quite different from the
printed order, and quite different, also, from the historical
order upon which the printed order is founded. But this third
order is not achieved; there is a clog, a stoppage, at the point
of crisis, and the Cantos fall back in the dismay of choices
that cannot be made. Climax, what happens when things

meet in a form and have ending, is rejected for the inchoate, the anecdotal, the deliberately confused, a jungle.

Jungle:
Glaze green and red feathers, jungle,
Basis of renewal, renewals;
Rising over the soul, green virid, of the jungle,
Lozenge of the pavement, clear shapes,
Broken, disrupted, body eternal,
Wilderness of renewals, confusion
Basis of renewals, subsistence,
Glazed green of the jungle; . . .

(Canto XX)

These phrases, upon which variations appear at least twice elsewhere in the Cantos, may, in association with the two passages quoted above about rag-bags and the subjects of conversation, be taken as Mr. Pound's declaration of doctrine. They make the "philosophic" basis, itself in anecdotal form, for the theory of sequence and structure observed in the Cantos. If the reader can accept this basis, or something like it, or can substitute for it an analogous feeling for confusion in his own soul, he will be able to accept most of the Cantos on their own terms. They will have become their own sub-ject-matter, their own end, and their own "philosophy." [9] Then the only test will be whether a passage put in question was or was not, by a saltatory action of the mind, an extension of the reader's own confusion. This view may appeal to many who take their art as the impact of experience regardless, and

[9] Mr. Pound is not a philosopher and the term is put in quotes to represent that something quite the opposite of a philosophy is being used as if it were one. A deep, but vague, feeling is made to act with the controlling power of a rigid, intellectual system. Both the depth and the vagueness are indicated when it is remembered that the Cantos accept Dante, the most orderly and rigidly systematic of poets, and that their object is in some sense analogous to that of the *Divine Comedy:* to array and judge centuries of years and individ-uals.

to whom the object of appreciation is inarticulate exhilaration. It has the extreme quality of all personal views; a quality whose maximal value is only established by surrender to it. Our concern here is only with Mr. Pound's demand that the view be taken, and we need merely grant a provisional assent to it, in order to judge the Cantos in spite of it.

Confusion, that is, is for Mr. Pound a deliberate element of procedure; but its success—such is the unitary character of language and hence of thought in language—will depend upon how well the things confused are known. Chaos is an absolute bliss which the mind may envisage but cannot reach in affirmation; there is a logic in the wildest association which the mind cannot help seizing when it sees it and which is ineffably irritating when, although suspected, it cannot be seized because it is unseen. The Malatesta Cantos furnish examples of confusion where the objects confused may at least be assumed as discoverable; and it is possible that the assumption is as good as the fact: the material is recorded history. In the following extract from Canto XXVIII no similar assumption can be made or if made cannot be similarly effective.

> And Mrs. Kreffle's mind was made up,
> Perhaps by the pressure of circumstance,
> She described her splendid apartment
> In Paris and left without paying her bill
> And in fact she wrote later from Sevilla
> And requested a shawl, and received it
> From the Senora at 300 pesetas cost to the latter
> (Also without remitting) which
> May have explained the lassitude of her daughter.

This, so far as can be determined, is one of Mr. Pound's completely personal contributions. He wrote it, or invented it, himself; and it has no probable source in literature or history. It is a pointless thumbnail sketch, one among the thirty-odd which in these Cantos represent our own age. It is Mr. Pound unsupported and insupportable: the pure anecdote; and there is nothing the reader can do about it.

The only assumption that can be made is that the anecdote meant something to Mr. Pound—something he didn't like but was mildly amused by. Seriously, it is a kind of dated journalism about which not enough can be known to make it important and which is not well enough written to permit enjoyment of the medium to replace knowledge of the subject. The subject failed to compel the craftsman and it came out flat. The translation from Ovid (*Metamorphoses* III, 580, ff.) in Canto III is equally anecdotal in treatment but it contains some of Mr. Pound's best writing and it has the existing literary monument to support the writing with subject and point. As soon as we know that it is about Bacchus we are at home and can appreciate as in the "Propertius" what Mr. Pound has done with the text. Mrs. Kreffle we cannot feel at home with because neither in literature nor in history did she give Mr. Pound anything to do.

The moral is plain. As our earlier comparison of "Propertius" and "Mauberley" suggested, Mr. Pound is at his best and most original when his talents are controlled by an existing text; and he is at his worst and, in the pejorative sense, most conventional, when he has to provide the subject as well as the workmanship.

We have examined the extremes of pure literature (the "Propertius" which may be thought of as resembling in this sense Cantos I and III), pure history (the Malatesta Cantos) and the personal contribution (Mrs. Kreffle). There remain certain combinations and modifications of these which exemplify the Cantos in their most interesting and important aspects.

Canto IV begins with an apostrophe to burning Troy, Apollo in his attribute as lord of the lyre (Anaxiforminges), Aurunculeia (the family name of the lady whose wedding is celebrated by Catullus in Carmen LXI), and Cadmus of Golden Prows who, among other things, was supposed to have invented the alphabet. Then follow two combinations of classical and Provençal material. The myth of Itys and Tereus (Ovid *Metam.* VI, 620, ff.) is combined with the story of the death of Cabestan, a Provençal troubadour who flourished about 1196. The story goes that Cabestan loved the lady Soremonda, and that her husband, Sir Raymond, discovering the intrigue, slew Cabestan and brought home his head and heart. The heart he roasted and seasoned with pepper. After his wife had eaten of the dish he told her what it was, showing her the head, whereupon she cast herself down from the balcony. The passage in Mr. Pound's Canto is not a version of this story but a reference to it; and the important thing about the reference is that it completes the references to the myth of Itys with which the Cabestan material is prefaced and concluded. Though description is complicated, Mr. Pound's verses are simple and once the objects of reference are known, immediately apprehensible.

The same Canto proceeds with a combination of the legend of Peire Vidal and the myth of Actaeon and Diana (Ovid, *Metam.* III, 170, ff.). Here the combination is carried further and becomes a uniting. Vidal mutters Ovid and identifies himself with Actaeon; which is perhaps Mr. Pound's explanation of Vidal's recorded behaviour. Loving a woman named Loba of Penautier, and being a little mad, Vidal called himself Lop, dressed as a wolf, ran wild in the mountains of Cabaret, where he was hunted down and brought in more dead than alive. Here again it is the comparison, the anthropological identification of different materials that is impor-

tant rather than the materials *per se*. No one not knowing
the original material could appreciate the point of these
verses. The allusions are not illustrative but indicative of a
subject.

In the next Canto begins Mr. Pound's treatment of the
assassination of Alessandro de' Medici by his cousin
Lorenzino, which is taken up or referred to throughout the
poem. This material is on a different plane and is worked up
with a different type of allusion from the two examples
above, but the intent is the same: analogous murders are
brought to bear on each other as if the verses had an anthropological bias and were at least as much a labour in comparative mythology as Ovid would have made them.

The narration is Mr. Pound's version of Benedetto Varchi's
original account. Varchi thinks of Brutus which would have
been natural to the contemporary student of Renaissance
murder, and Mr. Pound, as a classicist, as naturally thinks of
Agamemnon and quotes, in the Greek, from Aeschylus' play
parts of two lines dealing with Agamemnon's death. Later
appears the Italian phrase *Caina attende,* referring to Dante's
Inferno (XXXII) where those who commit Cain's sin are
found in a lake of ice. Then follows an allusion to the astro-
logical prophecy of the murder made in Perugia by Del
Carmine. And so on. The point for emphasis is that the
murder itself is not described; nor is more than the favourable
and alternative motive of patriotism indicated. What was
important for Mr. Pound was what the murder made it
possible to allude to. In this instance the connections are
comparatively ascertainable, or are superfluous, or can be
guessed. The verse, and especially its continuation at the end
of Canto VII, is vivid and excellent; the density of reference
and the clarity of image together give the effect of immitigable

substance, of which the particles, as it were, are in indefinable but necessary association.

This association, this tight cohesiveness, is the characteristic of the Cantos—it is almost their idiosyncrasy—upon which their success depends and from which result their many breaches with success. It is this effect which Mr. Pound uses instead of syllogistic logic, instead of narrative, and instead of plot. He leaves in disuse devices which would by their traditional force have ensured the strong and valuable effect of parade, of things coming one after another in an order more or less predictable by the reader's aroused expectation, and has chosen rather to depend on the device of a single method —the method of free ideogrammatic association.

Freedoms have their limits and invoke their own penalties. The Cantos overstep the one and are apparently oblivious of the other; which, while it may be one of the appropriate attitudes towards experiment, is not an attitude from which a poet can handle his work with any degree of certainty about the result. The helter-skelter appearance of the Cantos, the frequency with which they bring up or drop off short, their sudden leaps and pointless halts—these effects are not only wilful but are a necessary consequence of a method which, used exclusively, cannot but be misunderstood both by the poet and by his readers.

Let us examine the limitations as they proceed from a provisional declaration of principle. Mr. Pound wishes to bring together the subjects of intelligent conversation in such a way that their association will make the one significant in terms of the others, will make the one criticise the others, and so satisfy a purpose which amounts to the ethical in the issue of a hierarchy of values. He has himself set up his categories in a letter to *The New English Weekly* (Vol. III, No. 4. 11 May 1933). After denying that his poem has a dualistic basis and asserting that it should establish a hierarchy of values, he concludes: "If the reader wants three categories he can find them rather better in: permanent, recurrent, and merely haphazard or casual." Archetypes would perhaps be the myth of Itys and Terreus, the story of Cabestan, and, say, Mrs. Kreffle. The Malatesta Cantos mix all three categories into a fourth unnamed category. Another, equally useful set of archetypes would be the literary monument (Homer, Ovid, Dante), history (the Medici, the Malatesti), and journalism (Mrs. Kreffle, Baldy Bacon). A third set might be thought, act, and the merely phenomenal. The Cantos furnish evidence for numerous analogous triads. Two phrases quoted at important junctures in the Cantos are: *Formando di disio nuova persona* and *Et omniformis omnis intellectus est,* the first from Cavalcanti and the second from Psellos, each of which implies a triad in itself.

If with such categories in mind Mr. Pound wishes to combine his material as nearly as possible by the method of free association exclusively, it is fair to assume, leaving aside as obvious the questions of interest and ultimate cogency, that each such association should either contain, like the characters in a novel, a satisfying account of its terms, or should be immediately apperceptible to readers in a certain state of cultivation, or should be accompanied by a gloss. With the possible exception of the Malatesta Cantos and the longer translations from Homer and Ovid, Mr. Pound nowhere accounts for his material in the text. The poem, unlike the poems of Homer, Dante, and Milton, is addressed not to the general intelligence of its time, nor to an unusually cultivated class merely, but to a specially educated class alone, a class familiar with exactly the material Mr. Pound uses but does not present. And here the Cantos differ from such works as Joyce's *Ulysses,* the long poems of Blake, or the poetry of Crashaw, in that it is neither the structural framework and some of the ornament, nor the key to the meaning that is hidden in symbolism, complex allusion, and difficult thought, but the substance of the poem itself. The movement of the reader's mind is thus either from the poem as a unit to the verse as such, or from the poem to the material alluded to. Thus the poem is either lost in the original or becomes an attachment to it: is scholia not poetry.

Yet Mr. Pound must write and his poem must be read as if the poem were of first and only importance. That is where the limits of Mr. Pound's practice of association begin to exert themselves at least in a negative fashion. Those associations which come, not most readily to the ignorant but most keenly to the instructed mind are those which—like the combination of Ovidian myth and Provençal biography—are most susceptible to a complete gloss. The obscurity is so easily cleared up that it no longer seems to exist, and the reader comes away with the feeling that elements in his own mind have been so compounded as to add to his sensibility. For different readers different associations will be similarly successful, not so much because of different degrees of intelligence as because of different quantities of information. When the associations seem only to be a series of apostrophes, juxtapositions, and interpolations it will be the lack of appropriate information in the reader's mind that makes them seem so; and no amount of perspicuous good will can make up for that lack. To repeat: it is not the meaning but the very subject of the thing meant that must be hunted down. This is the positive limitation of Mr. Pound's method. The adequacy of his data to the ends he has in view must often depend on improbable accident. Let one example carry the weight of many arguments. At the end of Canto XXIII occur these lines in a context containing references to Troy and Anchises:

> "King Otreus, of Phrygia,
> That king is my father."

From Mr. Pound's point of view the use of this quotation, which in itself contains nothing remarkable and enlists no profound sentiment, is highly illuminating to the association he had in mind. When the exact origin is revealed the subject appears and the association is completed. But conjecture is almost a certainty that the reader not only will not know but will not exactly find out that the quotation comes from the first Hymn to Aphrodite and represents the goddess hiding her identity to Anchises before lying with him and becoming thus the mother of Aeneas. For such a reader the quotation is a breach of limits and the association fails because its technique demanded certainty of conditions external to the poem and inherently unpredictable: in this case an intensive and minute familiarity with the Homeric *Hymns to the Gods*.

Such are the limits that must needs be passed; the penalties of this technique are even more severe and arise from the same characteristics considered from another angle. As limitations are external and imposed from without, so penalties are internal and are a direct consequence of germinal character. The forms of expression are not rigid and their differences are perhaps not primitive. They may be reduced hypothetically to rudimentary agitations, signs of recognition or dismay; but the attempt, which Mr. Pound makes, to use a verbal language ideographically, to think in English words as if they carried the same sort of burden as Chinese characters,—such an attempt must not only often fail of objective form but even when it approximates that form, as in the Ovid-Provençal material, it is incapable of the higher effects

of either kind of expression used singly—much as hog-latin
is incapable of supplication. It is less that the familiar forms
of western logic are done away with than that they persist in
seeming to do work that they are not meant to do. The
western reader—at whom doubtless the Cantos are aimed—
will necessarily expect that the chief uses to which Mr. Pound
puts his language will be similar, or adjustable, to his own.
Neither the reader nor Mr. Pound can defeat these expectations by the assertion, however deliberate, that different
expectations are in order. The intent may be made clear but
the effect cannot transpire. In the passage from Canto XX
about the jungle quoted above, the reader may appreciate the
word "lozenge," can guess the seriousness of the intent, and
will know that the effect is of lesser dimension than the words
demanded. Here, as elsewhere where important matters are
in hand, the conclusion must be that Mr. Pound has described
his method, indicated his material, and used neither in terms
of the other.

It is irrelevant to speculate as to the possible success of an
ideographic method applied to ideographic symbols; Mr.
Pound has not made that experiment. He has proved, rather,
the impossibility of combining an ideographic structure and
a language whose logic is verbal without to a considerable
extent vitiating the virtues of both. And his successes may be
used against him. Whether his method be called free-association, ideography, or something else, where that method is
solely in evidence the result is unintelligible, trivial, or
vacantly conventional. Where the method is in abeyance, or
where in spite of its presence more familiar methods of
expression supersede it, Mr. Pound has written passages of
extraordinary beauty and clarity. If most of these passages
are to be found in translations, or where an original text has
been re-modelled, it only shows what a terrible penalty Mr.

Pound has imposed on work of his own invention by adopting his peculiar method, the penalty, in shortest description, of stultification. And the stultification arises of necessity because Mr. Pound has not seen that the idiosyncracy of thought in English is established by the idiosyncracy of the language itself.

The judgment that flows from this essay needs hardly be stated; it is judgment by description. But the description may be recapitulated and will perhaps gather point by condensation. Mr. Pound's poetry has had from the beginning one constant character which qualifies deeply and subordinates to it every other character. It has been deliberately constructed as a series of surfaces or *personae*; it is a mask of Mr. Pound's best craftsmanship through which the voices of old times and our own are meant to be heard. Because the medium is verse, and private, the voices are an integral part of the mask, but whether because of choice or some radical limitation of talent, the voices are as a rule given indirectly, by allusive quotation or analphabetical catalogue, and this is truer of Mr. Pound's original verse than of his translations. That is, the subject-matter of his verse is, as it were, behind the mask and apart from it in spite of the intention to the contrary, so that the reader is prevented from contact with the subject-matter through the verse.

The success of Mr. Pound's mask depends on the critical labour performed, in which, before the success is apparent, the reader must share. The reader must know the original or enough of it to apprehend the surface Mr. Pound has made for it, exactly as the Roman audience had to know the substance of the myths they heard recounted through the actor's *personae*. For Mr. Pound's verse is not something new, substantially on its own feet, it is a surface set upon something already existing.

When, as in "Mauberley" the subject begins by being something comparatively his own, a consequence of private experience, it is changed as rapidly as possible, not into something objective and independent, but into something conventional and hidden, wholly dependent for existence upon the surface under which it is hidden. In "Propertius" the procedure is contrary; the subject of what Mr. Pound does in his homage is the criticism of a subject rationally preserved in the verse. The fact of translation and the criticism involved in Mr. Pound's selective, condensing, emphatic method of translation together guarantee the original subject and make it Mr. Pound's own.

The Cantos may be most easily read as a combination, both as to method and subject, of "Mauberley" and "Propertius." The translations, under this view, secure the greatest success; the summaries such as the Malatesta Cantos rank second and the personal contributions third because the substance criticised, that is, given the form of a mask, is not sufficiently present in the parts which are not translation for the reader to apprehend it.

There is a secondary kind of success when the reader, by private research, is able to re-import the substance—as he may in the Ovid-Provençal episodes. The reader is not always able, and sometimes though able, as in the Malatesta Cantos, cannot grant the poem success because, again, Mr. Pound has not provided a critical enough surface for the substance, however acquired, to fill out. The reward of research cannot be guaranteed and the reader must choose whether or not to risk the work. This is because Mr. Pound while composing a poem of surfaces, a *persona,* has ignored the necessity that every convention have its second party subscribing to the terms on which the convention is laid down. The nature of conventions is agreement between the archetype and the instance and between the poet and his readers. Where a convention was initially successful as in the Medici-Agamemnon episode, failure for most readers was inevitable because of the free-association or ideographic method of subsequent treatment, wherein Mr. Pound became himself the victim of a method he could not use.

As suggested above the stultification of the Cantos as a whole rises from an intellectual attitude either insufficient or foreign to the idiosyncrasy of the English language. If the uses of language include expression, communication, and the clear exhibition of ideas, Mr. Pound is everywhere a master of his medium so long as the matter in hand is not his own, is translation or paraphrase; everywhere else, whether in putting his translations together or in original material, the language has an air of solipsism and bewildered intent. The contrast is too sharp and constant to explain as intermittence of talent, and must rather be due to an essential alteration, occurring when responsibility is removed, in the poet's attitude towards language itself. That is the judgment of this essay—upon which of course it may collapse—that Mr. Pound, however he may have stretched and sharpened his private sensibility, has by his raids upon ideograms and unsupported allusions, limited and dulled that of his poetry: the mask of the Cantos seems too often a camouflage.

There remain—and the pity is the greater because they are remnants—the actually hundreds of magnificent lines and passages. In an earlier version of the Cantos there was a line, now excised, which fits very well the whole poem: "A catalogue, his jewels of conversation." The Cantos are an anthology of such jewels and read as most people read anthologies, as indeed all but a few read any sort of poetry, for the felicity of line and phrase, for strangeness, or for an echoed aptness of sentiment, the reader can afford to forget the promise and ambition of which the poem cheated him. He will have been equally cheated in all but the smallest part of his reading.

1933

III

EXAMPLES OF WALLACE STEVENS

THE most striking if not the most important thing about
Mr. Stevens' verse is its vocabulary—the collection of
words, many of them uncommon in English poetry, which
on a superficial reading seems characteristic of the poems.
An air of preciousness bathes the mind of the casual reader
when he finds such words as fubbed, girandoles, curlicues,
catarrhs, gobbet, diaphanes, clopping, minuscule, pipping,
pannicles, carked, ructive, rapey, cantilene, buffo, fiscs, phylactery, princox, and funest. And such phrases as "thrum
with a proud douceur," or "A pool of pink, clippered with
lilies scudding the bright chromes," hastily read, merely
increase the feeling of preciousness. Hence Mr. Stevens has
a bad reputation among those who dislike the finicky, and a
high one, unfortunately, among those who value the ornamental sounds of words but who see no purpose in developing
sound from sense.

Both classes of reader are wrong. Not a word listed above
is used preciously; not one was chosen as an elegant substitute for a plain term; each, in its context, was a word
definitely meant. The important thing about Mr. Stevens'
vocabulary is not the apparent oddity of certain words, but
the uses to which he puts those words with others. It is the
way that Mr. Stevens combines kinds of words, unusual in a
single context, to reveal the substance he had in mind, which
is of real interest to the reader.

Good poets gain their excellence by writing an existing
language *as if* it were their own invention; and as a rule suc-

cess in the effect of originality is best secured by fidelity, in an extreme sense, to the individual words as they appear in the dictionary. If a poet knows precisely what his words represent, what he writes is much more likely to seem new and strange—and even difficult to understand—, than if he uses his words ignorantly and at random. That is because when each word has definite character the combinations cannot avoid uniqueness. Even if a text is wholly quotation, the condition of quotation itself qualifies the text and makes it so far unique. Thus a quotation made from Marvell by Eliot has a force slightly different from what it had when Marvell wrote it. Though the combination of words is unique it is read, if the reader knows his words either by usage or dictionary, with a shock like that of recognition. The recognition is not limited, however, to what was already known in the words; there is a perception of something previously unknown, something new which is a result of the combination of the words, something which is literally an access of knowledge. Upon the poet's skill in combining words as much as upon his private feelings, depends the importance or the value of the knowledge.

In some notes on the language of E. E. Cummings I tried to show how that poet, by relying on his private feelings and using words as if their meanings were spontaneous with use, succeeded mainly in turning his words into empty shells. With very likely no better inspiration in the life around him, Mr. Stevens, by combining the insides of those words he found fit to his feelings, has turned his words into knowledge. Both Mr. Stevens and Cummings issue in ambiguity—as any good poet does; but the ambiguity of Cummings is that of the absence of known content, the ambiguity of a phantom which no words could give being; while Mr. Stevens' ambiguity is that of a substance so dense with being, that it resists paraphrase and can be truly perceived only in the form of words in which it was given. It is the difference between poetry which depends on the poet and poetry which depends on itself. Reading Cummings you either guess or supply the substance yourself. Reading Mr. Stevens you have only to know the meanings of the words and to submit to the conditions of the poem. There is a precision in such ambiguity all the more precise because it clings so closely to the stuff of the poem that separated it means nothing.

Take what would seem to be the least common word in the whole of *Harmonium* [1]—funest (page 74, line 6.) The word means sad or calamitous or mournful and is derived from a French word meaning fatal, melancholy, baneful, and has to do with death and funerals. It comes ultimately from the latin *funus* for funeral. Small dictionaries do not stock it. The poem in which it appears is called "Of the Manner of addressing Clouds," which begins as follows:

> Gloomy grammarians in golden gowns,
> Meekly you keep the mortal rendezvous,
> Eliciting the still sustaining pomps
> Of speech which are like music so profound
> They seem an exaltation without sound.
> Funest philosophers and ponderers,
> Their evocations are the speech of clouds.
> So speech of your processionals returns
> In the casual evocations of your tread
> Across the stale, mysterious seasons. . . .

The sentence in which funest occurs is almost a parenthesis. It *seems* the statement of something thought of by the way, suggested by the clouds, which had better be said at once before it is forgotten. In such a casual, disarming way,

---

[1] The references are to the new edition of *Harmonium*. New York: Alfred A. Knopf, 1931. This differs from the first edition in that three poems have been cut out and fourteen added.

resembling the way of understatement, Mr. Stevens often introduces the most important elements in his poems. The oddity of the word having led us to look it up we find that, once used, funest is better than any of its synonyms. It is the essence of the funeral in its sadness, not its sadness alone, that makes it the right word: the clouds are going to their death, as not only philosophers but less indoctrinated ponderers know; so what they say, what they evoke, in pondering, has that much in common with the clouds. Suddenly we realise that the effect of funest philosophers is due to the larger context of the lines preceding, and at the same time we become aware that the statement about their evocations is central to the poem and illuminates it. The word pomps, above, means ceremony and comes from a greek word meaning procession, often, by association, a funeral, as in the phrase funeral pomps. So the pomps of the clouds suggests the funeral in funest.

The whole thing increases in ambiguity the more it is analysed, but if the poem is read over after analysis, it will be seen that *in the poem* the language is perfectly precise. In its own words it is clear, and becomes vague in analysis only because the analysis is not the poem. We use analysis properly in order to discard it and return that much better equipped to the poem.

The use of such a word as funest suggests more abstract considerations, apart from the present instance. The question is whether or not and how much the poet is stretching his words when they are made to carry as much weight as funest carries above. Any use of a word stretches it slightly, because any use selects from among many meanings the right one, and then modifies that in the context. Beyond this necessary stretching, words cannot perhaps be stretched without coming to nullity—as the popular stretching of awful, grand, swell, has more or less nullified the original senses of those words. If Mr. Stevens stretches his words slightly, as a live poet should and must, it is in such a way as to make them seem more precisely themselves than ever. The context is so delicately illuminated, or adumbrated, that the word must be looked up, or at least thought carefully about, before the precision can be seen. This is the precision of the expert pun, and every word, to a degree, carries with it in any given sense the puns of all its senses.

But it may be a rule that only the common words of a language, words with several, even groups of meanings, can be stretched the small amount that is possible. The reader must have room for his research; and the more complex words are usually plays upon common words, and limited in their play. In the instance above the word funest is not so much itself stretched by its association with philosophers as the word philosophers—a common word with many senses—stretches funest. That is, because Mr. Stevens has used the word funest, it cannot easily be detached and used by others. The point is subtle. The meaning so doubles upon itself that it can be understood only in context. It is the context that is stretched by the insertion of the word funest; and it is that stretch, by its ambiguity, that adds to our knowledge.

A use of words almost directly contrary to that just discussed may be seen in a very different sort of poem—"The Ordinary Women" (page 13). I quote the first stanza to give the tone:

> Then from their poverty they rose,
> From dry catarrhs, and to guitars
> They flitted
> Through the palace walls.

Then skipping a stanza, we have this, for atmosphere:

> The lacquered loges huddled there
> Mumbled zay-zay and a-zay, a-zay.
> The moonlight
> Fubbed the girandoles.

The loges huddled probably because it was dark or because they didn't like the ordinary women, and mumbled perhaps because of the moonlight, perhaps because of the catarrhs, or even to keep key to the guitars. Moonlight, for Mr. Stevens, is mental, fictive, related to the imagination and meaning of things; naturally it fubbed the girandoles (which is equivalent to cheated the chandeliers, was stronger than the artificial light, if any) . . . Perhaps and probably but no doubt something else. I am at loss, and quite happy there, to know anything literally about this poem. Internally, inside its own words, I know it quite well by simple perusal. The charm of the rhymes is enough to carry it over any stile. The strange phrase, "Fubbed the girandoles," has another charm, like that of the rhyme, and as inexplicable: the approach of language, through the magic of elegance, to nonsense. That the phrase is not nonsense, that on inspection it retrieves itself to sense, is its inner virtue. Somewhere between the realms of ornamental sound and representative statement, the words pause and balance, dissolve and resolve. This is the mood of Euphues, and presents a poem with fine parts controlled internally by little surds of feeling that save both the poem and its parts from preciousness. The ambiguity of this sort of writing consists in the double importance of both sound and sense where neither has direct connection with the other but where neither can stand alone. It is as if Mr. Stevens wrote two poems at once with the real poem somewhere between, unwritten but vivid.

A poem which exemplifies not the approach merely but actual entrance into nonsense is "Disillusionment of Ten

O'Clock" (page 88). This poem begins by saying that houses are haunted by white nightgowns, not nightgowns of various other colours, and ends with these lines:

> People are not going
> To dream of baboons and periwinkles.
> Only, here and there, an old sailor,
> Drunk and asleep in his boots,
> Catches tigers
> In red weather.

The language is simple and declarative. There is no doubt about the words or the separate statements. Every part of the poem makes literal sense. Yet the combination makes a nonsense, and a nonsense much more convincing than the separate sensible statements. The statement about catching tigers in red weather coming after the white nightgowns and baboons and periwinkles, has a persuasive force out of all relation to the sense of the words. Literally, there is nothing alarming in the statement, and nothing ambiguous, but by so putting the statement that it appears as nonsense, infinite possibilities are made terrifying and plain. The shock and virtue of nonsense is this: it compels us to scrutinise the words in such a way that we see the enormous ambiguity in the substance of every phrase, every image, every word. The simpler the words are the more impressive and certain is the ambiguity. Half our sleeping knowledge is in nonsense; and when put in a poem it wakes.

The edge between sense and nonsense is shadow thin, and in all our deepest convictions we hover in the shadow, uncertain whether we know what our words mean, nevertheless bound by the conviction to say them. I quote the second half of "The Death of a Soldier" (page 129):

> Death is absolute and without memorial,
> As in a season of autumn,

> When the wind stops,
> When the wind stops and, over the heavens,
> The clouds go, nevertheless,
> In their direction.

To gloss such a poem is almost impertinent, but I wish to observe that in the passage just quoted, which is the important half of the poem, there is an abstract statement, "Death is absolute and without memorial," followed by the notation of a natural phenomenon. The connection between the two is not a matter of course; it is syntactical, poetic, human. The point is, by combining the two, Mr. Stevens has given his abstract statement a concrete, sensual force; he has turned a conviction, an idea, into a feeling which did not exist, even in his own mind, until he had put it down in words. The feeling is not exactly in the words, it is because of them. As in the body sensations are definite but momentary, while feelings are ambiguous (with reference to sensations) but lasting; so in this poem the words are definite but instant, while the feelings they raise are ambiguous (with reference to the words) and have importance. Used in this way, words, like sensations, are blind facts which put together produce a feeling no part of which was in the data. We cannot say, abstractly, in words, any better what we know, yet the knowledge has become positive and the conviction behind it indestructible, because it has been put into words. That is one business of poetry, to use words to give quality and feeling to the precious abstract notions, and so doing to put them beyond words and beyond the sense of words.

A similar result from a different mode of the use of words may be noticed in such a poem as "The Emperor of Ice-Cream" (page 85):

> Call the roller of big cigars,
> The muscular one, and bid him whip

In kitchen cups concupiscent curds.
Let the wenches dawdle in such dress
As they are used to wear, and let the boys
Bring flowers in last month's newspapers.
Let be be finale of seem.
The only emperor is the emperor of ice-cream.

Take from the dresser of deal,
Lacking the three glass knobs, that sheet
On which she embroidered fantails once
And spread it so as to cover her face.
If her horny feet protrude, they come
To show how cold she is, and dumb.
Let the lamp affix its beam.
The only emperor is the emperor of ice-cream.

The poem might be called Directions for a Funeral, with
Two Epitaphs. We have a corpse laid out in the bedroom
and we have people in the kitchen. The corpse is dead; then
let the boys bring flowers in last month's (who would use
to-day's?) newspapers. The corpse is dead; but let the
wenches wear their everyday clothes—or is it the clothes
they are used to wear at funerals? The conjunction of a
muscular man whipping desirable desserts in the kitchen
and the corpse protruding horny feet, gains its effect because
of its oddity—not of fact, but of expression: the light
frivolous words and rapid metres. Once made the conjunction is irretrievable and in its own measure exact. Two ideas
or images about death—the living and the dead—have been
associated, and are now permanently fused. If the mind is a
rag-bag, pull out two rags and sew them together. If the
materials were contradictory, the very contradiction, made
permanent, becomes a kind of unison. By associating ambiguities found in nature in a poem we reach a clarity, a kind
of transfiguration even, whereby we learn *what* the ambiguity
was.

The point is, that the oddity of association would not have its effect without the couplets which conclude each stanza with the pungency of good epitaphs. Without the couplets the association would sink from wit to low humor or simple description. What, then, do the couplets mean? Either, or both, of two things. In the more obvious sense, "Let be be finale of seem," in the first stanza, means, take what ever seems to be, as really being; and in the second stanza, "Let the lamp affix its beam," means let it be plain that this woman is dead, that these things, impossibly ambiguous as they may be, are as they are. In this case, "The only emperor is the emperor of ice-cream," implies in both stanzas that the only power worth heeding is the power of the moment, of what is passing, of the flux.

The less obvious sense of the couplets is more difficult to set down because, in all its difference, it rises out of the first sense, and while contradicting and supplanting, yet guarantees it. The connotation is, perhaps, that ice-cream and what it represents is the only power *heeded,* not the only power there is to heed. The irony recoils on itself: what seems *shall* finally be; the lamp *shall* affix its beam. The only emperor is the emperor of ice-cream. The king is dead; long live the king.

The virtue of the poem is that it discusses and settles these matters without mentioning them. The wit of the couplets does the work.

Allied to the method of this poem is the method of much of "Le Monocle de mon Oncle." The light word is used with a more serious effect than the familiar, heavy words commonly chosen in poems about the nature of love. I take these lines from the first stanza (page 16):

> The sea of spuming thought foists up again
> The radiant bubble that she was. And then

> A deep up-pouring from some saltier well
> Within me, bursts its watery syllable.

The words foist and bubble are in origin and have remained
in usage both light. One comes from a word meaning to
palm false dice, and the other is derived by imitation from a
gesture of the mouth. Whether the history of the words was
present in Mr. Stevens' mind when he chose them is immaterial; the pristine flavour is still active by tradition and is
what gives the rare taste to the lines quoted. By employing
them in connection with a sea of spuming thought and the
notion of radiance whatever vulgarity was in the two words
is purged. They gain force while they lend their own lightness to the context; and I think it is the lightness of these
words that permits and conditions the second sentence in the
quotation, by making the contrast between the foisted bubble
and the bursting syllable possible.

Stanza IV of the same poem (pages 17-18) has a serious
trope in which apples and skulls, love and death, are closely
associated in subtle and vivid language. An apple, Mr.
Stevens says, is as good as any skull to read because, like the
skull, it finally rots away in the ground. The stanza ends
with these lines:

> But it excels in this, that as the fruit
> Of love, it is a book too mad to read
> Before one merely reads to pass the time.

The light elegance and conversational tone give the stanza
the cumulative force of understatement, and make it seem
to carry a susurrus of irony between the lines. The word
excels has a good deal to do with the success of the passage;
superficially a syntactical word as much as anything else,
actually, by its literal sense it saves the lines from possible
triviality.

We have been considering poems where the light tone increases the gravity of the substance, and where an atmosphere of wit and elegance assures poignancy of meaning. It is only a step or so further to that use of language where tone and atmosphere are very nearly equivalent to substance and meaning themselves. "Sea Surface Full of Clouds" (page 132) has many lines and several images in its five sections which contribute by their own force to the sense of the poem, but it would be very difficult to attach special importance to any one of them. The burden of the poem is the colour and tone of the whole. It is as near a tone-poem, in the musical sense, as language can come. The sense of single lines cannot profitably be abstracted from the context, and literal analysis does nothing but hinder understanding. We may say, if we like, that Mr. Stevens found himself in ecstasy—that he stood aside from himself emotionally—before the spectacle of endlessly varied appearances of California seas off Tehuantepec; and that he has tried to equal the complexity of what he saw in the technical intricacy of his poem. But that is all we can say. Neither the material of the poem nor what we get out of it is by nature susceptible of direct treatment in words. It might at first seem more a painter's subject than a poet's, because its interest is more obviously visual and formal than mental. Such an assumption would lead to apt criticism if Mr. Stevens had tried, in his words, to present a series of seascapes with a visual atmosphere to each picture. His intention was quite different and germane to poetry; he wanted to present the tone, in the mind, of five different aspects of the sea. The strictly visual form is in the background, merely indicated by the words; it is what the visual form gave off after it had been felt in the mind that concerned him. Only by the precise interweaving of association and suggestion, by the development of a delicate verbal pattern, could he secure the overtones that possessed him. A looser form would have captured nothing.

The choice of certain elements in the poem may seem arbitrary, but it is an arbitrariness without reference to their rightness and wrongness. That is, any choice would have been equally arbitrary, and, aesthetically, equally right. In the second stanza of each section, for example, one is reminded of different kinds of chocolate and different shades of green, thus: rosy chocolate and paradisal green; chop-house chocolate and sham-like green; porcelain chocolate and uncertain green; musky chocolate and too-fluent green; chinese chocolate and motley green. And each section gives us umbrellas variously gilt, sham, pied, frail, and large. The ocean is successively a machine which is perplexed, tense, tranced, dry, and obese. The ocean produces seablooms from the clouds, mortal massives of the blooms of water, silver petals of white blooms, figures of the clouds like blooms, and, finally, a wind of green blooms. These items, and many more, repeated and modified, at once impervious to and merging each in the other, make up the words of the poem. Directly they do nothing but rouse the small sensations and smaller feelings of atmosphere and tone. The poem itself, what it means, is somewhere in the background; we know it through the tone. The motley hue we see is crisped to "clearing opalescence."

> Then the sea
> And heaven rolled as one and from the two
> Came fresh transfigurings of freshest blue.

Here we have words used as a tone of feeling to secure the discursive evanescence of appearances; words bringing the senses into the mind which they created; the establishment of interior experience by the construction of its tone in words.

In "Tattoo" (page 108), we have the opposite effect, where the mind is intensified in a simple visual image. The tone existed beforehand, so to speak, in the nature of the subject.

> The light is like a spider.
> It crawls over the water.
> It crawls over the edges of the snow.
> It crawls under your eyelids
> And spreads its webs there—
> Its two webs.
>
> The webs of your eyes
> Are fastened
> To the flesh and bones of you
> As to rafters or grass.
> There are filaments of your eyes
> On the surface of the water
> And in the edges of the snow.

The problem of language here hardly existed: the words make the simplest of statements, and the poet had only to avoid dramatising what was already drama in itself, the sensation of the eyes in contact with what they looked at. By attempting *not* to set up a tone the tone of truth is secured for statements literally false. Fairy tales and Mother Goose use the same language. Because there is no point where the statements stop being true, they leap the gap unnoticed between literal truth and imaginative truth. It is worth observing that the strong sensual quality of the poem is defined without the use of a single sensual word; and it is that ambiguity between the words and their subject which makes the poem valuable.

There is nothing which has been said so far about Mr. Stevens' uses of language which might not have been said, with different examples, of any good poet equally varied and equally erudite [2]—by which I mean intensely careful of effects. We have been dealing with words primarily, and words are not limited either to an author or a subject. Hence they form unique data and are to be understood and commented on by themselves. You can hardly more compare two poets' use of a word than you can compare, profitably, trees to cyclones. Synonyms are accidental, superficial, and never genuine. Comparison begins to be possible at the level of more complicated tropes than may occur in single words.

Let us compare then, for the sake of distinguishing the kinds of import, certain tropes taken from Ezra Pound, T. S. Eliot, and Mr. Stevens.

From Mr. Pound—the first and third from the *Cantos* and the second from *Hugh Selwyn Mauberley:*

In the gloom, the gold gathers the light against it.

Tawn foreshores
Washed in the cobalt of oblivion.

A catalogue, his jewels of conversation.

From T. S. Eliot—one from *Prufrock,* one from *The Wasteland,* and one from *Ash Wednesday:*

I should have been a pair of ragged claws
Scuttling across the floors of silent seas.

[2] See *Words and Idioms,* by Logan Pearsall Smith, Boston: Houghton Mifflin, 1926, page 121. "One of the great defects of our critical vocabulary is the lack of a neutral, non-derogatory name for these great artificers, these artists who derive their inspiration more from the formal than the emotional aspects of their art, and who are more interested in the masterly control of their material, than in the expression of their own feelings, or the prophetic aspects of their calling." Mr. Smith then suggests the use of the words erudite and erudition and gives as reason their derivation "from *erudire* (E "out of," and *rudis,* "rude," "rough" or "raw"), a verb meaning in classical Latin to bring out of the rough, to form by means of art, to polish, to instruct." Mr. Stevens is such an *erudite;* though he is often more, when he deals with emotional matters as if they were matters for *erudition.*

The awful daring of a moment's surrender
Which an age of prudence can never retract.

Struggling with the devil of the stairs who wears
The deceitful face of hope and of despair.

The unequalled versatility of Ezra Pound (Eliot in a dedication addresses him as *Il Miglior Fabbro*) prevents assurance that the three lines quoted from him are typical of all his work. At least they are characteristic of his later verse, and the kind of feeling they exhibit may be taken as Pound's own. Something like their effect may be expected in reading a good deal of his work.

The first thing to be noticed is that the first two tropes are visual images—not physical observation, but something to be seen in the mind's eye; and that as the images are so seen their meaning is exhausted. The third trope while not directly visual acts as if it were. What differentiates all three from physical observation is in each case the nonvisual associations of a single word—*gathers,* which in the active voice has an air of intention; *oblivion,* which has the purely mental sense of forgetfulness; and less, obviously, *conversation,* in the third trope, which while it helps *jewels* to give the line a visual quality it does not literally possess, also acts to condense in the line a great many non-visual associations.

The lines quoted from T. S. Eliot are none of them in intention visual; they deal with a totally different realm of experience—the realm in which the mind dramatises, at a given moment, its feelings towards a whole aspect of life. The emotion with which these lines charge the reader's mind is a quality of emotion which has so surmounted the senses as to require no longer the support of direct contact with them. Abstract words have reached the intensity of thought and feeling where the senses have been condensed into abstraction. The first distich is an impossible statement which in its context is terrifying. The language has sensual elements but as such they mean nothing: it is the act of abstract dramatisation which counts. In the second and third distichs words such as *surrender* and *prudence, hope and despair,* assume, by their dramatisation, a definite sensual force.

Both Eliot and Pound condense; their best verse is weighted —Pound's with sensual experience primarily, and Eliot's with beliefs. Where the mind's life is concerned the senses produce images, and beliefs produce dramatic cries. The condensation is important.

Mr. Stevens' tropes, in his best work and where he is most characteristic, are neither visual like Pound nor dramatic like Eliot. The scope and reach of his verse are no less but are different. His visual images never condense the matter of his poems; they either accent or elaborate it. His dramatic statements, likewise, tend rather to give another, perhaps more final, form to what has already been put in different language.

The best evidence of these differences is the fact that it is almost impossible to quote anything short of a stanza from Mr. Stevens without essential injustice to the meaning. His kind of condensation, too, is very different in character and degree from Eliot and Pound. Little details are left in the verse to show what it is he has condensed. And occasionally, in order to make the details fit into the poem, what has once been condensed is again elaborated. It is this habit of slight re-elaboration which gives the firm textural quality to the verse.

Another way of contrasting Mr. Stevens' kind of condensation with those of Eliot and Pound will emerge if we remember Mr. Stevens' *intentional* ambiguity. Any observation, as between the observer and what is observed, is the notation of an ambiguity. To Mr. Stevens the sky, "the basal slate," "the universal hue," which surrounds us and is always upon us is the great ambiguity. Mr. Stevens associates two or more such observations so as to accent their ambiguities. But what is ambiguous in the association is not the same as in the things associated; it is something new, and it has the air of something condensed. This is the quality that makes his poems grow, rise in the mind like a tide. The poems cannot be exhausted, because the words that make them, intentionally ambiguous at their crucial points, are themselves inexhaustible. Eliot obtains many of his effects by the sharpness of surprise, Pound his by visual definition; they tend to exhaust their words in the individual use, and they are succesful because they know when to stop, they know when sharpness and definition lay most hold on their subjects, they know the maximal limit of their kinds of condensation. Mr. Stevens is just as precise in his kind; he brings ambiguity to the point of sharpness, of reality, without destroying, but rather preserving, clarified, the ambiguity. It is a difference in subject matter, and a difference in accent. Mr. Stevens makes you aware of how much is *already* condensed in any word.

The first stanza of "Sunday Morning" may be quoted (page 89). It should be remembered that the title is an integral part of the poem, directly affecting the meaning of many lines and generally controlling the atmosphere of the whole.

> Complacencies of the peignoir, and late
> Coffee and oranges in a sunny chair,
> And the green freedom of a cockatoo
> Upon a rug mingle to dissipate
> The holy hush of ancient sacrifice.
> She dreams a little, and she feels the dark

Encroachment of that old catastrophe,
As a calm darkens among water-lights.
The pungent oranges and bright, green wings
Seem things in some procession of the dead,
Winding across wide water, without sound.
The day is like wide water, without sound,
Stilled for the passing of her dreaming feet
Over the seas, to silent Palestine,
Dominion of the blood and sepulchre.

A great deal of ground is covered in these fifteen lines, and
the more the slow ease and conversational elegance of the
verse are observed, the more wonder it seems that so much
could have been indicated without strain. Visually, we have
a woman enjoying her Sunday morning breakfast in a sunny
room with a green rug. The image is secured, however, not
as in Pound's image about the gold gathering the light
against it, in directly visual terms, but by the almost casual
combination of visual images with such phrases as *"complacencies* of the peignoir," and "the green *freedom* of the
cockatoo," where the italicised words are abstract in essence
but rendered concrete in combination. More important, the
purpose of the images is to show how they dissipate the "holy
hush of ancient sacrifice," how the natural comfort of the
body is aware but mostly unheeding that Sunday is the
Lord's day and that it commemorates the crucifixion.

From her half awareness she feels the more keenly the
"old catastrophe" merging in the surroundings, subtly, but
deeply, changing them as a "calm darkens among water-
lights." The feeling is dark in her mind, darkens, changing,
the whole day. The oranges and the rug and the day all have
the quality of "wide water, without sound," and all her
thoughts, so loaded, turn on the crucifixion.

The transit of the body's feeling from attitude to attitude is
managed in the medium of three water images. These images

do not replace the "complacencies of the peignoir," nor change them; they act as a kind of junction between them and the Christian feeling traditionally proper to the day. By the time the stanza is over the water images have embodied both feelings. In their own way they make a condensation by appearing in company with and showing what was already condensed.

If this stanza is compared with the tropes quoted from Pound, the principal difference will perhaps seem that while Pound's lines define their own meaning and may stand alone, Mr. Stevens' various images are separately incomplete and, on the other hand, taken together, have a kind of completeness to which Pound's lines may not pretend: everything to which they refer is present. Pound's images exist without syntax, Mr. Stevens' depend on it. Pound's images are formally simple, Mr. Stevens' complex. The one contains a mystery, and the other, comparatively, expounds a mystery.

While it would be possible to find analogues to Eliot's tropes in the stanzas of "Sunday Morning," it will be more profitable to examine something more germane in spirit. Search is difficult and choice uncertain, for Mr. Stevens is not a dramatic poet. Instead of dramatising his feelings, he takes as fatal the drama that he sees and puts it down either in its least dramatic, most meditative form, or makes of it a simple statement. Let us then frankly take as pure a meditation as may be found, "The Snow Man" (page 12), where, again, the title is integrally part of the poem:

> One must have a mind of winter
> To regard the frost and the boughs
> Of the pine-trees crusted with snow;
>
> And to have been cold a long time
> To behold the junipers shagged with ice,
> The spruces rough in the distant glitter

Of the January sun; and not to think
Of any misery in the sound of the wind,
In the sound of a few leaves,

Which is the sound of the land
Full of the same wind
That is blowing in the same bare place

For the listener, who listens in the snow,
And, nothing himself, beholds
Nothing that is not there and the nothing that is.

The last three lines are as near as Mr. Stevens comes to the peculiar dramatic emotion which characterises the three tropes quoted from Eliot. Again, as in the passage compared to Pound's images, the effect of the last three lines depends entirely on what preceded them. The emotion is built up from chosen fragments and is then stated in its simplest form. The statement has the force of emotional language but it remains a statement—a modest declaration of circumstance. The abstract word *nothing,* three times repeated, is not in effect abstract at all; it is synonymous with the data about the winter landscape which went before. The part which is not synonymous is the emotion: the overtone of the word, and the burden of the poem. Eliot's lines,

The awful daring of a moment's surrender
Which an age of prudence can never retract,

like Pound's lines, for different reasons, stand apart and on their own feet. The two poets work in contrary modes. Eliot places a number of things side by side. The relation is seldom syntactical or logical, but is usually internal and sometimes, so far as the reader is concerned, fatal and accidental. He works in violent contrasts and produces as much by prestidigitation as possible. There was no reason in the rest of *Prufrock* why the lines about the pair of ragged claws should have appeared where they did and no reason, perhaps, why they should have appeared at all; but once they appeared they became for the reader irretrievable, complete in themselves, and completing the structure of the poem.

That is the method of a dramatic poet, who moulds wholes out of parts themselves autonomous. Mr. Stevens, not a dramatic poet, seizes his wholes only in imagination; in his poems the parts are already connected. Eliot usually moves from point to point or between two termini. Mr. Stevens as a rule ends where he began; only when he is through, his beginning has become a chosen end. The differences may be exaggerated but in their essence is a true contrast.

If a digression may be permitted, I think it may be shown that the different types of obscurity found in the three poets are only different aspects of their modes of writing. In Pound's verse, aside from words in languages the reader does not know, most of the hard knots are tied round combinations of classical and historical references. A passage in one of the *Cantos,* for example, works up at the same time the adventures of a Provençal poet and the events in one of Ovid's *Metamorphoses.* If the reader is acquainted with the details of both stories, he can appreciate the criticism in Pound's combination. Otherwise he will remain confused: he will be impervious to the plain facts of the verse.

Eliot's poems furnish examples of a different kind of reference to and use of history and past literature. The reader must be familiar with the ideas and the beliefs and systems of feeling to which Eliot alludes or from which he borrows, rather than to the facts alone. Eliot does not restrict himself to criticism; he digests what he takes; but the reader must know what it is that has been digested before he can appreciate the result. The Holy Grail material in *The*

Wasteland is an instance: like Tiresias, this material is a
dramatic element in the poem.

Mr. Stevens' difficulties to the normal reader present themselves in the shape of seemingly impenetrable words or
phrases which no wedge of knowledge brought from outside
the body of Mr. Stevens' own poetry can help much to split.
The wedge, if any, is in the words themselves, either in the
instance alone or in relation to analogous instances in the
same or other poems in the book. Two examples should
suffice.

In "Sunday Morning," there is in the seventh stanza (page
93) a reference to the sun, to which men shall chant their
devotion—

> Not as a god, but as a god might be,
> Naked among them, like a savage source.
> Their chant shall be a chant of paradise,
> Out of their blood, returning to the sky; . . .

Depending upon the reader this will or will not be obscure.
But in any case, the full weight of the lines is not felt until
the conviction of the poet that the sun is origin and ending
for all life is shared by the reader. That is why the god might
be naked among them. It takes only reading of the stanza,
the poem, and other poems where the fertility of the sun is
celebrated, to make the notion sure. The only bit of outside
information that might help is the fact that in an earlier
version this stanza concluded the poem.— In short, generally, you need only the dictionary and familiarity with the
poem in question to clear up a good part of Mr. Stevens'
obscurities.

The second example is taken from "The Man whose
Pharynx was Bad" (page 128):

> Perhaps, if winter once could penetrate
> Through all its purples to the final slate.

Here, to obtain the full meaning, we have only to consult the sixth stanza of "Le Monocle de mon Oncle" (page 18):

> If men at forty will be painting lakes
> The ephemeral blues must merge for them in one,
> The basic slate, the universal hue.
> There is a substance in us that prevails.

Mr. Stevens has a notion often intimated that the sky is the only permanent background for thought and knowledge; he would see things against the sky as a Christian would see them against the cross. The blue of the sky is the prevailing substance of the sky, and to Mr. Stevens it seems only necessary to look at the sky to share and be shared in its blueness.

If I have selected fairly types of obscurity from these poets, it should be clear that whereas the obscurities of Eliot and Pound are intrinsic difficulties of the poems, to which the reader must come well armed with specific sorts of external knowledge and belief, the obscurities of Mr. Stevens clarify themselves to the intelligence alone. Mode and value are different—not more or less valuable, but different. And all result from the concentrated language which is the medium of poetry. The three poets load their words with the maximum content; naturally, the poems remain obscure until the reader takes out what the poet puts in. What still remains will be the essential impenetrability of words, the bottomlessness of knowledge. To these the reader, like the poet, must submit.

Returning, this time without reference to Pound and Eliot, among the varieties of Mr. Stevens' tropes we find some worth notice which comparison will not help. In "Le Monocle de mon Oncle," the ninth stanza (page 20), has nothing logically to do with the poem; it neither develops the subject nor limits it, but is rather a rhetorical interlude set in the poem's midst. Yet it is necessary to the poem, because its rhetoric, boldly announced as such, expresses the feeling of the poet towards his poem, and that feeling, once expressed, becomes incorporated in the poem.

> In verses wild with motion, full of din,
> Loudened by cries, by clashes, quick and sure
> As the deadly thought of men accomplishing
> Their curious fates in war, come, celebrate
> The faith of forty, ward of Cupido.
> Most venerable heart, the lustiest conceit
> Is not too lusty for your broadening.
> I quiz all sounds, all thoughts, all everything
> For the music and manner of the paladins
> To make oblation fit. Where shall I find
> Bravura adequate to this great hymn?

It is one of the advantages of a non-dramatic, meditative style, that pure rhetoric may be introduced into a poem without injuring its substance. The structure of the poem is, so to speak, a structure of loose ends, spliced only verbally, joined only by the sequence in which they appear. What might be fustian ornament in a dramatic poem, in a meditative poem casts a feeling far from fustian over the whole, and the slighter the relation of the rhetorical interlude to the substance of the whole, the more genuine is the feeling cast. The rhetoric does the same thing that the action does in a dramatic poem, or the events in a narrative poem; it produces an apparent medium in which the real substance may be borne.

Such rhetoric is not reserved to set interludes; it often occurs in lines not essentially rhetorical at all. Sometimes it gives life to a serious passage and cannot be separated without fatal injury to the poem. Then it is the trick without

which the poem would fall flat entirely. Two poems occur
where the rhetoric is the vital trope—"A High-Toned Old
Christian Woman" (page 79), and "Bantams in Pine-
Woods" (page 101), which I quote entire:

> Chieftain Iffucan of Azcan in caftan
> Of tan with henna hackles, halt!
>
> Damned universal cock, as if the sun
> Was blackamoor to bear your blazing tail.
>
> Fat! Fat! Fat! I am the personal.
> Your world is you. I am my world.
>
> You ten-foot poet among inchlings. Fat!
> Begone! An inchling bristles in these pines,
>
> Bristles, and points their Appalachian tangs,
> And fears not portly Azcan nor his hoos.

The first and last distichs are gauds of rhetoric; nevertheless
they give not only the tone but the substance to the poem.
If the reader is deceived by the rhetoric and believes the poem
is no more than a verbal plaything, he ought not to read
poetry except as a plaything. With a different object, Mr.
Stevens' rhetoric is as ferociously comic as the rhetoric in
Marlowe's *Jew of Malta,* and as serious. The ability to handle
rhetoric so as to reach the same sort of intense condensation
that is secured in bare, non-rhetorical language is very rare,
and since what rhetoric can condense is very valuable it
ought to receive the same degree of attention as any other
use of language. Mr. Stevens' successful attempts in this
direction are what make him technically most interesting.
Simple language, dealing obviously with surds, draws emotion
out of feelings; rhetorical language, dealing rather, or apparently, with inflections, employed with the same seriousness,
creates a surface *equivalent* to an emotion by its approximately

complete escape from the purely communicative function of language.[3]

We have seen in a number of examples that Mr. Stevens uses language in several different ways, either separately or in combination; and I have tried to imply that his success is due largely to his double adherence to words and experience as existing apart from his private sensibility. His great labour has been to allow the reality of what he felt personally to pass into the superior impersonal reality of words. Such a transformation amounts to an access of knowledge, as it raises to a condition where it may be rehearsed and understood in permanent form that body of emotional and sensational experience which in its natural condition makes life a torment and confusion.

With the technical data partly in hand, it ought now to be possible to fill out the picture, touch upon the knowledge itself, in Mr. Stevens' longest and most important poem, "The Comedian as the Letter C." Everywhere characteristic of Mr. Stevens' style and interests, it has the merit of difficulty—difficulty which when solved rewards the reader beyond his hopes of clarity.

Generally speaking the poem deals with the sensations and images, notions and emotions, ideas and meditations, sensual adventures and introspective journeyings of a protagonist called Crispin. More precisely, the poem expounds the shifting of a man's mind between sensual experience and its

[3] There is a point at which rhetorical language resumes its communicative function. In the second of "Six Significant Landscapes" (page 98), we have this image.

> A pool shines
> Like a bracelet
> Shaken at a dance,

which is a result of the startling associations induced by an ornamental, social, rhetorical style in dealing with nature. The image perhaps needs its context to assure its quality.

imaginative interpretation, the struggle, in that mind, of the imagination for sole supremacy and the final slump or ascent where the mind contents itself with interpreting plain and common things. In short, we have a meditation, with instances, of man's struggle with nature. The first line makes the theme explicit: "Nota: man is the intelligence of his soil, the sovereign ghost." Later, the theme is continued in reverse form: "His soil is man's intelligence." Later still, the soil is qualified as suzerain, which means sovereign over a semi-independent or internally autonomous state; and finally, at the end of the poem, the sovereignty is still further reduced when it turns out that the imagination can make nothing better of the world (here called a turnip), than the same insoluble lump it was in the beginning.

The poem is in six parts of about four pages each. A summary may replace pertinent discussion and at the same time preclude extraneous discussion. In Part I, called the World without Imagination, Crispin, who previously had cultivated a small garden with his intelligence, finds himself at sea, "a skinny sailor peering in the sea-glass." At first at loss and "washed away by magnitude," Crispin, "merest minuscule in the gales," at last finds the sea a vocable thing,

> But with a speech belched out of hoary darks
> Noway resembling his, a visible thing,
> And excepting negligible Triton, free
> From the unavoidable shadow of himself
> That elsewhere lay around him.

The sea "was no help before reality," only "one vast subjugating final tone," before which Crispin was made new. Concomitantly, with and because of his vision of the sea, "The drenching of stale lives no more fell down."

Part II is called Concerning the Thunder-Storms of Yucatan, and there, in Yucatan, Crispin, a man made vivid by the sea, found his apprehensions enlarged and felt the need to fill his senses. He sees and hears all there is before him, and writes fables for himself

> Of an aesthetic tough, diverse, untamed,
> Incredible to prudes, the mint of dirt,
> Green barbarism turned paradigm.

The sea had liberated his senses, and he discovers an earth like "A jostling festival of seeds grown fat, too juicily opulent," and a "new reality in parrot squawks." His education is interrupted when a wind "more terrible than the revenge of music on bassoons," brings on a tropical thunder-storm. Crispin, "this connoisseur of elemental fate," identifies himself with the storm, finding himself free, which he was before, and "more than free, elate, intent, profound and studious" of a new self:

> the thunder, lapsing in its clap
> Let down gigantic quavers of its voice
> For Crispin to vociferate again.

With such freedom taken from the sea and such power found in the storm, Crispin is ready for the world of the imagination. Naturally, then, the third part of the poem, called Approaching Carolina, is a chapter in the book of moonlight, and Crispin "a faggot in the lunar fire." Moonlight is imagination, a reflection or interpretation of the sun, which is the source of life. It is also, curiously, this moonlight, North America, and specifically one of the Carolinas. And the Carolinas, to Crispin, seemed north; even the spring seemed arctic. He meditates on the poems he has denied himself because they gave less than "the relentless contact he desired." Perhaps the moon would establish the necessary liaison between himself and his environment. But perhaps not. It seemed

> Illusive, faint, more mist than moon, perverse,
> Wrong as a divagation to Peking. . . .
> The moonlight was an evasion, or, if not,
> A minor meeting, facile, delicate.

So he considers, and teeters back and forth, between the sun and moon. For the moment he decides against the moon and imagination in favor of the sun and his senses. The senses, instanced by the smell of things at the river wharf where his vessel docks, "round his rude aesthetic out" and teach him "how much of what he saw he never saw at all."

> He gripped more closely the essential prose
> As being, in a world so falsified,
> The one integrity for him, the one
> Discovery still possible to make,
> To which all poems were incident, unless
> That prose should wear a poem's guise at last.

In short, Crispin conceives that if the experience of the senses is but well enough known, the knowledge takes the form of imagination after all. So we find as the first line of the fourth part, called The Idea of a Colony, "Nota: his soil is man's intelligence," which reverses the original statement that man is the intelligence of his soil. With the new distinction illuminating his mind, Crispin plans a colony, and asks himself whether the purpose of his pilgrimage is not

> to drive away
> The shadows of his fellows from the skies,
> And, from their stale intelligence released,
> To make a new intelligence prevail?

The rest of the fourth part is a long series of synonymous tropes stating instances of the new intelligence. In a torment of fastidious thought, Crispin writes a prologomena for his colony. Everything should be understood for what it is and should follow the urge of its given character. The spirit of things should remain spirit and play as it will.

The man in Georgia waking among pines
Should be pine-spokesman. The responsive man,
Planting his pristine cores in Florida,
Should prick thereof, not on the psaltery,
But on the banjo's categorical gut.

And as for Crispin's attitude toward nature, "the melon
should have apposite ritual" and the peach its incantation.
These "commingled souvenirs and prophecies,"—all images
of freedom and the satisfaction of instinct,—compose Crispin's idea of a colony. He banishes the masquerade of
thought and expunges dreams; the ideal takes no form from
these. Crispin will be content to "let the rabbit run, the cock
declaim."

In Part V, which is A Nice Shady Home, Crispin dwells in
the land, contented and a hermit, continuing his observations
with diminished curiosity. His discovery that his colony has
fallen short of his plan and that he is content to have it fall
short, content to build a cabin,

who once had planned
Loquacious columns by the ructive sea,

leads him to ask whether he should not become a philosopher
instead of a coloniser.

Should he lay by the personal and make
Of his own fate an instance of all fate?

The question is rhetorical, but before it can answer itself,
Crispin, sapped by the quotidian, sapped by the sun, has no
energy for questions, and is content to realise, that for all
the sun takes

it gives a humped return
Exchequering from piebald fiscs unkeyed.

Part VI, called And Daughters with Curls, explains the

implications of the last quoted lines. The sun, and all the new
intelligence which it enriched, mulcted the man Crispin, and
in return gave him four daughters, four questioners and four
sure answerers. He has been brought back to social nature,
has gone to seed. The connoisseur of elemental fate has
become himself an instance of all fate. He does not know
whether the return was "Anabasis or slump, ascent or chute."
His cabin—that is the existing symbol of his colony—seems
now a phylactery, a sacred relic or amulet he might wear in
memorial to his idea, in which his daughters shall grow up,
bidders and biders for the ecstasies of the world, to repeat his
pilgrimage, and come, no doubt, in their own cabins, to the
same end.

Then Crispin invents his doctrine and clothes it in the
fable about the turnip:

> The world, a turnip once so readily plucked,
> Sacked up and carried overseas, daubed out
> Of its ancient purple, pruned to the fertile main,
> And sown again by the stiffest realist,
> Came reproduced in purple, family font,
> The same insoluble lump. The fatalist
> Stepped in and dropped the chuckling down his craw,
> Without grace or grumble.

But suppose the anecdote was false, and Crispin a profitless
philosopher,

> Glozing his life with after-shining flicks,
> Illuminating, from a fancy gorged
> By apparition, plain and common things,
> Sequestering the fluster from the year,
> Making gulped potions from obstreperous drops,
> And so distorting, proving what he proves
> Is nothing, what can all this matter since
> The relation comes, benignly, to its end.

So may the relation of each man be clipped.

The legend or subject of the poem and the mythology it develops are hardly new nor are the instances, intellectually considered, very striking. But both the clear depth of conception and the extraordinary luxuriance of rhetoric and image in which it is expressed, should be at least suggested in the summary here furnished. Mr. Stevens had a poem with an abstract subject—man as an instance of fate,—and a concrete experience—the sensual confusion in which the man is waylaid;—and to combine them he had to devise a form suitable to his own peculiar talent. The simple statement—of which he is a master—could not be prolonged to meet the dimensions of his subject. To the dramatic style his talents were unsuitable, and if by chance he used it, it would prevent both the meditative mood and the accent of intellectual wit which he needed to make the subject his own. The form he used is as much his own and as adequate, as the form of *Paradise Lost* is Milton's or the form of *The Wasteland* is Eliot's. And as Milton's form filled the sensibility of one aspect of his age, Mr. Stevens' form fits part of the sensibility —a part which Eliot or Pound or Yeats do little to touch— of our own age.

I do not know a name for the form. It is largely the form of rhetoric, language used for its own sake, persuasively to the extreme. But it has, for rhetoric, an extraordinary content of concrete experience. Mr. Stevens is a genuine poet in that he attempts constantly to transform what is felt with the senses and what is thought in the mind—if we can still distinguish the two—into that realm of being, which we call poetry, where what is thought is felt and what is felt has the strict point of thought. And I call his mode of achieving that transformation rhetorical because it is not lyric or dramatic or epic, because it does not transcend its substance, but is a reflection upon a hard surface, a shining mirror of rhetoric.

In its nature depending so much on tone and atmosphere, accenting precise management of ambiguities, and dealing with the subtler inflections of simple feelings, the elements of the form cannot be tracked down and put in order. Perhaps the title of the whole poem, "The Comedian as the Letter C," is as good an example as any where several of the elements can be found together. The letter C is, of course, Crispin, and he is called a letter because he is small (he is referred to as "merest minuscule," which means small letter, in the first part of the poem) and because, though small, like a letter he stands for something—his colony, cabin, and children—as a comedian. He is a comedian because he deals finally with the quotidian (the old distinction of comedy and tragedy was between every day and heroic subject matter), gorged with apparition, illuminating plain and common things. But what he deals with is not comic; the comedy, in that sense, is restricted to his perception and does not touch the things perceived or himself. The comedy is the accent, the play of the words. He is at various times a realist, a clown, a philosopher, a coloniser, a father, a faggot in the lunar fire, and so on. In sum, and any sum is hypothetical, he may be a comedian in both senses, but separately never. He is the hypothesis of comedy. He is a piece of rhetoric—a persona in words—exemplifying all these characters, and summing, or masking, in his persuasive style, the essential prose he read. He is the poem's guise that the prose wears at last.

Such is the title of the poem, and such is the poem itself. Mr. Stevens has created a surface, a texture, a rhetoric in which his feelings and thoughts are preserved in what amounts to a new sensibility. The contrast between his subjects—the apprehension of all the sensual aspects of nature as instances of fate,—and the form in which the subjects are expressed is what makes his poetry valuable. Nature becomes nothing but words and to a poet words are everything.

1931

IV

D. H. LAWRENCE AND EXPRESSIVE FORM

As a poet, and only to a less degree as a novelist, Lawrence
belongs to that great race of English writers whose
work totters precisely where it towers, collapses exactly in its
strength: work written out of a tortured Protestant sensibility
and upon the foundation of an incomplete, uncomposed
mind: a mind without defences against the material with
which it builds and therefore at every point of stress horribly
succumbing to it. Webster, Swift, Blake, and Coleridge—
perhaps Donne, Sterne, and Shelley, and on a lesser plane
Marston, Thompson (of the Dreadful Night), and Beddoes—
these exemplify, in their different ways, the deracinated,
unsupported imagination, the mind for which, since it lacked
rational structure sufficient to its burdens, experience was too
much. Their magnitude was inviolate, and we must take
account of it not only for its own sake but also to escape its
fate; it is the magnitude of ruins—and the ruins for the most
part of an intended life rather than an achieved art.

Such judgment—such prediction of the terms of appreciation—may seem heavy and the operation of wilful prejudice
(like that of our dying Humanism), but only if the reader
refuses to keep in mind that of which he can say more.
Criticism, the effort of appreciation, should be focused upon
its particular objects, not limited to them. Shakespeare,
Dante, and Milton, for example, remain monuments (not
ruins) of the imagination precisely in what is here a relevant
aspect. Their work, whatever the labours of exegesis, remains
approximately complete in itself. The work of Shakespeare,

even the Sonnets, is not for us an elongation of the poet's self, but is independent of it because it has a rational structure which controls, orders, and composes in external or objective form the material of which it is made; and for that effect it is dependent only upon the craft and conventions of the art of poetry and upon the limits of language. We criticise adversely such work where it fails of objective form or lacks unarticulated composition, as in the Sonnets or *Hamlet*. We criticise *Lycidas* because the purpose of the digressions is not articulated and so there is injury to the composition—the growing together into an independent entity—of the poem. And this is the right meat for criticism; this is the kind of complaint to which poetry is of its own being subject; the original sin of which no major work is entirely free.

This essay proposes to outline an attack upon Lawrence as a poet on the grounds just laid out; that the strength of his peculiar insight lacks the protection and support of a rational imagination, and that it fails to its own disadvantage to employ the formal devices of the art in which it is couched. Thus the attack will be technical. No objections will be offered to the view of life involved—which is no more confused than Dostoieffsky's, and no less a mirror than Shakespeare's; only admiration for its vigour, regret that it did not, and argument that in the technical circumstances it could not, succeed. For it should be remembered that the structure of the imagination no less than the sequence of rhyme is in an important sense a technical matter.

Perhaps our whole charge may be laid on the pretension, found in the Preface to the *Collected Poems,* that the radical imperfection of poetry is a fundamental virtue. That is not how Lawrence frames it; he says merely that certain of his early poems failed "because the poem started out to be something it didn't quite achieve, because the young man interfered with his demon"; which seems harmless enough until we read that he regards many of his poems as a fragmentary biography, asks us to remember in reading them the time and circumstance of his life, and expresses the wish that in reading the Sonnets we knew more about Shakespeare's self and circumstance. After consideration, I take the young man in the quotation to be just what Lawrence thought he was not, the poet as craftsman, and the demon was exactly that outburst of personal feeling which needed the discipline of craft to become a poem. As for Shakespeare's Sonnets, if we did know more about Shakespeare's self, we should only know a little more clearly where he failed as a poet; the Sonnets themselves would be not a whit improved. A statement of which—since there is always a necessary baggage of historical and intellectual background—I wish to assert only the comparative or provisional truth.

However wrong Lawrence was about the young man, the demon, and Shakespeare's self, the point here is that his remarks explain why there is so little to say about his important poems as poetry, and they characterise the seed of personal strength, which, nourished exclusively, became his weakness, and ultimately brought about his disintegration and collapse as a poet. Lawrence was the extreme victim of the plague afflicting the poetry of the last hundred and fifty years —the plague of expressive form.

You cannot talk about the art of his poetry because it exists only at the minimum level of self-expression, as in the later, more important poems, or because, as in the earlier accentual rhymed pieces written while he was getting under way, its art is mostly attested by its badness. The ordering of words in component rhythms, the array of rhymes for prediction, contrast, transition and suspense, the delay of ornament, the anticipation of the exactly situated dramatic trope, the

development of image and observation to an inevitable end—
the devices which make a poem cohere, move, and shine
apart—these are mostly not here, or are present badly and at
fault. This absence of the advantages of craft is not particularly due to the inability to use them, but to a lack of
interest. Lawrence hardly ever, after the first, saw the use of
anything that did not immediately devour his interest,
whether in life or in art. (Poetry, it may be remarked, is
never an immediate art but always of implication.)

And he had besides, to control his interests, a special blind-
ing light of his own, and it was only what this light struck
or glared on that captured his interest, and compelled, by a
kind of automatism, the writing hand. If a good deal else
got in as well, it was not from concession or tactical motives,
but by accident and willy-nilly, or because Lawrence was
deceived and thought his demon illuminated him when not
present at all. This is the presumptive explanation of the long
reaches of dead-level writing. When you depend entirely upon
the demon of inspiration, the inner voice, the inner light, you
deprive yourself of any external criterion to show whether
the demon is working or not. Because he is yours and you
wilfully depend on him, he will seem to be operating with
equal intensity at every level of imagination. That is the
fallacy of the faith in expressive form—the faith some aspects
of which we have been discussing, that if a thing is only
intensely enough felt its mere expression in words will give
it satisfactory form, the dogma, in short, that once material
becomes words it is its own best form. By this stultifying
fallacy you cannot ever know whether your work succeeds or
fails as integral poetry, can know only and always that what
you have said symbolises and substitutes for your experience
to you, whatever it substitutes for in the minds of your readers. That Lawrence was aware of this fallacy, only thinking

it a virtue, is I think evident; he would not otherwise have pled with his readers to put themselves in his place, to imagine themselves as suffering his experience, while reading the long section of his poems called "Look! We have come through!"; which is a plea, really, for the reader to do the work the poet failed to do, to complete the poems of which he gave only the expressive outlines.

There is a further vitiating influence of Lawrence's dogma as he seems to hold it, whether you take it as the demon of enthusiastic inspiration or the reliance on expressive form; it tends, on the least let-up of particularised intensity, to the lowest order of the very formalism which it was meant to escape: the formalism of empty verbiage, of rhodomontade, masquerading as mystical or philosophical poetry. If you become content, even tormentedly, with self-expression, the process of education no less than that of taste ceases, and anything may come to stand, and interchangeably, for anything else. On the one hand the bare indicative statement of experience seems equivalent to insight into it, and on the other the use of such labels as God or Evil, however accidentally come by, seems to have the force of the rooted concepts which they may, when achieved by long labour or genuine insight, actually possess. Thus a dog's dying howl may be made to express in itself the whole tragedy of life, which it indeed may or may not do, depending on the reach of the imagination, of represented experience, you bring to bear on it. In Lawrence's later poems, where he is most ambitious, there is more of this empty formalism, unknown to him, than in any poet of similar potential magnitude. Whatever happened in his own mind, what transpires in the poems is the statement without the insight, the label without the seizable implied presence of the imaginative reach. The pity is that had Lawrence matured an external form to anywhere near the degree that he intensified his private apprehension, that form would have persuaded us of the active presence of the insight and the imagination which we can now only take on trust or *ipse dixit*.

These radical defects in Lawrence's equipment and in his attitude towards his work, may be perhaps exhibited in certain of the early poems when he had not deliberately freed himself from those devices of form which, had he mastered them, might have saved him. He began writing in the ordinary way, using to express or discover his own impulses the contemporary models that most affected him. The freshness of his personal life, the process of personal awakening (since he had something to awaken) provided, by rule, a copious subject-matter; and the freshness, to him, of other men's conventions amply supplied him and even, again by rule, sometimes overwhelmed him with forms. Occasionally, still in the natural course of a poet's progress, there was in his work a material as well as a formal influence, but rather less frequently than in most poets. For instance, "Lightning" and "Turned Down" are so strongly under the influence of the Hardy of *Time's Laughing Stocks* and *Satires of Circumstances,* that there was very little room for Lawrence himself in the poems; Hardy's sensibility as well as Hardy's form crowded him out. By apparent paradox, the value of the poems to Lawrence was personal; as renderings of Hardy they add nothing. Where the influence was less apparent, it was more genuine because more digested, and far more successful, as, for example, in the two quatrains called "Gipsy." Hardy was the only then practicing poet who was in the hard-earned habit of composing so much implication in so brief a space and upon the nub of a special circumstance. It was from Hardy that Lawrence learned his lesson. (The nub

of circumstance is of course the gipsy's traditional aversion to
entering a house.)

> I, the man with a red scarf,
>> Will give thee what I have, this last week's earnings.
> Take them and buy thee a silver ring
>> And wed me, to ease my yearnings.

> For the rest, when thou art wedded
>> I'll wet my brow for thee
> With sweat, I'll enter a house for thy sake,
>> Thou shalt shut doors on me.

Thus houses and doors become "really" houses and doors.
The poem is for that quality worth keeping in the early
Lawrence canon; but its importance here is in the technical
faults—by which I mean its radical and unnecessary variations from the norm of its model. It represents, I think
(subject to correction), about as far as Lawrence ever went in
the direction of strict accentual syllabic form; which is not
very far. Hardy would have been ashamed of the uneven,
lop-sided metrical architecture and would never have been
guilty (whatever faults he had of his own) of the disturbing
inner rhyme in the second quatrain. Lawrence was either
ignorant or not interested in these matters; at any rate he
failed to recognise the access of being which results from a
perfected strict form. He preferred, in this poem, to depend
on the best economical statement of his subject with the least
imposition of external form, strict or not. This is an example
of the fallacy of expressive form; because, granted that he
used a set form at all, it is his substance, what he had to say
and was really interested in, that suffers through his failure
to complete the form. If the reader compares this poem with
say Blake's "To the Muses," which is not a very strict poem
in itself, the formal advantage will be plain.

A more important poem, a poem which measurably captured more of Lawrence's sensibility, and as it happens more of ours, will illustrate the point, at least by cumulation, more clearly. Take the first poem preserved in the collected edition, "The Wild Common." We have here, for Lawrence says that it was a good deal re-written, the advantage of an early and a late poem at once. It is, substantially, in its present form, one of the finest of all Lawrence's poems. It presents the pastoral scene suggested by the title, proceeds to describe a naked man (the narrator) watching his white shadow quivering in a sheep-dip; either actually or imaginatively the man enters the water and the shadow is resolved with the substance and is identified; the poem ends with the affirmation, confirmed by singing larks and a lobbing rabbit, that "all that is good, all that is God takes substance!" The feeling is deep and particularised and the emotion is adequate to the material presented. The point here is that in gaining his ends Lawrence used an extraordinary combination of inconsistent modes and means. I ask only, for the sake of the argument, that the reader look at the poem with the same attention to craft as is customary (and is indeed the common proof of appreciation) in the examination of a drawing or a fugue: that he look and read *as if* he had a trained mind. Take the matter of rhymes. Whether by weakness of sound, weakness of syntactical position, lack of metrical propulsion or, as the case is, restraint, superfluity with regard to sense, or the use of mere homonym for true rhyme—the rhyme words not only fail as good rhymes but because of the distortions they bring about injure the substance and disfigure the outline of the poem. (In other poems such as "Discord in Childhood" the exigencies of rhyme misunderstood dictate actually inconsistent images and tropes.) That is a formal defect; there are also faults in the combinations of the modes of language. In this same poem, without dramatic change to warrant the variation, there are examples of fake "poetic" language, explicit direct presentation, the vague attribute and the precise attribute, colloquial language, and plain empty verbiage. It is as if in one drawing you found employed to the disadvantage of each the modes of outline and inner marking, chiaroscuro, and total visual effect.

Another poem, "Love on a Farm," has the special power of a dramatic fiction; it employs, dramatically, a violent but credible humanitarianism to force the feeling of death into the emotion of love. But it would have been better expanded and proved in prose. There is nothing in the poem to praise as poetry between the image of the intention and the shock of the result. Lawrence simply did not care in his verse— and, after *Sons and Lovers,* in many reaches of his more characteristic prose—for anything beyond the immediate blue-print expression of what he had in mind. The consequence is this. Since he wilfully rejected as much as he could of the great mass of expressive devices which make up the craft of poetry, the success of his poems depends, not so much on his bare statements, as upon the constant function of communication which cannot be expunged from the language.

Only the articulate can be inarticulately expressed, even under the dogma of expressive form, and Lawrence was, within the limits of his obsessive interests, one of the most powerfully articulate minds of the last generation. Since he used language straightforwardly to the point of sloppiness, without ever wilfully violating the communicative residue of his words, so much of his intention is available to the reader as is possible in work that has not been submitted to the completing persuasiveness of a genuine form. That much is a great deal; its capacity is the limit of greatness in the human personality. Being human, Lawrence could not escape in his

THE DOUBLE AGENT

least breath the burden of human experience, and, using language in which to express himself *for* himself, could not help often finding the existing, readily apprehensible word-forms the only suitable ones. That is a discipline by implication upon the soul of which the purest Protestant, as Lawrence was, cannot be free: the individual can contribute only infinitesimally even to his own idea of himself. In addressing even his most private thoughts he addresses a stranger and must needs find a common tongue between them. Thus Lawrence at his most personal, where he burrowed with most savage rapacity into himself, stood the best chance of terminating his passion in common experience. The language required, the objects of analogy and the tropes of identification, necessarily tended to the commonplace. This is at least negatively true of Lawrence's later, prophetic poems (as it is true on a level of greater magnitude in the prophetic poems of Blake); the fundamental declarations of insight, what Lawrence was after, in the Tortoise poems, could not help appearing in language commonplace for everything except its intensity. Here again it may be insisted, since such insistence is the object of this essay, that had Lawrence secured the same intensity in the process of his form as came naturally to him in seizing his subject, the poems would have escaped the inherent weakness of the commonplace (the loss of identity in the reader's mind) in the strength of separate being.

Before proceeding, as we have lastly to do, to measure and provisionally characterise the driving power in Lawrence's most important work, let us first examine, with a special object, one of the less important but uniquely successful poems. This is the poem called "Corot." It is written at the second remove from the experience involved. Not so much does it deal with a particular picture by Corot, or even with

[112]

the general landscape vision of Corot, as it attempts a thinking back, by Lawrence, through Corot, into landscape itself at a major mode of insight. Corot—the accumulation of impressions, attitudes, and formal knowledge with which Corot furnishes the attentive mind—is the medium through which the poem transpires. It is perhaps the only poem of its kind Lawrence wrote; a poem with a deliberately apprehended external scaffolding. We know that most poems about pictures, and most illustrations of literature, stultify themselves by keeping to the terms of the art they re-represent—or else come to mere minor acts of appreciation—come, in short, in either case, pretty much to nothing. Something very different took place here. By finding his material at a second remove —the remove of Corot past the remove of language—Lawrence provided himself, for once, with a principle of objective form; which in the fact of this poem composed his material better than he was ever able to compose in terms of mere direct apprehension however intense. Despite the cloudy words—we have the word "dim" used imprecisely three times in thirty-six lines—despite the large words and phrases such as Life and Time, goal, purpose, and mighty direction—and despite the inconsistent metres, Lawrence nevertheless was able to obtain merely because of the constant presence of an external reference ("Corot"), a unity of effect and independence of being elsewhere absent in his work. That the poem may have been as personal for Lawrence as anything he ever wrote makes no difference; for the reader the terms of conception are objective, and the poem could thus not help standing by itself.

The poem is small, its value merely illustrative, and if it is remembered at all it will be so only in the general context of Lawrence; but I have emphasised the principle of its compositional success because it is on similar principles that most great poetry has been composed; or at least—a more prudent statement—similar principles may be extracted from most of the poetry we greatly value: the principle that the reality of language, which is a formal medium of knowledge, is superior and anterior to the reality of the uses to which it is put, and the operative principle, that the chaos of private experience cannot be known or understood until it is projected and ordered in a form external to the consciousness that entertained it in flux. Of the many ways in which these principles may be embodied, Lawrence's poetry enjoys the advantage of but few, and those few by accident, as in "Corot," or because he could not help it, as in the constant reliance on the communicative function of language mentioned above. But he worked in the poverty of apparent riches and felt no need. There was a quality in his apprehension of the experience that obsessed him that in itself sufficed to carry over the reality of his experience in the words of his report—always for him and sometimes for the reader. This I think, for lack of a better word, may be called the quality of hysteria.

Hysteria comes from the Greek word for womb, and, formerly limited to women, was the name given to extraordinary, disproportionate reactions to the shock of experience. In hysteria the sense of reality is not annulled, resort is not to fancy or unrelated illusion; the sense of reality is rather heightened and distorted to a terrifying and discomposing intensity. The derangement of the patient is merely the expression, through a shocked nervous system, of the afflicting reality. But hysteria is not limited in its expressive modes to convulsions and shrieking. We have hysterias which express themselves in blindness, deafness, paralysis, and even secondary syphilis (lacking of course the appropriate bacteria). Some forms of romantic love may be called habit-hysterias of a comparatively benign character. In all these modes what is expressed has an apparent overwhelming reality. The blind man is really blind, the deaf deaf, and the paralytic cannot move—while hysteria lasts.

Now I do not wish to introduce Lawrence as a clinical example of hysteria; it would be inappropriate and unnecessary to any purpose of literary criticism; but I think it can be provisionally put that the reality in his verse, and in his later prose (from *The Rainbow* to *Mornings in Mexico* if not in *Lady Chatterly's Lover*) is predominantly of the hysterical order. Hysteria is certainly one of the resources of art—as it represents an extreme of consciousness; and it is arguable that much art is hysteria controlled—that is, restored to proportion by seizure in objective form. And the reader should remember that in a life so difficult to keep balanced, plastic, and rational, the leaning towards the expressive freedom of hysteria may often be intractable. The pretence or fact of hysteria is an ordinary mode of emotional expression. The reality of what is expressed is intense and undeniable, and is the surest approach to the absolute. But what is expressed in hysteria can never be wholly understood until the original reality is regained either by analysis or the imposition of limits. Otherwise, and in art, the hysteria is heresy and escapes the object which created it. That is how I think Lawrence worked; he submitted the obsessions of his experience to the heightening fire of hysteria and put down the annealed product just as it came. His special habit of hysteria is only a better name for the demon, the divinity, referred to in the Preface to the *Collected Poems*; and there is no reason to suppose that Lawrence would himself reject the identification. The reality persists, and is persuasive to those who catch the clue and accept the invitation by its very enormity.

Certainly it is in terms of some such notion that we must explain Lawrence's increasing disregard of the control of rationally conceived form and his incipient indifference, in the very last poems, to the denotive functions of language. So also we may explain the extraordinary but occasional and fragmentary success of his poetry as expression: by the enormity of the reality exposed. As it happens, Lawrence's obsessions ran to sex, death, the isolation of the personality, and the attempt at mystical fusion. Had he run rather to claustrophobia, fetish-worship, or some of the more obscure forms of human cowardice, his method of expression would have been less satisfactory: since it would not have commanded the incipient hysteria of sympathy. The normal subject-matter, in the sense of a sturdy pre-occupation with ordinary interests, kept his enormity of expression essentially accessible in most of his poems, although there are some places, for example in "The Ship of Death" or "Sicilian Cyclamens" where the hysteric mode carries the pathetic fallacy and the confusion of symbols beyond any resolution.

But normal subject-matter was not the only saving qualification; there is in the best poems a kind of furious underlying honesty of observation—the very irreducible surd that makes the hysteria an affair of genius not of insanity. One aspect of this honesty is perhaps most clearly seen in the poem called "She Said as Well to Me," which I think marks the climax of the long series called "Look! We Have Come Through!" There Lawrence manages to present, for all the faults of the work he did not do, and merely by the intensified honesty of the observation, the utter dignity of the singleness and isolation of the individual. Later in "Medlars and Sorb Apples," the hysteria is increased and the observation becomes vision, and leaves, perhaps, the confines of poetry.

> Orphic farewell, and farewell, and farewell
> And the *ego sum* of Dionysos

D. H. LAWRENCE AND EXPRESSIVE FORM

> The *sono io* of perfect drunkenness
> Intoxication of final loneliness.

It became, in fact, ritual frenzy; a matter to which we shall return. But first let us examine the eighteen pages of the poems about tortoises. Here we have the honesty working the other way round. In "She Said as Well to Me" and in all the poems of "Look! We have Come Through!" which make up Lawrence's testament of personal love, the movement is from the individual outward: it is the report or declaration, made unequivocally, of an enormously heightened sense of self. The self, the individual, is the radial point of sensibility. The six tortoise poems (which I take as the type of all the later poems) have as their motive the effort to seize on the plane of self-intoxication the sense of the outer world. The exhilarated knowledge of the self is still the aim, but here the self is the focal, not the radial, point of sensibility. The bias, the predicting twist of the mind, is no longer individual love, but the sexual, emergent character of all life; and in terms of that bias, which is the controlling principle, the seed of reality, in the hysteria of expression, Lawrence brings every notation and association, every symbolic suggestion he can find, to bear upon the shrieking plasm of the self. I quote the concluding lines of "Tortoise Shout."

The cross,
The wheel on which our silence first is broken,
Sex, which breaks up our integrity, our single inviolability,
    our deep silence,
Tearing a cry from us.

Sex, which breaks us into voice, sets us calling across the
    deeps, calling, calling for the complement,
Singing and calling, and singing again, being answered, hav-
    ing found.

Torn, to become whole again, after long seeking what is lost,
The same cry from the tortoise as from Christ, the Osiris-cry
  of abandonment,
That which is whole, torn asunder,
That which is in part, finding its whole again throughout the
  universe.[1]

Here again the burden of honesty is translated or lost in the
condition of ritual, of formal or declarative prayer and mystical identification; which is indeed a natural end for emotions
of which the sustaining medium is hysteria. To enforce the
point, let us take "The Fish" (the poems of the four Evan-
gelistic Beasts would do as well), which represented for
Lawrence, in the different fish he observes, the absolute,
untouchable, unknowable life, "born before God was love, or
life knew loving," "who lies with the waters of his silent
passion, womb-element," and of whom he can write, finally:

> In the beginning
> Jesus was called the Fish . . .
> And in the end.

Per omnia saecula saeculorum. The Fish and likewise the
Tortoise are acts of ceremonial adoration, in which the reader,
if he is sympathetic, because of the intensity of the act, cannot

---

[1] May I suggest that the reader compare this passage from Lawrence with
the following lines from T. S. Eliot's *Ash Wednesday* as a restorative to the
sense of *controlled* hysteria. The two poems have nearly the same theme.

Lady of silences	The greater torment
Calm and distressed	Of love satisfied
Torn and most whole	End of the endless
Rose of memory	Journey to no end
Rose of forgetfulness	Conclusion of all that
Exhausted and life-giving	Is inconclusible
Worried reposeful	Speech without word and
The single Rose	Word of no speech
Is now the Garden	Grace to the Mother
Where all loves end	For the Garden
Terminate torment	Where all love ends.
Of love unsatisfied	

help sharing. Lawrence was by consequence of the type of his insight and the kind of experience that excited him, a religious poet. His poetry is an attempt to declare and rehearse symbolically his pious recognition of the substance of life. The love of God for him was in the declaration of life in the flux of sex. Only with Lawrence the piety was tortured—the torture of incomplete affirmation. The great mystics saw no more profoundly through the disorder of life than Lawrence their ultimate vision but they saw within the terms of an orderly insight. In them, reason was stretched to include disorder and achieved mystery. In Lawrence, the reader is left to supply the reason and the form; for Lawrence only expresses the substance.

The affirmation to which the more important poems of Lawrence mount suffers from incompleteness for the same reasons that the lesser poems examined in the first part of this essay suffered. On the one hand he rejected the advantage of objective form for the immediate freedom of expressive form, and on the other hand he preferred the inspiration of immediate experience to the discipline of a rationally constructed imagination. He had a powerful sensibility and a profound experience, and he had the genius of insight and unequivocal honesty: he was in contact with the disorder of life. In his novels and tales the labour of creating and opposing characters, the exigencies of narrative, all the detail of execution, combined to make his works independent, controlled entities to a great extent. But in his poetry, the very intensity of his self-expression overwhelmed all other considerations, and the disorder alone prevailed.

The point at issue, and the pity of it, can be put briefly. Lawrence the poet was no more hysterical in his expressive mode than the painter Van Gogh. But where Van Gogh developed enough art to control his expression objectively, and so left us great paintings, Lawrence developed as little art as possible, and left us the ruins of great intentions; ruins which we may admire and contemplate, but as they are ruins of a life merely, cannot restore as poetry. Art was too long for Lawrence; life too close.

1935

V

NEW THRESHOLDS, NEW ANATOMIES

NOTES ON A TEXT OF HART CRANE

IT IS a striking and disheartening fact that the three most ambitious poems of our time should all have failed in similar ways: in composition, in independent objective existence, and in intelligibility of language. *The Wasteland,* *The Cantos,* and *The Bridge* all fail to hang together structurally in the sense that "Prufrock," "Envoi," and "Praise for an Urn"—lesser works in every other respect—do hang together. Each of the three poems requires of the reader that he supply from outside the poem, and with the help of clues only, the important, *controlling* part of what we may loosely call the meaning. And each again deliberately presents passages, lines, phrases, and single words which no amount of outside work can illumine. The fact is striking because, aside from other considerations of magnitude, relevance, and scope, these are not the faults we lay up typically against the great dead. The typical great poet is profoundly rational, integrating, and, excepting minor accidents of incapacity, a master of ultimate verbal clarity. Light, radiance, and wholeness remain the attributes of serious art. And the fact is disheartening because no time could have greater need than our own for rational art. No time certainly could surrender more than ours does daily, with drums beating, to fanatic politics and despotically construed emotions.

But let us desert the disheartening for the merely striking aspect, and handle the matter, as we can, within the realm of poetry, taking up other matters only tacitly and by implication. Let us say provisionally that in their more important works Eliot, Pound, and Crane lack the ultimate, if mythical, quality of aseity, that quality of completeness, of independence, so great that it seems underived and an effect of pure creation. The absence of aseity may be approached variously in a given poet; but every approach to be instructive, even to find the target at all, must employ a rational mode and the right weapon. These notes intend to examine certain characteristic passages of Hart Crane's poems as modes of language and to determine how and to what degree the effects intended were attained. The rationale is that of poetic language; the weapons are analysis and comparison. But there are other matters which must be taken up first before the language itself can be approached at all familiarly.

Almost everyone who has written on Crane has found in him a central defect, either of imagination or execution, or both. Long ago, in his Preface to *White Buildings,* Allen Tate complained that for all his talent Crane had not found a suitable theme. Later, in his admirable review of *The Bridge,* Yvor Winters brought and substantiated the charge (by demonstrating the exceptions) that even when he had found a theme Crane could not entirely digest it and at crucial points simply was unable to express it in objective form. These charges hold; and all that is here said is only in explication of them from a third point of view.

Waldo Frank, in his Introduction to the *Collected Poems,* acting more as an apologist than a critic, proffers two explanations of Crane's incompleteness as a poet, to neither of which can I assent, but of which I think both should be borne in mind. Mr. Frank believes that Crane will be understood and found whole when our culture has been restored from revolutionary collectivism to a predominant interest in the person; when the value of expressing the personal in the terms of the cosmic shall again seem supreme. This hypothesis would seem untenable unless it is construed as relevant to the present examination; when it runs immediately into the hands of the obvious but useful statement that Crane was interested in persons rather than the class-struggle. Mr. Frank's other explanation is that Crane's poetry was based upon the mystical perception of the "organic continuity between the self and a seemingly chaotic world." Crane "was too virile to deny the experience of continuity; he let the world pour in; and since his nuclear self was not disciplined to detachment from his nerves and passions, he lived exacerbated in a constant swing between ecstasy and exhaustion." I confess I do not understand "organic continuity" in this context, and all my efforts to do so are defeated by the subsequent word "detachment." Nor can I see how this particular concept of continuity can be very useful without the addition and control of a thorough supernaturalism. The control for mystic psychology is theology, and what is thereby controlled is the idiosyncrasy of insight, not the technique of poetry.

What Mr. Frank says not-rationally can be usefully re-translated to that plane on which skilled readers ordinarily read good poetry; which is a rational plane; which is, on analysis, the plane of competent technical appreciation. Such a translation, while committing grave injustice on Mr. Frank, comes nearer doing justice to Crane. It restores and brings home the strictures of Tate and Winters, and it brings judgment comparatively back to the minute particulars (Blake's phrase) which are alone apprehensible. To compose the nuclear self and the seemingly chaotic world is to find a suitable theme, and the inability so to compose rises as much from immaturity and indiscipline of the major poetic uses of language as from personal immaturity and indiscipline.

Baudelaire only rarely reached the point of self-discipline and Whitman never; but Baudelaire's language is both disciplined and mature, and Whitman's sometimes so. *Les Fleurs du Mal* are a profound poetic ordering of a life disorderly, distraught, and deracinated, a life excruciated, in the semantic sense of that word, to the extreme. And Whitman, on his side, by a very different use of language, gave torrential expression to the romantic disorder of life in flux, whereas his private sensibility seems either to have been suitably well-ordered or to have felt no need of order.

Whitman and Baudelaire are not chosen with reference to Crane by accident but because they are suggestively apposite. The suggestion may be made, not as blank truth but for the light there is in it, that Crane had the sensibility typical of Baudelaire and so misunderstood himself that he attempted to write *The Bridge* as if he had the sensibility typical of Whitman. Whitman characteristically let himself go in words, in any words and by all means the handiest, until his impulse was used up. Baudelaire no less characteristically caught himself up in his words, recording, ordering, and binding together the implications and tacit meanings of his impulse until in his best poems the words he used are, as I. A. Richards would say, inexhaustible objects of meditation. Baudelaire aimed at control, Whitman at release. It is for these reasons that the influence of Whitman is an impediment to the *practice* (to be distinguished from the reading) of poetry, and that the influence of Baudelaire is re-animation itself. (It may be noted that Baudelaire had at his back a well-articulated version of the Catholic Church to control the moral aspect of his meanings, where Whitman had merely an inarticulate pantheism.)

To apply this dichotomy to Crane is not difficult if it is done tentatively, without requiring that it be too fruitful, and without requiring that it be final at all. The clue or nexus is found, aside from the poems themselves, in certain prose statements. Letters are suspect and especially letters addressed to a patron, since the aim is less conviction by argument than the persuasive dramatisation of an attitude. It is therefore necessary in the following extract from a letter to Otto Kahn that the reader accomplish a reduction in the magnitude of terms.

Of the section of *The Bridge* called "The Dance" Crane wrote: "Here one is on the pure mythical and smoky soil at last! Not only do I describe the conflict between the two races in this dance—I also became identified with the Indian and his world before it is over, which is the only method possible of ever really possessing the Indian and his world as a cultural factor." Etc. I suggest that, confronted with the tight, tense, intensely personal lyric quatrains of the verse itself, verse compact with the deliberately inarticulate interfusion of the senses, Crane's statement of intention has only an *ipse dixit* pertinence; that taken otherwise, taken as a living index of substance, it only multiplies the actual confusion of the verse and impoverishes its achieved scope. Taken seriously, it puts an impossible burden on the reader: the burden of reading two poems at once, the one that appears and the "real" poem which does not appear except by an act of faith. This would be reading by legerdemain, which at the moment of achievement must always collapse, self-obfuscated.

Again, in the same letter, Crane wrote that, "The range of *The Bridge* has been called colossal by more than one critic who has seen the ms., and though I have found the subject to be vaster than I had at first realised, I am still highly confident of its final articulation into a continuous and eloquent span . . . *The Aeneid* was not written in two years—nor in four, and in more than one sense I feel justified in comparing the historical and cultural scope of *The Bridge* to that great work. It is at least a symphony with an epic theme, and a work of considerable profundity and inspiration."

The question is whether this was wishful thinking of the vague order commonest in revery, convinced and sincere statement of intention, or an effect of the profound duplicity —a deception in the very will of things—in Crane's fundamental attitudes towards his work; or whether Crane merely misunderstood the logical import of the words he used. I incline to the notion of duplicity, since it is beneath and sanctions the other notions as well; the very duplicity by which the talents of a Baudelaire appear to their possessor disguised and disfigured in the themes of a Whitman, the same fundamental duplicity of human knowledge whereby an accustomed disorder seems the order most to be cherished, or whereby a religion which at its heart denies life enriches living. In the particular reference, if I am right, it is possible to believe that Crane laboured to perfect both the strategy and the tactics of language so as to animate and manœuver his perceptions—and then fought the wrong war and against an enemy that displayed, to his weapons, no vulnerable target. He wrote in a language of which it was the virtue to accrete, modify, and interrelate moments of emotional vision— moments at which the sense of being gains its greatest access, —moments at which, by the felt nature of knowledge, the revealed thing is its own meaning; and he attempted to apply his language, in his major effort, to a theme that required a sweeping, discrete, indicative, anecdotal language, a language in which, by force of movement, mere cataloguing can replace and often surpass representation. He used the private lyric to write the cultural epic; used the mode of intensive contemplation, which secures ends, to present the mind's actions, which have no ends. The confusion of tool and purpose not only led him astray in conceiving his themes; it obscured at crucial moments the exact character of the work he was actually doing. At any rate we find most impenetrable and ineluctable, in certain places, the very matters he had the genius to see and the technique to clarify: the matters which are the substance of rare and valid emotion. The confusion, that is, led him to content himself at times with the mere cataloguing statement, enough for him because he knew the rest, of what required completely objective embodiment.

Another, if ancillary, method of enforcing the same suggestion (of radical confusion) is to observe the disparity between Crane's announced purpose and the masters he studied. Poets commonly profit most where they can borrow most, from the poets with whom by instinct, education, and accident of contact, they are most nearly unanimous. Thus poetic character is early predicted. In Crane's case, the nature of the influences to which he submitted himself remained similar from the beginning to the end and were the dominant ones of his generation. It was the influence of what we may call, with little exaggeration, the school of tortured sensibility—a school of which we perhaps first became aware in Baudelaire's misapprehension of Poe, and later, in the hardly less misapprehending resurrection of Donne. Crane benefited, and was deformed by, this influence both directly and by an assortment of indirection; but he never surmounted it. He read the modern French poets who are the result of Baudelaire, but he did not read Racine of whom Baudelaire was himself a product. He read Wallace Stevens, whose strength and serenity may in some sense be assigned to the combined influence of the French moderns and, say, Plato; but he did not, at least affectively, read Plato. He read Eliot, and through and in terms of him, the chosen Elizabethans—though more in Donne and Webster than in Jonson and

Middleton; but he did not, so to speak, read the Christianity from which Eliot derives his ultimate strength, and by which he is presently transforming himself. I use the word *read* in a strong sense; there is textual evidence of reading throughout the poems. The last influence Crane exhibited is no different in character and in the use to which he put it than the earliest: the poem called "The Hurricane" derives immediately from the metric of Hopkins but not ultimately from Hopkins' integrating sensibility. Thus Crane fitted himself for the exploitation of the peculiar, the unique, the agonised and the tortured perception, and he developed language-patterns for the essentially incoherent aspects of experience: the aspects in which experience assaults rather than informs the sensibility. Yet, granting his sensibility, with his avowed epic purpose he had done better had he gone to school to Milton and Racine, and, in modern times, to Hardy and Bridges—or even Masefield—for narrative sweep.

Crane had, in short, the wrong masters for his chosen fulfilment, or he used some of the right masters in the wrong way: leeching upon them, as a poet must, but taking the wrong nourishment, taking from them not what was hardest and most substantial—what made them great poets—but taking rather what was easiest, taking what was peculiar and idiosyncratic. That is what kills so many of Crane's poems, what must have made them impervious, once they were discharged, even to himself. It is perhaps, too, what killed Crane the man,—because in a profound sense, to those who use it, poetry is the only means of putting a tolerable order upon the emotions. Crane's predicament—that his means defeated his ends—was not unusual, but his case was extreme. In more normal form it is the predicament of immaturity. Crane's mind was slow and massive, a cumulus of substance; it had, to use a word of his own, the synergical quality, and with time it might have worked together, clarified, and become its own meaning. But he hastened the process and did not survive to maturity.

Certainly there is a hasty immaturity in the short essay on Modern Poetry, reprinted as an appendix to the *Collected Poems,* an immaturity both in the intellectual terms employed and in the stress with which the attitude they rehearse is held. Most of the paper tilts at windmills, and the lance is too heavy for the wielding hand. In less than five pages there is deployed more confused thinking than is to be found in all his poems put together. Poetry is not, as Crane says it is, an architectural art—or not without a good deal of qualification; it is a linear art, an art of succession, and the only art it resembles formally is plain song. Nor can Stravinsky and the cubists be compared, as Crane compares them, in the quality of their abstractions with the abstractions of mathematical physics: the aims are disparate; expression and theoretic manipulation can never exist on the same plane. Nor can psychological analyses, in literature, be distinguished in motive and quality from dramatic analyses. Again, and finally, the use of the term *psychosis* as a laudatory epithet for the substance of Whitman, represents to me the uttermost misconstruction of the nature of poetry: a psychosis is a mental derangement not due to an organic lesion or neurosis. A theory of neurosis (as, say, Aiken has held it in *Blue Voyage*) is more tenable scientifically; but neither it seems to me has other than a stultifying critical use. Yet, despite the confusion and positive irrationality of Crane's language the general tendency is sound, the aspiration sane. He wanted to write good poetry and his archetype was Dante; that is enough. But in his prose thinking he had the wrong words for his thoughts, as in his poetry he had often the wrong themes for his words.

II

So far, if the points have been maintained at all, what I have written adds up to the suggestion that in reading Hart Crane we must make allowances for him,—not historical allowances as we do for Shakespeare, religious allowances as for Dante and Milton, or philosophical as for Goethe and Lucretius,—but fundamental allowances whereby we agree to supply or overlook what does not appear in the poems, and whereby we agree to forgive or guess blindly at those parts of the poems which are unintelligible. In this Crane is not an uncommon case, though the particular allowances may perhaps be unique. There are some poets where everything is allowed for the sake of isolated effects. Sedley is perhaps the supreme example in English; there is nothing in him but two lines, but these are famous and will always be worth saving. Waller is the more normal example, or King, where two or three poems are the whole gist. Crane has both poems and passages; and in fact there is hardly a poem of his which has not something in it, and a very definite something, worth saving.

The nature of that saving quality, for it saves him no less than ourselves, Crane has himself most clearly expressed in a stanza from the poem called "Wine Menagerie."

> New thresholds, new anatomies! Wine talons
> Build freedom up about me and distill
> This competence—to travel in a tear
> Sparkling alone, within another's will.

I hope to show that this stanza illustrates almost inexhaustibly, to minds at all aware, both the substance and the aspiration of Crane's poetry, the character and value of his perceptions, and his method of handling words to control them. If we accept the stanza as a sort of declaration of policy and apply it as our own provisional policy to the sum of his work, although we limit its scope we shall deepen and articulate our appreciation,—a process, that of appreciation, which amounts not to wringing a few figs from thistles but to expressing the wine itself.

Paraphrase does not greatly help. We can, for the meat of it, no more be concerned with the prose sense of the words than Crane evidently was. Crane habitually re-created his words from within, developing meaning to the point of idiom; and that habit is the constant and indubitable sign of talent. The meanings themselves are the idioms and have a twist and life of their own. It is only by ourselves meditating on and *using* these idioms,—it is only by emulation,—that we can master them and accede to their life.

Analysis, however, does help, and in two directions. It will by itself increase our intimacy with the words as they appear; and it will as the nexus among comparisons disclose that standard of achievement, inherent in this special use of poetic language, by which alone the value of the work may be judged. (Analysis, in these uses, does not cut deep, it does not cut at all: it merely distinguishes particulars; and the particulars must be re-seen in their proper focus before the labour benefits.)

Moving in the first direction, towards intimacy, we can say that Crane employed an extreme mode of free association; that operation among words where it is the product rather than the addition that counts. There was, for example, no logical or emotional connection between thresholds and anatomies until Crane verbally juxtaposed them and tied them together with the cohesive of his metre. Yet, so associated, they modify and act upon each other mutually and produce a fresh meaning of which the parts cannot be segregated.

Some latent, unsuspected part of the cumulus of meaning in each word has excited, so to speak, and affected a corresponding part in the others. It is the juxtaposition which is the agent of selection, and it is a combination of metre and the carried-over influence of the rest of the poem, plus the as yet undetermined expectations aroused, which is the agent of emphasis and identification. It should be noted that, so far as the poem is concerned, the words themselves contain and do not merely indicate the feelings which compose the meaning; the poet's job was to put the words together like bricks in a wall. In lesser poetry of the same order, and in poetry of different orders, words may only indicate or refer to or substitute for the feelings; then we have the poetry of vicarious statement, which takes the place of, often to the highest purpose, the actual complete presentation, such as we have here. Here there is nothing for the words to take the place of; they are their own life, and have an organic continuity, not with the poet's mind nor with the experience they represent, but with themselves. We see that thresholds open upon anatomies: upon things to be explored and understood and felt freshly as an adventure; and we see that the anatomies, what is to be explored, are known from a new vantage, and that the vantage is part of the anatomy. The separate meanings of the words fairly rush at each other; the right ones join and those irrelevant to the juncture are for the moment—the whole time of the poem—lost in limbo. Thus the association "New Thresholds, new anatomies!" which at first inspection might seem specious or arbitrary (were we not used to reading poetry) not only does not produce a distortion but, the stress and strain being equal, turns out wholly natural and independently alive.

In the next phrase the association of the word "talons" with the context seems less significantly performed. So far as it refers back and expresses a seizing together, a clutching by a bird of prey, it is an excellent word well-chosen and spliced in. The further notion, suggested by the word "wine," of release, would also seem relevant. There is, too, an unidentifiable possibility—for Crane used words in very special senses indeed—of "talons" in the sense of cards left after the deal; and there is even, to push matters to the limit, a bare chance that some element of the etymon—ankle, heel—has been pressed into service. But the possibilities have among them none specially discriminated, and whichever you choose for use, the dead weight of the others must be provisionally carried along, which is what makes the phrase slightly fuzzy. And however you construe "wine talons" you cannot, without distorting what you have and allowing for the gap or lacuna of what you have not, make your construction fit either or both of the verbs which it governs. Talons neither build nor distill even when salvation by rhyme is in question. If Crane meant—as indeed he may have—that wines are distilled and become brandies or spirits, then he showed a poverty of technique in using the transitive instead of the intransitive form. Objection can be carried too far, when it renders itself nugatory. These remarks are meant as a kind of exploration; and if we now make the allowance for the unidentified distortion and supply with good will the lacuna in the very heart of the middle phrases, the rest of the stanza becomes as plain and vivid as poetry of this order need ever be. To complete the whole association, the reader need only remember that Crane probably had in mind, and made new use of Blake's lines:

> For a Tear is an Intellectual Thing,
> And a Sigh is the Sword of an Angel King.

It is interesting to observe that Blake was talking against war and that his primary meaning was much the same as that expressed negatively in "Auguries of Innocence" by the following couplet:

> He who shall train the Horse to War
> Shall never pass the Polar Bar.

Crane ignored the primary meaning, and extracted and emphasised what was in Blake's image a latent or secondary meaning. Or possibly he combined—made a free association of—the intellectual tear with

> Every Tear from Every Eye
> Becomes a Babe in Eternity;

only substituting the more dramatic notion of will for intellect. What is important to note is that, whatever its origin, the meaning as Crane presents it is completely transformed and subjugated to the control of the "new thresholds, new anatomies!"

The stanza we have been considering is only arbitrarily separated from the whole poem—just as the poem itself ought to be read in the context of the whole "White Buildings" section. The point is, that for appreciation—and for denigration—all of Crane should be read thoroughly, at least once, with similar attention to detail. That is the way in which Crane worked. Later readings may be more liberated and more irresponsible—as some people read the Bible for what they call its poetry or a case-history for its thrill; but they never get either the poetry or the thrill without a preliminary fundamental intimacy with the rational technique involved. Here it is a question of achieving some notion of a special poetic process. The principle of association which controls this stanza resembles the notion of wine as escape, release, father of insight and seed of metamorphosis, which controls the poem; and, in its turn, the notion of extra-logical, intoxicated metamorphosis of the senses controls and innervates Crane's whole sensibility.

To illustrate the uniformity of approach, a few examples are presented, some that succeed and some that fail. In "Lachrymae Christi" consider the line

> Thy Nazarene and tinder eyes.

(Note, from the title, that we are here again concerned with tears as the vehicle-image of insight, and that, in the end, Christ is identified with Dionysus.) Nazarene, the epithet for Christ, is here used as an adjective of quality in conjunction with the noun tinder also used as an adjective; an arrangement which will seem baffling only to those who underestimate the seriousness with which Crane remodelled words. The first three lines of the poem read:

> Whitely, while benzine
> Rinsings from the moon
> Dissolve all but the windows of the mills.

Benzine is a fluid, cleansing and solvent, has a characteristic tang and smart to it, and is here associated with the light of the moon, which, through the word "rinsings," is itself modified by it. It is, I think, the carried-over influence of benzine which gives startling aptness to Nazarene. It is, if I am correct for any reader but myself, an example of suspended association, or telekinesis; and it is, too, an example of syllabic interpenetration or internal punning as habitually practiced in the later prose of Joyce. The influence of one word on the other reminds us that Christ the Saviour cleanses and solves and has, too, the quality of light. "Tinder" is a simpler instance of how Crane could at once isolate a word and bind it in, impregnating it with new meaning. Tinder is used to kindle fire, powder, and light; a word incipient and bristling with the action proper to its being. The association is completed when it is remembered that tinder is very nearly a homonym for tender and, *in this setting,* puns upon it.

Immediately following, in the same poem, there is a parenthesis which I have not been able to penetrate with any certainty, though the possibilities are both fascinating and exciting. The important words in it do not possess the excluding, limiting power over themselves and their relations by which alone the precise, vital element in an ambiguity is secured. What Crane may have meant privately cannot be in question—his words may have represented for him a perfect tautology; we are concerned only with how the words act upon each other—or fail to act—so as to commit an appreciable meaning. I quote the first clause of the parenthesis.

> Let sphinxes from the ripe
> Borage of death have cleared my tongue
> Once and again . . .

It is syntax rather than grammar that is obscure. I take it that "let" is here a somewhat homemade adjective and that Crane is making a direct statement, so that the problem is to construe the right meanings of the right words in the right references; which will be an admirable exercise in exegesis, but an exercise only. The applicable senses of "let" are these: neglected or weary, permitted or prevented, hired, and let in the sense that blood is let. Sphinxes are inscrutable, have secrets, propound riddles to travellers and strangle those who cannot answer. "Borage" has at least three senses: something rough (sonally suggestive of barrage and barrier), a blue-flowered, hairy-leaved plant, and a cordial made from the plant. *The Shorter Oxford Dictionary* quotes this jingle from Hooker: "I Borage always bring courage." One guess is that Crane meant something to the effect that if you meditate enough on death it has the same bracing and warming effect as drinking a cordial, so that the riddles of life (or death) are answered. But something very near the contrary may have been intended; or both. In any case a guess is ultimately worthless because, with the defective syntax, the words do not verify it. Crane had a profound feeling for the hearts of words, and how they beat and cohabited, but here they overtopped him; the meanings in the words themselves are superior to the use to which he put them. The operation of selective cross-pollination not only failed but was not even rightly attempted. The language remains in the condition of that which it was intended to express: in the flux of intoxicated sense; whereas the language of the other lines of this poem here examined—the language, not the sense—is disintoxicated and candid. The point is that the quality of Crane's success is also the quality of his failure, and the distinction is perhaps by the hair of accident.

In the part of *The Bridge* called "Virginia," and in scores of places elsewhere, there is a single vivid image, of no structural importance, but of great delight as ornament: it both fits the poem and has a startling separate beauty of its own, the phrase: "Peonies with pony manes." [1] The freshness has nothing to do with accurate observation, of which it is devoid, but has its source in the arbitrary character of the association: it is created observation. Another example is contained in

> Down Wall, from girder into street noon leaks,
> A rip-tooth of the sky's acetylene;

which is no more forced than many of Crashaw's best images. It is, of course, the pyramiding associations of the word acetylene that create the observation: representing as it does

---

[1] Compare Marianne Moore's "the lion's ferocious chrysanthemum head."

an intolerable quality of light and a torch for cutting metal, and so on.

Similarly, again and again, both in important and in ornamental phrases, there are effects only half secured, words which are not the right words but only the nearest words. E.g.: "What eats the pattern with *ubiquity*. . . . Take this *sheaf* of dust upon your tongue . . . Preparing *penguin* flexions of the arms . . . [A tugboat] with one *galvanic* blare . . . I heard the *hush of lava wrestling* your arms." Etc. Not that the italicized words are wrong but that they fall short of the control and precision of impact necessary to vitalise them permanently.

There remains to consider the second help of analysis (the first was to promote intimacy with particulars), namely, to disclose the standard of Crane's achievement in terms of what he actually accomplished; an effort which at once involves comparison of Crane with rendered possibilities in the same realm of language taken from other poets. For Crane was not alone; style, like knowledge, of which it is the expressive grace, is a product of collaboration; and his standard, whether consciously or not, was outside himself, in verse written in accord with his own bent: which the following, if looked at with the right eye, will exemplify.

Sunt lacrimae rerum mortalia tangunt.—Vergil.

Lo giorno se n'andava, e l'aer bruno
    toglieva gli animai, che sono in terra,
    dalle fatiche loro.—Dante.

A brittle glory shineth in his face;
As brittle as the glory is the face.—Shakespeare.

Adieu donc, chants du cuivre et soupirs de la flûte!
Plaisirs, ne tentez plus un coeur sombre et boudeur!
Le Printemps adorable a perdu son odeur!—Baudelaire.

But Love has pitched his mansion in
The place of excrement;
For nothing can be sole or whole
That has not been rent.—Yeats.

She dreams a little, and she feels the dark
Encroachment of that old catastrophe,
As a calm darkens among water-lights.—Stevens.

The relevant context is assumed to be present, as we have been assuming it all along with Crane. Every quotation, except that from Yeats which is recent, should be well known. They bring to mind at once, on one side, the sustaining, glory-breeding power of magnificent form joined to great intellect. Before that impact Crane's magnitude shrinks. On the other side, the side of the particulars, he shrinks no less. The significant words in each selection, and so in the lines themselves, will bear and require understanding to the limit of analysis and limitless meditation. Here, as in Crane, words are associated by the poetic process so as to produce a new and living, an idiomatic, meaning, differing from and surpassing the separate factors involved. The difference—which is where Crane falls short of his standard—is this. Crane's effects remain tricks which can only be resorted to arbitrarily. The effects in the other poets—secured by more craft rather than less—become, immediately they are understood, permanent idioms which enrich the resources of language for all who have the talent to use them. It is perhaps the difference between the immediate unbalance of the assaulted, intoxicated sensibility and the final, no less exciting, clarity of the sane, mirroring sensibility.

It is said that Crane's inchoate heart and distorted intellect only witness the disease of his generation; but I have cited two poets, if not of his generation still his contemporaries, who escaped the contagion. It is the stigma of the first order of poets (a class which includes many minor names and deletes some of the best known) that they master so much of life as they represent. In Crane the poet succumbed with the man.

What judgment flows from these strictures need not impede the appreciation of Crane's insight, observation, and intense, if confused, vision, but ought rather to help determine it. Merely because Crane is imperfect in his kind is no reason to give him up; there is no plethora of perfection, and the imperfect beauty, like life, retains its fascination. And there is about him, too—such were his gifts for the hearts of words, such the vitality of his intelligence—the distraught but exciting splendour of a great failure.

1935

VI

THE METHOD OF MARIANNE MOORE

IN MAKING a formal approach to Marianne Moore, that is in
deliberately drawing back and standing aside from the
flux and fabric of long reading to see where the flux flowed
and how the fabric was made, what at once predominates is
the need for special terms and special adjustments to meet
the texture and pattern of her poems. So only can the substance be reconciled and brought home to the general body
of poetry; so only, that is, can the substance be made available
and availing. The facts are clear enough and many of them
even obvious to a wakened attention; the problem is to
name them with names that both discriminate her work and
relate it—if only in parallel—to other work with which it is
cognate. Time and wear are the usual agents of this operation, whereby mutual interpenetration is effected between the
new and old—always to be rediscriminated for closer contact—
and the new becomes formally merely another resource of the
art. Here we may assist and provisionally anticipate a little
the processes of time and wear. What we make is a fiction to
school the urgency of reading; no more; for actually we must
return to the verse itself in its own language and to that felt
appreciation of it to which criticism affords only overt clues.

In making up our own fiction let us turn first to some of
those with which Miss Moore herself supplies us; which we
may do all the more readily and with less wariness because she
is so plainly responsible and deliberate in her least use of language—being wary only not to push illustrations past inten-

tion, insight, and method, into the dark. Substance is the dark, otherwise to be known.[1] And this is itself the nub of the first illustration. I quote complete "The Past is the Present." [2]

If external action is effete
 and rhyme is outmoded,
  I shall revert to you,
 Habakkuk, as on a recent occasion I was goaded
   into doing by XY, who was speaking of unrhymed
    verse.
This man said—I think that I repeat
 his identical words:
  'Hebrew poetry is
 prose with a sort of heightened consciousness.' Ecstasy
   affords
  the occasion and expediency determines the form.

It is a delicate matter to say here only the guiding thing, both to avoid expatiation and to point the issue. I wish of course to enforce the last period, very possibly in a sense Miss Moore might not expect, yet in Miss Moore's terms too. A poem, so far as it is well-made for its own purpose, predicts much of which the author was not aware; as a saw cannot be designed for *all* its uses. Nor do the predictions emerge by devilling scripture, but rather by observation of the organic

---

[1] As Matthew Arnold distinguished between descriptions of nature written in "the Greek way" and those written in "the faithful way," and made his distinction fruitful, we might, without being too solemn about it, distinguish between the content of verse taken on a rational, conventional plane, and the content, itself non-rational and unique, which can be reached only *through* the rational form and conventional scaffold.

[2] Text of all quotations from *Selected Poems,* with an Introduction by T. S. Eliot, New York, The Macmillan Co., 1935. This differs from the earlier *Observations* (New York, The Dial Press, 1925) by the addition of eight poems and the omission of fourteen. Most of the reprinted poems have been revised slightly, one or two considerably, and one is entirely re-written and much expanded.

development of the words as they play upon each other. A poem is an idiom and surpasses the sum of its uses.[3]

For ease of approach let us take the last and slightest fact first. In Miss Moore's work inverted commas are made to perform significantly and notably and with a fresh nicety which is part of her contribution to the language. Besides the normal uses to determine quotation or to indicate a special or ironic sense in the material enclosed or as a kind of minor italicisation, they are used as boundaries for units of association which cannot be expressed by grammar and syntax. They are used sometimes to impale their contents for close examination, sometimes to take their contents as in a pair of tongs for gingerly or derisive inspection, sometimes to gain the isolation of superiority or vice versa—in short for all the values of setting matter off, whether in eulogy or denigration. As these are none of them arbitrary but are all extensions and refinements of the common uses, the reader will find himself carried along, as by rhyme, to full appreciation. Which brings us with undue emphasis to the inverted commas in this poem. In earlier versions the last three lines were enclosed; here the second sentence, which is crucial to the poem, stands free, and thus gains a strength of isolation without being any further from its context, becoming in fact nearer and having a more direct relation to the *whole* poem: so much so that the earlier pointing must seem to have been an oversight. Once part of what the man said, part of his identical words, it is now Miss Moore's or the poem's com-

[3] Put the other way round we can borrow, for what it is worth, a mathematician's definition of number and apply it to poetry. A poem is, we can say, like any number, "the class of all classes having the properties of a given class"; it is ready for all its uses, but is itself "only" the class to which the uses belong. The analogue should not be pushed, as its virtue is in its incongruity and as afterthought.

ment on what the man said and the conclusion of the poem. So read, we have in this sentence not only a parallel statement to the statement about Hebrew poetry but also a clue to the earlier lines. It is what the rest of the poem builds to and explains; and it in its turn builds back and explains and situates the rest of the poem. And it is the pointing, or at any rate the comparison of the two pointings, which makes this clear. If it were a mere exercise of Miss Moore's and our own in punctuation, then as it depended on nothing it would have nothing to articulate. But Miss Moore's practice and our appreciation are analogous in scope and importance to the score in music. By a refinement of this notion Mr. Eliot observes in his introduction that "many of the poems are in exact, and sometimes complicated formal patterns, and move with the elegance of a minuet." It is more than that and the very meat of the music, and one need not tire of repeating it because it *ought* to be obvious. The pattern establishes, situates, and organises material which without it would have no life, and as it enlivens it becomes inextricably a part of the material; it participates as well as sets off. The only difficulty in apprehending this lies in our habit of naming only the conventional or abstract aspects of the elements of the pattern, naming never their enactment.[4]

So far we exemplify generally that ecstasy affords the occasion and expediency determines the form. We perceive the occasion and seize the nearest peg to hang the form on, which happened to be the very slight peg of inverted commas. Working backwards, we come on Hebrew Poetry and Habakkuk, one of its more rhetorical practitioners. Hebrew poetry (not to say the Bible) is used throughout Miss Moore's work

---

[4] Whether this is a defect of language or of thinking I leave to I. A. Richards who alone has the equipment (among critics) and the will to determine.

as a background ideal and example of poetic language, an
ideal, however, not directly to be served but rather kept in
mind for impetus, reference, and comparison. A good part
of the poem "Novices" is eulogy of Hebrew poetry. Here,
in this poem, we have Habakkuk, who has a special as well
as a representative business. As a poet Habakkuk was less
than the Psalmist or Solomon or Job; nor had he pith of the
Proverbs or the serenity of Ecclesiastes. His service here is in
the fact that he was a prophet of the old school, a praiser of
gone times, a man goaded, as Miss Moore is, into crying out
against the spiritual insufficience and formal decay of the
times. The goading was the occasion of his ecstasy; anathema
and prayer his most expedient—his most satisfactory—form.
Miss Moore is speaking of matters no less serious; she couples
external action and rhyme; and for her the expedient form
is a pattern of elegant balances and compact understatement.
It is part of the virtue of her attack upon the formless in life
and art that the attack should show the courtesy and aloof-
ness of formal grace. There is successful irony, too, in resort-
ing through masterly rhymes to Habakkuk, who had none,
and who would no doubt have thought them jingling and
effete. (The rhymes have also the practical function of binding the particles of the poem. The notions which compound
the poem mutually modify each other, as Coleridge and Mr.
Richards would prescribe, and reach an equivalence; and the
medium in which the modifications flow or circulate is
emphasised and echoed in the rhymes.)

We note above that external action and rhyme are coupled,
a juxtaposition which heightens the importance of each. If
we conceive Habakkuk presiding upon it the import of the
association should become clear. In the first line, "If external
action is effete," the word *effete* is a good general pejorative,
would have been suitable for Habakkuk in his capacity of

goaded prophet. External action is the bodying forth of social life and when we call it effete we say the worst of it. Effete is a word much used of civilisations in decline— Roman, Byzantine, Persian—to represent that kind of sophistication which precedes the relapse into barbarism. What is effete may yet be bloody, stupid, and cruel, and its very refinements are of these. In the effete is the *flowering* of the vicious, a flowering essentially formless because without relation to the underlying substance. Thus, by Habakkuk, we find the morals implicit in the poem. Again, the poem may be taken declaratively (but only if it is tacitly held to include the implicit); if society and literature are in such shape that I cannot follow immediate traditions, well, I shall appeal to something still older. It is all the same. Ecstasy affords the occasion and expediency determines the form, whether I think of life or art.

I have, I think, laid out in terms of a lowered consciousness, a good deal of the material of this poem; but the reader need not think the poem has disappeared or its least fabric been injured. It is untouched. Analysis cannot touch but only translate for preliminary purposes the poem the return to which every sign demands. What we do is simply to set up clues which we can name and handle and exchange whereby we can make available all that territory of the poem which we cannot name or handle but only envisage. We emphasise the technique, as the artist did in fact, in order to come at the substance which the technique employed. Naturally, we do not emphasise all the aspects of the technique since that would involve discussion of more specific problems of language than there are words in the poem, and bring us, too, to all the problems of meaning which are *not* there.[5] We

[5] A perspective of just such a literally infinite labour is presented in I. A. Richards' *Mencius and the Mind,* which is fascinating but engulfing; as the

select, rather, those formal aspects which are most readily demonstrable: matters like rhyme and pattern and punctuation, which appear to control because they accompany a great deal else; and from these we reach necessarily, since the two cannot be detached except in the confusion of controversy, into the technical aspects, the conventional or general meanings of the words arranged by the form: as exemplified here by Habakkuk and the word effete. We show, by an analysis which always conveniently stops short, a selection of the ways in which the parts of a poem bear on each other; and we believe, by experience, that we thereby become familiar with what the various tensions produce: the poem itself. This belief is of an arbitrary or miraculous character, and cannot be defended except by customary use. It should perhaps rather be put that as the poet requires his technique (which is not his knowledge) before he can put his poem on paper, so the reader requires a thorough awareness of technique (which again is not *his* knowledge) before he can read the poem. However that may be—and the best we can do is a doubtful scaffold of terms—the point here is that all that can ever actually be brought into the discussion of a poem is its technical aspects. Which happens in all but the best poetry to be very near the whole of it. Here, in Miss Moore's poem, "The Past is the Present," we might provisionally risk the assertion that the last line is the surd of the "poetry" in it. The rest both leads up to it and is suffused by it. The rest is nothing without it; and it would itself remain only a dislocated aphorism, lacking poetry, without

---

opposite perspective is presented by the same author (with C. K. Ogden) in various works on Basic English, which combines the discipline of ascetic poverty with the expansiveness of, in a few hundred words, verbal omniscience. But I quote from Miss Moore's "Picking and Choosing," with I hope no more solemnity than the text affords: "We are not daft about the meaning but this familiarity with wrong meanings puzzles one."

the rest. "Ecstasy affords the occasion and expediency determines the form."

As it happens the line is actually pertinent as a maxim for Miss Moore's uncollected poetics; its dichotomy is at the intellectual base of all her work; and if we examine next the poem called "Poetry" we shall find Miss Moore backing us up in carefully measured understatement neatly placed among expedient ornament. But let us put off examination of the poem as such, and consider first what there is in it that may be translated to intellectual terms. The poem will outlast us and we shall come to it perhaps all the more sensitively for having libelled it; and it may indeed luckily turn out that our libel is the subject of the poem: that certainly will be the underlying set of argument. To translate is to cross a gap and the gap is always dark. Well then, whatever the injustice to the poem and to Miss Moore as an aesthetician, the following notions may be abstracted from the text for purposes of discourse and amusement. Since these purposes are neither dramatic nor poetic the order in which the notions are here displayed is not that in which they appear in the poem.

Miss Moore's poem says, centrally, that we cannot have poetry until poets can be "literalists of the imagination." The phrase is made from one in W. B. Yeats' essay, "William Blake and the Imagination." The cogent passage in Yeats reads: "The limitation of his [Blake's] view was from the very intensity of his vision; he was a too literal realist of the imagination, as others are of nature; and because he believed that the figures seen by the mind's eye, when exalted by inspiration, were 'eternal essences,' symbols or divine essences, he hated every grace of style that might obscure their lineaments." Yeats first printed his essay in 1897; had he written it when he wrote his postscript, in 1924, when he, too, had come to hate the graces which obscure, he would, I think, have

adopted Miss Moore's shorter and wholly eulogistic phrase and
called Blake simply a "literalist of the imagination,"[6] and
found some other words to explain Blake's excessively arbitrary symbols. At any rate, in Miss Moore's version, the
phrase has a bearing on the poem's only other overt reference, which is to Tolstoi's exclusion of "business documents
and school books" from the field of poetry. Here her phrase
leads to a profound and infinitely spreading distinction.
Poets who can present, as she says they must, "imaginary
gardens with real toads in them," ought also to be able to
present, and indeed will if their interest lies that way, real
school books and documents. The whole flux of experience
and interpretation is appropriate subject matter to an imagination *literal* enough to see the poetry in it; an imagination,
that is, as intent on the dramatic texture (on what is involved,
is tacit, is immanent) of the quotidian, as the imagination of
the painter is intent, in Velasquez, on the visual texture of
lace. One is reminded here, too, of T. S. Eliot's dogma in
reverse: "The spirit killeth; the letter giveth life"; and as
with Eliot the result of his new trope is to refresh the original
form by removing from it the *dead* part of its convention, so
Miss Moore's object is to exalt the imagination at the expense
of its conventional appearances. Her gardens are imaginary,
which makes possible the reality of her toads. Your commonplace mind would have put the matter the other way round—
with the good intention of the same thing—and would have
achieved nothing but the sterile assertion of the imagination
as a portmanteau of stereotypes: which is the most part of
what we are used to see carried, by all sorts of porters, as poetic
baggage.

[6] My quotation is taken from the collected edition of Yeats' Essays, New
York, 1924, page 147; Miss Moore's reference, which I have not checked, was
to the original *Ideas of Good and Evil,* printed some twenty years earlier by
A. H. Bullen.

It is against them, the porters and their baggage, that Miss Moore rails when she begins her poem on poetry with the remark: "I, too, dislike it: there are things that are important beyond all this fiddle." But in the fiddle, she discovers, there is a place for the genuine. Among the conventions of expression there is the possibility of vivid, particularised instances:

> Hands that can grasp, eyes
> that can dilate, hair that can rise
> if it must,

and so on. Such hands, hair, and eyes, are, we well know, props and crises of poetastry, and are commonly given in unusable, abstract form, mere derivative gestures we can no longer feel; as indeed their actual experience may also be. They remain, however, exemplars of the raw material of poetry. If you take them literally and make them genuine in the garden of imagination, then, as the poem says, "you are interested in poetry." You have seen them in ecstasy, which is only to say beside themselves, torn from their demeaning context; and if you are able to give them a new form or to refresh them with an old form—whichever is more expedient—then you will have accomplished a poem.

Perhaps I stretch Miss Moore's intentions a little beyond the pale; but the process of her poem itself I do not think I have stretched at all—have merely, rather, presented one of the many possible descriptions by analogue of the poetic process she actually employs. The process, like any process of deliberate ecstasy, involves for the reader as well as the writer the whole complex of wakened sensibility, which, once awakened, must be both constrained and driven along, directed and freed, fed and tantalised, sustained by reason to the very point of seeing, in every rational datum—I quote from another poem, "Black Earth"—the "beautiful element of unreason under it." The quotidian, having been shown as genuine, must be shown no less as containing the strange, as saying more than appears, and, even more, as containing the print of much that cannot be said at all. Thus we find Miss Moore constantly presenting images the most explicit but of a kind containing inexhaustibly the inexplicable—whether in gesture or sentiment. She gives what we know and do not know; she gives in this poem, for example, "elephants pushing, a wild horse taking a roll, a tireless wolf under a tree," and also "the base-ball fan, the statistician." We can say that such apposites are full of reminding, or that they make her poem husky with unexhausted detail, and we are on safe ground; but we have not said the important thing, we have not named the way in which we are illuminated, nor shown any sign at all that we are aware of the major operation performed— in this poem (elsewhere by other agents)—by such appositions. They are as they succeed the spring-boards—as when they fail they are the obliterating quicksands—of ecstasy. In their variety and their contrasts they force upon us two associated notions; first we are led to see the elephant, the horse, the wolf, the base-ball fan, and the statistician, as a group or as two groups detached by their given idiosyncrasies from their practical contexts, we see them beside themselves, for them-selves alone, like the lace in Velasquez or the water-lights in Monet; and secondly, I think, we come to be aware, whether consciously or not, that these animals and these men, are themselves, in their special activities, obsessed, freed, and beside themselves. There is an exciting quality which the pushing elephant and the base-ball fan have in common; and our excitement comes in feeling that quality, so integral to the apprehension of life, as it were beside and for itself, not in the elephant and the fan, but in terms of the apposition in the poem.

Such matters are not credibly argued and excess of statement perhaps only confuses import and exaggerates value. As it happens, which is why this poem is chosen rather than another, the reader can measure for himself exactly how valuable this quality is; he can read the "same" poem with the quality dominant and again with the quality hardly in evidence. On page 31 in *Observations* the poem appears in thirteen lines; in *Selected Poems* it has either twenty nine or thirty, depending on how you count the third stanza. For myself, there is the difference between the poem and no poem at all, since the later version delivers—where the earlier only announces—the letter of imagination. But we may present the differences more concretely, by remarking that in the earlier poem half the ornament and all the point are lacking. What is now clearly the dominant emphasis—on poets as literalists of the imagination—which here germinates the poem and gives it career, is not even implied in the earlier version. The poem did not get that far, did not, indeed, become a poem at all. What is now a serious poem on the nature of aesthetic reality remained then a half-shrewd, half-pointless conceit against the wilfully obscure. But it is not, I think, this rise in level from the innocuous to the penetrating, due to any gain in the strength of Miss Moore's conception. The conception, the idea, now that we know what it is, may be as readily inferred in the earlier version as it is inescapably felt in the later, but it had not in the earlier version been articulated and composed, had no posture to speak of, had lacked both development and material to develop: an immature product. The imaginary garden was there but there were no real toads in it.

What we have been saying is that the earlier version shows a failure in the technique of making a thought, the very substantial failure to know when a thought is complete and when it merely adverts to itself and is literally insufficient. There is also—as perhaps there must always be in poetry that fails—an accompanying insufficience of verbal technique, in this instance an insufficience of pattern and music as compared to the later version. Not knowing, or for the moment not caring, what she had to do, Miss Moore had no way of choosing and no reason for using the tools of her trade. Miss Moore is to an extent a typographic poet, like Cummings or Hopkins; she employs the effects of the appearance and arrangement of printed words as well as their effects sounding in the ear: her words are in the end far more *printed* words than the words of Yeats, for example, can ever be. And this is made clear by the earlier version which lacks the *printed* effect rather than by the later version which exhibits it. When we have learned how, we often do not notice what we appreciate but rather what is not there to *be* appreciated.

But if we stop and are deliberate, by a stroke cut away our intimacy with the poem, and regard it all round for its physiognomy, an object with surfaces and signs, we see immediately that the later version looks better on the page, has architecture which springs and suggests deep interiors; we notice the rhymes and the stanza where they are missing and how they multiply heavily, *both to the ear and the eye,* in the last stanza; we notice how the phrasing is marked, how it is shaded, and how, in the nexus of the first and second stanzas, it is momentarily confused: we notice, in short, not how the poem was made—an operation intractable to any description —but what about it, now that it is made, will strike and be felt by the attentive examiner. Then turning back to the earlier version, knowing that it has pretty much the same heart, gave as much occasion for ecstasy, we see indefeasibly why it runs unpersuasively through the mind, and why the later, matured version most persuasively invades us. It is no use saying that Miss Moore has herself matured—as evidence the notion is inadmissible; the concept or idea or thought of the poem is not difficult, new or intense, but its presentation, in the later version, is all three. She found, as Yeats would say, the image to call out the whole idea; that was one half. The other half was finding how to dress out the image to its best advantage, so as to arouse, direct, sustain, and consolidate attention.

That is not, or hardly at all, a question of Miss Moore's personal maturity; as may be shown, I think, if we consult two poems, presumably more or less as early as the earlier version of "Poetry." One is a poem which Miss Moore omits from her *Selected Poems,* but which Mr. Eliot neatly reprints in his Introduction, called "The Talisman." In the light of what we have been saying, Miss Moore was right in omitting it (as she was mainly right in omitting thirteen other poems); it lacks the fundamental cohesiveness of a thing made complete: with a great air of implying everything, it implies almost nothing. Yet Mr. Eliot was right in quoting it, and for the reasons given; it shows a mastery of heavy rhyme which produces its fatal atmosphere, and it shows that authoritative manner of speech-English which is one device to achieve persuasion. But the omission is more justifiable than the quotation; the substantial immaturity of the poem diseases the maturity of the form and makes it specious, like the brightness of fevered eyes.

The other poem, "Silence," which I quote, Miss Moore reprints verbatim except for the addition of a single letter to perfect the grammar and the omission of double quotes in the next to last line.

My father used to say,
'Superior people never make long visits,
have to be shown Longfellow's grave

or the glass flowers at Harvard.
Self-reliant like the cat—
that takes its prey to privacy,
the mouse's limp tail hanging like a shoelace from its mouth—
they sometimes enjoy solitude,
and can be robbed of speech
by speech that has delighted them.
The deepest feeling always shows itself in silence;
not in silence, but restraint.'
Nor was he insincere in saying, 'Make my house your inn.'
Inns are not residences.

There was no reason for change, only for scruples maintained
and minute scrutiny; for the poem reaches that limit of being
—both in the life of what it is about and in that other, musical
life which is the play of a special joining of words—which
we call maturity. It is important to emphasise here what commonly we observe last, namely the magnitude or scope of the
poem; otherwise the sense of its maturity is lost. The magnitude is small but universal within the universe of those who
distinguish cultivated human relations, which leaves us all the
room we need to grow while reading the poem; and which
signifies, too, that we should only diminish the value and
injure the genuineness of the poem if we held its magnitude
greater, its reach further. Thus the reader must contribute
his sense of its maturity to the poem before it can be situated,
before, as Wallace Stevens says, we can "let be be the finale
of seem."

There is here the spirit of an old controversy which we
need not re-enter, but which we ought to recognise in order
to pass it by: the controversy about young men writing great
poems and old men going to seed, about Wordsworth of the
Lyrical Ballads and Wordsworth wordsworthian. It is a
popular controversy in various senses of that adjective. A
more pertinent phrasing of the seminal problem, by which we

should escape the false controversy, is, I think, a phrasing in terms of the question of maturity; and the point is that there are various orders of maturity with complex mutually related conditions required to produce each. There are the broad and obvious classes of conditions which we list under the heads of technical competence and underlying import; but we do not, in actual poems, ever have import without competence or competence without import. Trouble rises from the confusion of import with intellectually demonstrable content, and technical competence with *mere* skill of execution. The music of words alone may lift common sentiment to great import, e.g. Take, O take those lips away; or at any rate we are faced with much great poetry which has only commonplace intellectual content and yet affects our fundamental convictions. Again—and I do not mean to leave the realm of poetry—we have, as an example of half-way house, such things as the best speeches in *The Way of the World,* where an effect like that of music and like that of thought, too, is had without full recourse to either, but rather through the perfection of the spoken word alone. And at the other end we have the great things in the great poets that do not *appear* to depend upon anything but their own barest bones. It is hard here to give an example beyond suspicion. There is Paolo's speech at the end of *Inferno* V, Blake's Time is the Mercy of eternity, Shakespeare's Ripeness is all, perhaps the Epilogue to *The Poetaster.* The point is that a balance must be struck of complex conditions so that nothing is too much and nothing not enough; but most of all it must be remembered that the balance of conditions which produced maturity in one place will not necessarily produce it in another. Nor is it just to judge the maturity of one poem by standards brought from another order of poetry; nor, lastly, does the maturity of a poem alone determine its magnitude. Drayton's "The Part-

ing," the ballad "Waly Waly," and *Anthony and Cleopatra,*
are all, and equally, mature poetry. *Hamlet,* we say, has a
sick place in it, and for us the first part of the first act of
King Lear is puerile; but we do not judge *Hamlet* and *Lear*
in terms of Drayton or the balladist, although we may, for
certain purposes, apply to them the special perfection of
Anthony. Maturity is the touchstone of achievement, not of
magnitude.

Returning to Miss Moore's "Silence," let us see if we can
what balance it is she has struck to bring it to a maturity
which makes the question of magnitude for the moment
irrelevant. The outer aids and props familiar in her best
verse are either absent or negligible. The poem has no
imposed, repetitive pattern, no rhyme for emphasis or sound,
it calls particularly neither upon the eye nor the ear; it
ignores everywhere the advantage of referring the reader, for
strength, to any but the simplest elements of overt form—
the rudiment of continuous iambic syllabification, which pre-
vails in all but one line. Only one phrase—that about the
mouse's limp tail—is specifically characteristic of Miss Moore;
all the rest of the phrasing represents cultivated contemporary idiom, heightened, as we see at first glance, because set
apart.

Here is one of the secrets—perhaps we ought to say one of
the dominant fixed tropes—of Miss Moore's verse; and it is
here what she has relied upon almost altogether. She resorts,
or rises like a fish, continually to the said thing, captures it,
sets it apart, points and polishes it to bring out just the special
quality she heard in it. Much of her verse has the peculiar,
unassignable, indestructible authority of speech overheard—
which often means so much precisely because we do not know
what was its limiting, and dulling, context. The quality in
her verse that carries over the infinite possibilities of the over-

heard, is the source and agent of much of her power to give a sense of invading reality; and it does a good deal to explain what Mr. Eliot, in his Introduction, calls her authoritativeness of manner—which is a different thing from a sense of reality.

It does not matter that Miss Moore frequently works the other way round, abstracting her phrase from a guidebook, an advertisement, or a biography; what matters is that whatever her sources she treats her material as if it were quoted, isolated speech, and uses it, not as it was written or said—which cannot be known—but for the purpose which, taken beside itself, seems in it paramount and most appropriate. In "Silence" she takes phrases from Miss A. M. Homans and from Prior's life of Edmund Burke, and combines them in such a way that they declare themselves more fully, because isolated, emphasised, and lit by the incongruous image of the cat and the mouse, than either could have declared themselves in first context. The poet's labour in this respect is similar to that of a critical translation where, by selection, exclusion, and rearrangement a sense is emphasised which was found only on a lower level and diffusely in the original; only here there is no damage by infidelity but rather the reward of deep fidelity to what, as it turns out, was really there waiting for emphasis.

But besides the effect of heightened speech, Miss Moore relies also and as deeply upon the rhetorical device of understatement—by which she gains, as so many have before her, a compression of substance which amounts to the fact of form. Form is, after all, the way things are put, and it may be profitably though not finally argued that every device of saying is an element in the form of what is said, whether it be detachable and predictable like the stress of a syllable or inextricable and innate like the tone of a thought. Understatement is a misnomer in every successful instance, as it achieves exactly what it pretends not to do: the fullest possible order of statement consonant with the mode of language employed. In such classic examples as Shakespeare's "The rest is silence," or Wordsworth's "But oh, the difference to me!" who shall suggest that more could have been said another way? who rather will not believe that it is in phrases such as these that the radical failure of language (its inability ever explicitly to *say* what is in a full heart) is overcome? Never, surely, was there a poorer name for such a feat of imagination: what we call understatement is only secured when we have charged ordinary words with extraordinary content, content not naturally in words at all. But they must be the right words nonetheless. Did not Shakespeare and Wordsworth really state to the limit matters for which there are no large words, matters which must, to be apprehended at all, be invested in common words?

Such is the archetype, the seminal expectation of understatement, and Miss Moore's poem, on its special plane, subscribes to it. But we are here concerned more with its subordinate, its ancillary uses—with its composition with operative irony and with its use to avoid a *conventional form* while preserving the conventional intention in all freshness. These are the uses with which we are familiar in daily life—crassly in sarcasm and finely in shrewd or reasonable wit; and it is on the plane of daily life and what might be said there—only heightened and rounded off for inspection—that this poem is written. It is part of the understatement, in the sense here construed, that superior people should be compared not to the gods accredited to the great world but to the cat carrying a mouse into a corner. The advantage is double. By its very incongruity—its quaintness, if you will—the comparison forces into prominence the real nature of the following notion of chosen solitude. We cut away immediately all that does not belong to the business of the poem; and find ourselves possessed of a new point of view thrown up and "justified" by the contrast. By a proud irony, content barely to indicate itself, the conventional views of solitude and intimacy are both destroyed and re-animated. A similar effect is secured in the last two lines—perhaps most emphatically in the choice of the word *residences,* itself, in this context, an understatement for the emotional word *homes* that detonates far more than the word *homes* could have done.

Finally, it is perhaps worth noting that "Make my house your inn" is both an understatement and a different statement of Burke's intention. Burke did not have the glass flowers, nor cats proud with mice, preceding his invitation: "Throw yourself into a coach," said he. "Come down and make my house your inn." But Miss Moore heard the possibility and set it free with all it implied. That is the poem. As the reader agrees that it is successful without recourse to the traditional overt forms of the art, he ought perhaps to hold that its virtue rises from recourse to the mystery, the fount of implication, in the spoken word combined with a special use of understatement. It makes a sample of the paradigm in its purest order, but hardly its least complex. The ecstasy was of speech, the expediency the greatest economy of means—as it happened in this poem, understatement. Yet as it is genuine, the spirit of its imagination is seen through the letter of what the speech might say.

All this is meant to be accepted as a provisional statement of Miss Moore's practical aesthetic—to denominate the ways her poems are made and to suggest the variety of purposes they serve. As it is acceptable, subject to modification and growth in any detail, it should be applicable elsewhere in her work, and if applied make intimacy easier. It may be profitable in that pursuit to examine lightly a selection of the more complex forms—both outward and inward—in which her work is bodied. Miss Moore is a poet bristling with notable facts—especially in the technical quarter—and it would be shameful in an essay at all pretentious not to make some indication of their seductiveness and their variety.

She is an expert in the visual field at compelling the incongruous association to deliver, almost startlingly to ejaculate, the congruous, completing image: e.g., in the poem about the pine tree called "The Monkey Puzzle,"—"It knows that if a nomad may have dignity, Gibraltar has had more"; "the lion's ferocious chrysanthemum head seeming kind in comparison"; and "This porcupine-quilled, complicated starkness." The same effect is seen with greater scope in the first stanza of "The Steeple-Jack."

> Dürer would have seen a reason for living
>   in a town like this, with eight stranded whales
> to look at; with the sweet sea air coming into your house
> on a fine day, from water etched
>   with waves as formal as the scales
> on a fish.

Here the incongruity works so well as perhaps to be imperceptible. The reader beholds the sea as it is for the poem, but also as it never was to a modern (or a sailor's) eye, with the strength and light of all he can remember of Dürer's water-etchings, formal and "right" as the scales on a fish. It is the same formal effect, the Dürer vision, that sets the continuing tone, as the moon sets the tide (with the sun's help), for the whole poem, bringing us in the end an emotion as clean, as ordered, as startling as the landscape which yields it.

> It could not be dangerous to be living
>   in a town like this, of simple people,
> who have a steeple-jack placing danger signs by the church

while he is gilding the solid-
      pointed star, which on a steeple
stands for hope.

In "The Hero," which is complementary to "The Steeple-
Jack" and with it makes "Part of a Novel, Part of a Poem,
Part of a Play," [7] we have another type of association, on the
intellectual plane, which *apparently* incongruous, is at heart
surprising mainly because it is so exact. Some men, says
Miss Moore, have been "lenient, looking upon a fellow crea-
ture's error with the feelings of a mother—a woman or a cat."
The "cat" refines, selects and—removing the sentimental
excess otherwise associated with "mother" in similar contexts
—establishes the gesture and defines, in the apposition, the
emotion. It is a similar recognition of identic themes in the
apparently incongruous—though here the example is more
normal to poetic usage—that leads to her defining statement
about the Hero.

              He's not out
   seeing a sight but the rock
   crystal thing to see—the startling El Greco
   brimming with inner light—that
covets nothing that it has let go.

What Mr. Eliot puts into his Introduction about Miss
Moore's exploitation of some of the less common uses of
rhyme—besides stress-rhyme, rhyme against the metric, internal auditory rhyme, light rhyme—should excite the reader
who has been oblivious to pursuit and the reader who has
been aware to perusal. Here let us merely re-enforce Mr.

[7] Something a hasty reader might miss is that (page 2, bottom) the Steeple-
Jack, so orderly in his peril, might be part of a novel, and that the frock-coated
negro (page 5, top) might, with his sense of mystery, be part of a play. The
text is "part of a poem." Miss Moore's titles are often the most elusive parts
of her poems.

Eliot with an example or so, and half an addition to his categories.

In the stanza from "The Hero" just quoted there is the paradigm for a rhyme-sound refrain which the well-memoried ear can catch. The first and last two lines of this and every other stanza rhyme on the sound of long "o," some light and some heavy. It is a question whether devices of this order integrally affect the poem in which they occur. If they do affect it, it must be in a manner that can neither be named nor understood, suffusing the texture unascertainably. But such devices do not need to be justified as integrating forces. It is enough for appreciation that this example should set up, as it does, a parallel music to the strict music of the poem which cannot be removed from it once it is there any more than it can be surely brought into it. It is part of the poem's weather. The Provençal poets worked largely in this order of rhyme, and in our own day Wallace Stevens has experimented with it.

Although many of the poems are made on intricate schemes of paired and delayed rhymes—there being perhaps no poem entirely faithful to the simple quatrain, heroic, or couplet structure—I think of no poem which for its rhymes is so admirable and so alluring as "Nine Nectarines and Other Porcelain." Granting that the reader employs a more analytical pronunciation in certain instances, there is in the last distich of each stanza a rhyme half-concealed and half overt. These as they are first noticed perhaps annoy and seem, like the sudden variations, trills, mordents and turns in a Bach Fugue, to distract from the theme, and so, later, to the collected ear, seem all the more to enhance it, when the pleasure that may be taken in them for themselves is all the greater. More precisely, if there be any ears too dull, Miss Moore rhymes the penultimate syllable of one line with the ultimate syllable of the next. The effect is of course cumulative; but the cumulus is of delicacy not mass; it is cumulative, I mean, in that in certain stanzas there would be no rhyme did not the precedent pattern make it audible. If we did not have

> a bat is winging. It
> is a moonlight scene, bringing . . .

we should probably not hear

> and sets of Precious things
> dare to be conspicuous.

What must be remembered is that anyone can arrange syllables, the thing is to arrange syllables at the same time you write a poem, and to arrange them as Miss Moore does, on four or five different planes at once. Here we emphasise mastery on the plane of rhyme. But this mastery, this intricacy, would be worthless did the poem happen to be trash.

Leaving the technical plane—at least in the ordinary sense of that term—there is another order of facts no less beguiling, the facts of what Miss Moore writes about—an order which has of course been touched on obliquely all along. What we say now must be really as oblique as before, no matter what the immediacy of approach; there is no meeting Miss Moore face to face in the forest of her poems and saying This is she, this is what she means and is: tautology is not the right snare for her or any part of her. The business of her poetry (which for us is herself) is to set things themselves delicately conceived in relations so fine and so accurate that their qualities, mutually stirred, will produce a new relation: an emotion. Her poems answer the question, What will happen in poetry, what emotion will transpire, when these things have been known or felt beside each other? The things are words and have qualities that may be called on apart from the qualities of the objects they name or connect. Keats' odes are composed on the same method, and Milton's *Lycidas*. But there are differences which must be mastered before the identity can be seen.

For Keats the Nightingale was a touchstone and a liberating symbol; it let him pour himself forth and it gave him a free symbol under which to subsume his images and emotions; the nightingale was a good peg of metonomy, almost, when he was done, a good synechdoche. For his purposes, the fact that he had a nightingale to preside over his poem gave the poem a suffusing order; and in the end everything flows into the nightingale.

With Miss Moore, in such poems as "An Octopus," "England," "The Labours of Hercules," "The Monkeys," and "The Plumet Basilisk," there is less a freeing of emotions and images under the aegis of the title notion, that there is a deliberate delineation of specific poetic emotions with the title-notion as a starting point or spur: a spur to develop, compare, entangle, and put beside the title-notion a series of other notions, which may be seen partly for their own sakes in passing, but more for what the juxtapositions conspire to produce. Keats' emotions were expansive and general but given a definite symbolic form; Miss Moore's emotions are special and specific, producing something almost a contraction of the given material, and so are themselves their own symbols. The distinction is exaggerated, but once seized the reader can bring it down to earth. Put another way, it is comparatively easy to say what Keats' poem is about, or what it is about in different places: it is about death and love and nostalgia, and about them in ways which it is enough to mention to understand. It is not easy to say what one of Miss Moore's longer poems is about, either as a whole or in places. The difficulty is not because we do not know but precisely because we do know, far more perfectly and far more specifically than we know anything about Keats' poem. What it is about is what it does, and not at any one place but all along. The parts stir each other up (where Keats put stirring things in sequence) and the aura of agitation resulting, profound or light as it may be, is what it is about. Naturally, then, in attempting to explain one of these poems you find yourself reading it through several times, so as not to be lost in it and so that the parts will not only follow one another as they must, being words, but will also be beside one another as their purpose requires them to be. This perhaps is why Miss Moore could write of literature as a phase of life: "If one is afraid of it, the situation is irremediable; if one approaches it familiarly what one says of it is worthless."

It is a method not a formula; it can be emulated not imitated; for it is the consequence of a radical leaning, of more than a leaning an essential trope of the mind: the forward stress to proceed, at any point, to proceed from one thing to another, crossing all gaps regardless, but keeping them all in mind. The poem called "The Monkeys" (in earlier versions "My Apish Cousins") has monkeys in the first line only. We proceed at once to "zebras supreme in their abnormality," and "elephants with their fog-coloured skin"; proceed, that is, with an abstract attribution and a beautifully innervated visual image. But the monkeys were not there for nothing; they signify the zoo and they establish an air for the poem that blows through it taking up a burden, like seeds, as it passes. I cannot say how the monkeys perform their function. But if it could be told it would not help; no more than it helps to say that the poem is composed not only on a rhyme and a typographic but also on a rigidly syllabic pattern. The first line of each stanza has fifteen syllables and the second sixteen; the third lines have ten, and the last, with which they balance, ten; and the fifth lines, except in the third stanza with thirteen, have fifteen. The fact of syllabic pattern has a kind of tacit interest, but we cannot say whether we can appreciate it, because we do not know whether even the trained ear can catch the weight of variations of this order. The monkeys are in a different position, and even if we cannot say in blueprint words what it is, we know that the interest is functional because we can report the fact of its experience.

More could be said—and in description a poem merely difficult and complex enough to require deep and delicately adjusted attention might seem a labyrinth; but let us rather move to a different poem, "An Octopus," and there select for emphasis a different aspect of the same method. This is a poem, if you like, about the Rocky Mountain Parks, Peaks, Fauna, and Flora; it is also about the Greek mind and language, and a great deal else. It contains material drawn from illustrated magazines, travel books, Cardinal Newman, Trollope, Richard Baxter's *The Saint's Everlasting Rest* (a book used in a dozen poems), W. D. Hyde's *Five Great Philosophies,* the Department of the Interior Rules and Regulations, and a remark overheard at the circus. Composed in free rhythm, natural cadence, and lines terminated by the criteria of conversational or rhetorical sense, it has a resemblance in form and typical content to certain of the Cantos of Ezra Pound; a resemblance strong enough to suggest that Pound may have partly derived his method from Miss Moore. The dates do not make derivation impossible, and the changes in structure from the earlier to the later Cantos confirm the suggestion. The pity in that case is that Pound did not benefit more; for there is a wide difference in the level and value of the effects secured. The elements in Pound's Cantos, especially the later ones, remain as I have argued elsewhere essentially disjunct because the substance of them is insufficiently present in the text; whereas in Miss Moore's poems of a similar order, and especially in "An Octopus," although themselves disjunct and even inviolate, coming from different countries of the mind, the substances are yet sufficiently present in the poem to compel conspiracy and cooperation. You cannot look in the words of a poem and see two objects really side by side without seeing a third thing, which will be specific and unique. The test, if reference can again be made to "Poetry," is in the genuineness of the presentation of the elements: [8] there must be real toads in the imaginary garden. Miss Moore has a habit of installing her aesthetics in her poems as she goes along, and in "An Octopus" she pleads for neatness of finish and relentless accuracy, both in mountains and in literature; and the mountain has also, what literature ought to have and Miss Moore does have, a capacity for fact. These notions only refine the notion of the letter of the imagination. The point here is that the notions about the treatment of detail explain why Pound's later Cantos seem diffuse in character and intangible in import and why Miss Moore's poem has a unity that grows with intimacy.

There are more aspects of Miss Moore's method as there are other lights in which to see, but enough has been touched on here to show what the method is like, that it is not only pervasive but integral to her work. It is integral to the degree that, with her sensibility being what it is, it imposes limits more profoundly than it liberates poetic energy. And here is one reason—for those who like reasons—for the astonishing fact that none of Miss Moore's poems attempt to be major poetry, why she is content with smallness in fact so long as it suggests the great by implication. Major themes are not sus-

[8] Mr. Eliot in his Introduction and Mr. Kenneth Burke in a review agree in finding genuineness paramount in Miss Moore's work.

ceptible of expression through a method of which it is the virtue to produce the idiosyncratic in the fine and strict sense of that word. Major themes, by definition of general and predominant interest, require for expression a method which produces the general in terms not of the idiosyncratic but the specific, and require, too, a form which seems to *contain* even more than to *imply* the wholeness beneath. The first poem in the present collection, "Part of a Novel, Part of a Poem, Part of a Play," comes as near to major expression as her method makes possible; and it is notable that here both the method and the content are more nearly "normal" than we are used to find. Elsewhere, though the successful poems achieve their established purposes, her method and her sensibility, combined, transform her themes from the normal to the idiosyncratic plane. The poem "Marriage," an excellent poem, is never concerned with either love or lust, but with something else, perhaps no less valuable, but certainly, in a profound sense, less complete.

Method and sensibility ought never, in the consideration of a poet, to be kept long separate, since the one is but the agent of growth and the recording instrument of the other. It is impossible to ascertain the stress of sensibility within the individual and it is an injustice to make the attempt; but it is possible to make at least indications of the sensibility informing that objective thing a body of poetry. Our last observation, that there is in the poem "Marriage" no element of sex or lust, is one indication. There is no sex anywhere in her poetry. No poet has been so chaste; but it is not the chastity that rises from an awareness—healthy or morbid—of the flesh, it is a special chastity aside from the flesh—a purity by birth and from the void. There is thus, by parallel, no contact by disgust in her work, but rather the expression of a cultivated distaste; and this is indeed appropriate, for within the context of purity disgust would be out of order. Following the same train, it may be observed that of all the hundreds of quotations and references in her poems none is in itself stirring, although some are about stirring things; and in this she is the opposite of Eliot, who as a rule quotes the thing in itself stirring; and here again her practice is correct. Since her effects are obtained partly by understatement, partly by ornament, and certainly largely by special emphasis on the quiet and the quotidian, it is clear that to use the thing obviously stirring would be to import a sore thumb, and the "great" line would merely put the poem off its track. Lastly, in this train, and to begin another, although she refers eulogistically many times to the dazzling colour, vivid strength, and torrential flow of Hebrew poetry, the tone of her references is quiet and conversational.

By another approach we reach the same conclusion, not yet named. Miss Moore writes about animals, large and small, with an intense detached intimacy others might use in writing of the entanglements of people. She writes about animals as if they were people minus the soilure of overweeningly human preoccupations, to find human qualities freed and uncommitted. Compare her animal poems with those of D. H. Lawrence. In Lawrence you feel you have touched the plasm; in Miss Moore you feel you have escaped and come on the idea. The other life is there, but it is round the corner, not so much taken for granted as obliviated, not allowed to transpire, or if so only in the light ease of conversation: as we talk about famine in the Orient in discounting words that know all the time that it *might* be met face to face. In Miss Moore life is remote (life as good *and* evil) and everything is done to keep it remote; it is reality removed, but it is nonetheless reality, because we *know* that it is removed. This is perhaps another way of putting Kenneth Burke's hypothesis:

"if she were discussing the newest model of automobile, I think she could somehow contrive to suggest an antiquarian's interest." Let us say that everything she gives is minutely precise, immediately accurate to the witnessing eye, but that both the reality under her poems and the reality produced by them have a nostalgic quality, a hauntedness, that cannot be reached, and perhaps could not be borne, by these poems, if it were.

Yet remembering that as I think her poems are expedient forms for ecstasies apprehended, and remembering, too, both the tradition of romantic reticence she observes and the fastidious thirst for detail, how could her poems be otherwise, or more? Her sensibility—the deeper it is the more persuaded it cannot give itself away—predicted her poetic method; and the defect of her method, in its turn, only represents the idiosyncrasy of her sensibility: that it, like its subject matter, constitutes the perfection of standing aside.

It is provisionally worth noting that Miss Moore is not alone but characteristic in American literature. Poe, Hawthorne, Melville (in *Pierre*) Emily Dickinson, and Henry James, all—like Miss Moore—shared an excessive sophistication of surfaces and a passionate predilection for the genuine —though Poe was perhaps not interested in too much of the genuine; and all contrived to present the conviction of reality best by making it, in most readers' eyes, remote.

1935

VII

THE DANGERS OF AUTHORSHIP

M R. COWLEY and Mr. Eliot are looking [1]—but neither together nor in the same direction—for a living standard
of approach to literature. Neither, in the books before us, is
primarily a literary critic—as indeed their subtitles attest;
neither attacks his problem from within the field of literature
as an art that finds autonomy in its practice, and neither forti-
fies himself in any logic of aesthetics. Each, rather, regards
literature as it interprets life rightly or wrongly, with reference to a general, complete view of life as distinguished from
the free, uncontrolled, merely literary view. Each deeply real-
ises that literature does not ever in fact—at least in the degree
that it is serious—escape into thin air without first influencing
the moral and spiritual life of its readers; and each therefore
requires that literature assent, for its own salvation, or at least
to secure its best possibilities, to a definite intellectual and
spiritual discipline. Mr. Eliot asserts the discipline of Christian orthodoxy and provides examples of the evils that result
from ignoring it. Mr. Cowley suggests a discipline that rises
from an honest recognition of the class-struggle and all its
implications in economic and political life; and he provides
us with a comparative history of recent literary futility as it
resulted from a distorted emphasis upon the individual. It
should be observed that neither Mr. Eliot nor Mr. Cowley

[1] *Exile's Return.* A narrative of ideas. By Malcolmn Cowley. New
York: W. W. Norton & Company, Inc. $3.00.
   After Strange Gods. A primer of modern heresy. By T. S. Eliot. New
York: Harcourt, Brace and Company. $1.25.

is an absolutist; both allow for great art outside the fold, but not the greatest.

Here they have each a cause to serve; each wishes to correct the living author from the dangers of the unguided pursuit of his profession; they want to save him from confusion, from irrelevance, from dishonesty, and from the corruption of moral or social diabolism. Nobler, and rasher, intentions could not be conceived; their object is to solve the dilemma of those who lack convictions and faith but who feel increasingly the urgency of both. The rashness consists in what I take to be the tacit assumption of both men that any particular frame of faith, political, moral, or religious, can fit any large body of men at any one time, or even, what is more important, the abler minds among it. That is the risk the apologist must always take and upon which he is eventually defeated; his success lies elsewhere, and in the interim, while men deceive themselves that the dogma in question is flexible, plastic, hierarchic, and universal.

Let us examine first the idea of Christian orthodoxy that Mr. Eliot brings forward. Here there is no proffered gambit. Mr. Eliot (I think because of the magic element which inheres in orthodoxy) assumes we are already initiate. He finds it necessary to presuppose that we know a good deal about Christianity and are able to distinguish roughly what in our experience, in our prejudices and prepared attitudes, is Christian in origin or direction and what is not; and this regardless of the presence or absence of specific faith; when the plain fact is that most of us—and I include atheists, Jews, and the multitude of the indifferent—merely have something of Christianity in our blood and no more know what it is than we do the fear and the animal hope which are also there. Other generations may have differed, may have possessed a general, persuasive sense of Christianity in which every sentiment and

every event of the mind found its orderly—or its disorderly—
place; our own generation I think has only analytic and separated notions, and therefore, since faith is whole or nothing,
can only draw back cheated of understanding at what I take
to be the critical sentence of the book:—"What I have been
leading up to is the following assertion: that when morals
cease to be a matter of tradition and orthodoxy—that is, of
the habits of the community formulated, corrected, and elevated by the continuous thought and direction of the Church
—and when each man is to elaborate his own, then *personality*
becomes a thing of alarming importance." That the Church
is catholic, not Roman Catholic but the Church of England
and hence to a large part of the Christian world seems schis-
matic and heretical and to another part seems something
worse, formalistic and idolatrous, and that in any case the
same Church is known in America under the style of Protestant Episcopal—these considerations only contribute to the
confusion with which the outsider must greet the word. We
simply do not know what is meant by the Church in the
crucial sense in which Mr. Eliot refers to it.

Two further sentences will specify the difficulty. "It should
hardly be necessary to add that the 'classical' is just as unpredictable as the romantic, and that most of us would not recognise a classical writer if he appeared, so queer and horrifying
he would seem even to those who clamour for him." Mr.
Eliot has previously suggested, with the peculiar emphasis of
understatement characteristic of his method, that there is an
analogue between the orthodox and the classical, the heretical
and the romantic; and I wish here tentatively to substitute
the theological terms for the literary in Mr. Eliot's sentence.
We would not know an orthodox writer if he appeared, nor, I
think, could the writer know himself to be orthodox. The
second sentence is Mr. Eliot's statement concerning the rift

some critics have observed between his poetry and his essays. "I should say that in one's prose reflexions one may be legitimately occupied with ideals, whereas in the writing of verse one can deal only with actuality." The sentiment is admirable and as an antithesis it helps explain Mr. Eliot's verse, which indeed constantly requires explanation; but it seems, to an outsider, the opposite of the orthodox position. As orthodoxy it is at least startling and requires a development Mr. Eliot does not give it before it can be digested under the "continuous thought and direction of the Church."

Objections not altogether captious might proceed much further. We might inquire, for example, whether a writer might not be unable to accept the thirty-nine articles and the spiritual authority of the bishops, and yet exercise complete orthodoxy in morals. We might inquire whether, like Athanasius in Mr. Eliot's example, there might not be a single orthodox writer unheeded and all the rest heretical. And so on; Mr. Eliot makes room for these inquiries. And not all the armour of his wit will defend him from this inquiry: whether, when he says that "reasons of race and religion combine to make any large number of free-thinking Jews undesirable," he means that he has no objections to any number of orthodox Jews, or whether he means that there is an optimum salt of agnosticism. But such objections only make Mr. Eliot's viewpoint more difficult to follow; they introduce that element of personality which he finds so alarming.

The major predicament in which Mr. Eliot leaves us is this. With a seductive vigour of speech and a persuasive air of authority he sets up for our use in evaluating literature the criterion of an orthodox Christianity which the greater part of us have lost, surrendered, or denied—if indeed we ever had it. He then reminds us that all men are naturally impure, that most writers, even the most orthodox, are somewhat heretical, and that orthodoxy, which is a consensus of the living and the dead, unlike tradition exists whether there be any who know it or not. He further implies that in his own case orthodoxy appears in his verse only through the irony that its ideal form is absent. The predicament would hardly be worth formulating and we could safely leave Mr. Eliot to his private adventure, were it not that this very ineluctable orthodoxy again and again brings its apologist to the point of keen judgment and profound feeling. It is something to be able to judge for oneself of the good and evil in life and its mirror art, and it is a great deal to be able to affirm that judgment persuasively over others; and if it is the "continuous thought and direction of the Church" that has given Mr. Eliot his access of critical strength we must respect the mystery to which we cannot assent.

But it may be there is another explanation, which the outsider, in his own interest, cannot help suggesting. Perhaps it is not the orthodoxy witnessed by the Church which imbues Mr. Eliot's critical blood, so that his Christianity, as such, only lends a colour of terminology to his thought without affecting its substance, as when he criticises the sentimental melodrama of Thomas Hardy under the head of diabolism. As Mr. Eliot once observed in speaking of Wordsworth, "the difference between revolution and reaction may be by the breadth of a hair"; and the difference between the orthodoxy of Mr. Eliot's criticism and that of his Church may be even finer, and equally profound, by the mere split of a hair. He uses, or at least we may recognise in him when he avoids theology and handles the literature before him, an orthodoxy which flows merely on the application of the whole intelligence. His judgments of Yeats and Pound and Hopkins, Joyce and Mansfield and Lawrence, have a merit and a utility upon which the conviction of the Church only intrudes. The criteria he actually applies are not canonical; he measures his men rather by the degree of their honesty and the depth of their sensibility.

Mr. Eliot would deny this explanation and find its purview blind. "I doubt," he observes during his discussion of diabolism, "whether what I am saying can convey very much to anyone for whom the doctrine of Original Sin is not a very real and tremendous thing." Mr. Eliot may be right and if so it represents a grave loss for him as well as for ourselves. In other words, by insisting on his terms and retreating upon his Church he limits our understanding of him and deforms his own approach. Mr. Eliot may be right, too, of course, in another sense: he may be speaking inspired and literal truth. But we can neither act upon nor controvert matters where there is no fundamental agreement. Few men have a capacity for religion, fewer still can find it animate in the arms of the Church; and this though all equally be saved or damned; these few must walk alone, or suffer the terrible punishment of being followed by the empty, the vain, and the foolish. But why should we put aside a man who can distinguish the peculiarity of great poetry as "merely a peculiar honesty, which, in a world too frightened to be honest, is peculiarly terrifying"; who can remark that "morals for the saint are only a preliminary matter; for the poet a secondary matter"; and who can describe thus the essential advantages for a poet: "it is to be able to see beneath both beauty and ugliness; to see the boredom, the horror, and the glory." Certainly not because he and a few others nourish their intelligence upon a Church which stultifies so many. Only, as we admire him, we cannot follow him.

So it is in a very different way with Mr. Cowley. He does not offer us a Church or insist upon terms which he is sure we do not understand; and he does not retreat at all. He writes robustly, freshly, and with a kind of vivid candour what might well have been a serious and carefully articulated private journal of the literary life—including and indeed accenting the personal—of his time; which was also, measurably and recognisably, our time; a time which for both has ended. He has, I think, a double object, of which the more important aspect looms everywhere behind the other. On the surface, Mr. Cowley deals with the personality and geography of his own generation of writers; beneath or behind or upon the horizon looms not only what happened but what had to happen to that generation as it aged or weakened; it had to return, to be converted, to a functional position in a society conceived organically—or it had to die. The prospect, the necessity, and the fact of this conversion, as it came to be realised, or as, for some, it could not be realised and brought death for terminus, is everywhere under and at the heart of the book. It is with this aspect of the book that we are here concerned.

Mr. Cowley narrates the history of the young artist of our time; and the object of the narrative is to represent, to *show* —not to prove whether by logic or doctrine—the social choice which has become inevitable for the artist at all awake. It is not the specific choice that Mr. Cowley recommends that is so important, but the specific necessity, in our predicament, of some choice. The reasons for the necessity are analogous to those which forced Mr. Eliot *back* upon the Church: the reasons of felt want, or a felt ethical weakness, the nausea of centrifugal or perimetric motion.

We need a burden of moral discipline and the forward stress of directed insight in order to be strong, and not only for ourselves as private individuals, but also as artists requiring to take advantage of the opportunities before us. Mr. Eliot would liberate us in the ethical image of Christian Orthodoxy; Mr. Cowley would liberate us a little nearer home by a right understanding of the society in economic and political process before us. It is the difference between the ethical climate of the *Criterion* and that of the *New Republic*. Mr. Eliot's ethics are revealed and have a stable beating heart capable of any burden of circumstance; Mr. Cowley's ethics are current and have a principle in view rather than an ideal behind. It is the difference between an ideal derived from a supernatural order—that is, from historical theological insight—and an ideal that flows from the process of the natural world, and has, as derivation, the surviving portion of inherited natural insight. These phrases of distinction are subject to correction and elaboration; but they witness certainly a radical distinction between ideals of heavenly origin and those which are *of* something in the natural world. The two may be at heart the same, since we cannot escape our limiting humanity, but the alternative emphases make all the difference in action. Mr. Eliot unearths the sanctions of the Conservative; Mr. Cowley envisages the necessities of whatever it may be that is the opposite of the Conservative—liberal, radical, communist, agnostic, or whatnot. I should like to suggest the phrase: deliberately plastic intelligence, but that might give the impression that Mr. Eliot has not a vital intelligence, which is false; so I leave the phrase as a merely provisional parallel, put in by an outsider, as a rhetorical plane of reference for both.

There is this further, really subordinate, difference between the two men, which at first strikes us as predominant and weighting the balance for Mr. Cowley. To achieve Mr. Eliot's point of view you have to work hard; or at least I have to work hard to remove my interests to a supernatural plane, and try as I may I cannot be sure, remembering Mr. Eliot's admonition on Original Sin, that I have at all usefully succeeded. I *think* I know what Mr. Eliot means when he puts

the artist's prime business as moral conflict in terms of Chris-
tion Orthodoxy; but I may have imperilled my soul in thinking so. With Mr. Cowley you do not need to work hard;
you need to think what has happened to you since 1914; you
need to read history. And if you read the history Mr. Cowley
gives you you will find it easy to share his point of view.
You may even find it too easy and think it your duty as a
good agnostic to draw back a little, on the proved rule that
when history seems easy—as when it seems authoritative—it
may turn out to have been glib. Authority and ease are the
signs of mastery not truth. But if you look in Mr. Cowley
again you will find it is not the history that is easy but the
conclusion it forces.

His account of Eliot, Joyce, and Valéry, his description of
Edmund Wilson's Symbolist movement (to be distinguished
from Arthur Symons') and his objections thereto, his analysis
of the post-war disintegration into either absolutism or the
ineluctable or both—these are pertinent, provisional, and critical; and these, when you remember his plain honesty and his
intelligence—these are qualifications enough. When you
couple his literary history with the economic and political
history of the same period the ease of his conclusion is just
and acceptable. The artist suddenly found "that society was
not a dull abstraction." His explanation (which is his conclusion) is simple. "Once a writer had recognised that society
contained hostile classes, that the result of their conflict was
uncertain and would affect his own fortunes, then he ceased
to believe that political action was silly: he became 'political-
ised.' If he also decided that the class whose interests lay
closest to his own was the working class, that the home he
was seeking lay with them, he became a radical. When the
change took place, it was almost as simple as that."

The day of the individual was gone (it is always gone);

the escape of the Protestant's dream of escape had turned out an exile in which nothing flourished but negation and desperation. The writer, if he was to amount to anything like the scene before him in his work, if he was, furthermore, to preserve himself as an individual (it was only the authority and the isolation—that is, the myth—of the individual which needed destruction)—this writer found it necessary to take up his social and political responsibilities. His imagination had to assume a deliberate ethical bias, and acquire social material, in order to get any work done at all.

Mr. Cowley's statement of the predicament of the American writer, if taken provisionally and for these years, seems to me correct. He must make a choice. And I agree that the implication of the wrong choice is death; but it need not be made under Mr. Cowley's eagle alone. It need not be made under any eagle at all. With Mr. Cowley's politics I am, I think, pretty much in accord, and with most of his specific views on literature; but with some of what I take to be the implications of his statement I cannot agree—I mean, I suppose, that I resent the implications I know others will find; all those whose political convictions, being kept brand-new, overwhelm and in fact replace the sturdy sensibility of which Mr. Cowley is himself an exponent.

In making a political choice, and in ordering your mind so as to make that choice of genuine consequence, it does not follow that if you are a writer your new politics will directly influence the substance you write of. Nor, if you are a critic, does it follow that you have uncovered political exigency as a prime standard. The writer, the artist of any kind, is, so far as he has any will in the matter, an independent mirror of the processes of life which happen to absorb him; he creates by showing, by representing; and his only weapons for change are the irony of the intelligence that can be brought to bear on the contemptible and the stupid, and the second irony of a second point of view, implicit in his work, but alien to that of his subject-matter. (In this reference there is a remark of Mr. Eliot's about Shakespeare to the effect that a good mirror is worth any amount of transcendence.) It may so happen that an artist's political convictions are fundamental to his work, when they will appear in it more likely with a tacit than a hortatory strength, as a radical qualification of the blood-stream; and it may happen not. The artist must always reserve the right to exhibit what he sees and feels of the human predicament, and the only thing we may require of him is that he does not exhibit what he neither sees nor feels but only thinks, for political or other reasons, that he ought to. Here Mr. Eliot's remark about the ideal in criticism and the actual in verse, seem to apply. If the political passions of this day cannot secure, as the Christians with their Dante, their cathedrals, and their Madonnas once did, the propaganda of great art, it need reflect the ignominy neither of the artist nor of the politics; it is misfortune only, and I think we may escape it; but in either case we may yet have great art.

Mr. Cowley may think my argument of implication is thin air; and for himself he is right: he has made only the apologist's mistake in believing that is is possible that others will be as sound with his own ideas as he is himself. The recent criticism of literature in terms of the (Marxian) class-struggle as performed by Mr. Hicks, Mr. Gregory and others, both in the absolutism of their rejections and the generosity of their enthusiasms, by example prove him wrong;—as the literary criticism of the House of Bishops would tend to prove Mr. Eliot deluded.

As I began by saying, these essays are meant to save the author from the dangers of his profession; and though I follow Mr. Cowley rather than Mr. Eliot, I think both have done something much better. They have shown us dangers which, being met, will improve our stature as citizens— whether of God or State—and which, overcome, and forced into their own domain, will add to the stature of our independence as artists.

1934

VIII

T. S. ELIOT

IF YOU want a text to head and animate a discussion of Mr.
Eliot's work from *Ash Wednesday* to *Murder in the Cathedral*, there is none better—for exactness, for ambiguity, and
for a capacity to irritate those unlikely otherwise to respond—
than the following sentence drawn from *After Strange Gods*,
which summarises Mr. Eliot's answer to the charge of in-
coherence between his verse and his critical prose. "I should
say that in one's prose reflexions one may be legitimately
occupied with ideals, whereas in the writing of verse one can
only deal with actuality." Here Mr. Eliot shows his characteristic talent for making statements of position which mis-
lead some, drive others to laboured exegesis, but end by
seeming self-evident and a piece with the body of his work.
In this instance what is misleading is not in the words but
in the common and not always tacit assumption that poetry
aims to transcend or idealise the actual; which may be so of
some poetry, of official poetry for example, but cannot well be
so without vitiating it, of poetry like Mr. Eliot's which has a
dramatic or moral cast. Conflict of character, mixture of
motive, and the declaration of human purpose and being,
cannot be presented (however much they may be argued)
except in terms of good and evil, which makes the most actual
realm we know.

It is the criterion of the actual, of the important orders
among it, and the means of approach that differ; and if we
call the differences verbal, intending to belittle them, it is

because we wish to escape the pressure of imaginative labour inherent in any genuine picture of the actual—as if the actual were free and ascertainable to all comers at the turn of a tap, instead of being, as it is, a remaining mystery even when long ardour has won knowledge of it. The actual, for poetry, or for Mr. Eliot's poetry, resides perhaps among "the deeper, un-named feelings which form the substratum of our being, to which we rarely penetrate"; a notion, and Mr. Eliot's phrasing of it, to which this essay will return. Now, you might say that for the realm of the actual so conceived the psychoanalysts have a means of approach but no criterion, and the Nazis have a criterion which for their purpose makes means of approach superfluous. Mr. Eliot has a criterion and a means which may be disentangled but which cannot be separated. But it is not a criterion that many can adopt to-day. As it happens, the three major adequate criteria of the actual—the Church of the great Christians, philosophy as it includes Plato, Mon-taigne, and Spinoza, and, third, that nameless tradition of the supernatural in daily life which includes folk-magic and extra-Christian religion; as it happens all three are in our day either taken as modes of escape or their animating influence is ignored. This is because of the tireless human genius for evasion and the inexhaustible human appetite for facts of the kinds that have use but cannot declare meaning: the statistical facts of science; it has nothing to do with the adequacy of the criteria themselves. Which indicates only that a man must achieve his own criterion individually and that it may appear disguised.

Mr. Eliot's criterion is the Christianity of the Church of England; and he is in the process of achieving it for himself. He provides us with an example of a powerful poetic imag-ination feeding on a corpus of insight either foreign or stulti-fying to the imaginative habit of most of us, and sustained by an active and inclusive discipline beyond our conscious needs. He is as far from us as Mr. Yeats, our one indubitable major poet, is with his fairies and lunar phases; and as close, in his best work, as Mr. Yeats in his, in an immitigable grasp of reality. It is a question which is the outsider. Mr. Yeats finds Christianity as unsatisfying for himself, finally, as any Huxley;[1] and Mr. Eliot has emphasised, with reference to Mr. Yeats, that you cannot take heaven by magic, has argued in several places recently that you cannot substitute a private for an institutional religion or philosophy. Both men write verse with the authority and the application of an orthodoxy. It may be that both are outsiders, if we conceive, as it may be fruitful to do, that the prevailing essences of English and American civilisation are heterodox—when the mere sight of any orthodoxy, of any whole view, may be entertained as dramatic and profoundly tragic. Some such notion was perhaps tacitly present in Mr. Eliot's mind when he wrote the following sentence. "At the moment when one writes, one is what one is, and the damage of a lifetime, and of having been born into an unsettled society, cannot be repaired at the moment of composition." At least it is in terms derived from such notion that the spectator can see the tragedy in the lives of such writers as D. H. Lawrence and Hart Crane—perhaps no less in the life of Dante—though the writers themselves may have seen only the pursuit of a task.[2]

[1] I hope to consider in another place the extraordinary strength in representing reality which Mr. Yeats derives from his own resort to the supernatural; a strength so great that it corrects every *material* extravagance of his doctrine. Here I merely quote three lines addressed to a modern Catholic.

Homer is my example and his unchristened heart.

The lion and the honeycomb, what has Scripture said?

So get you gone, Von Hügel, though with blessings on your head.

[2] It is notable that from another point of view Henry James saw the artist as an interesting theme for fiction only in his guise as a failure; his success was wholly in his work. See the Prefaces to *The Tragic Muse*, *The Author of Beltraffio*, and *The Lesson of the Master*.

Here two interesting and fundamental problems are raised
—that of the truth of an orthodoxy and that of the tragedy
of an orthodox mind in a heterodox world; one is for theology
and the other for imaginative representation; but neither can
be here our concern. Our own problem is no less interesting
and I think no less fundamental; the problem of the moral
and technical validity of Mr. Eliot's Christianity as it labours
to seize the actual for representation in his poetry. Validity is
not truth in an ascertainable sense, but amounts to truth in a
patent sense. We are faced in Mr. Eliot's recent verse with a
new and rising strength patently connected with his Christianity; and the Christian discipline is dominant and elemental in the two plays, *The Rock* and *Murder in the Cathedral*. It might formerly have been thought odd to call
attention to a writer's religion as still earlier his religious
conformity would have been the final test of his value. Now
a man's religion is the last thing we can take for granted
about him, which is as it should be; and when a writer shows'
the animating presence of religion in his work, and to the
advantage of his work, the nature of that presence and its
linkage deserve at least once our earnest examination. Interest
will be clearly seen if the statement can be accepted that there
has hardly been a poet of similar magnitude in English whose
work, not devotional in character, shows the operative, dramatic presence of Christianity. Many poets have relied, like
Wordsworth, upon a religion to which they did not adhere,
and many have used such a religion provisionally as a foil
from the rack; but there are only rarely examples of poets or
poems where deliberate affirmative use is made of religion
for dramatic purposes. It is true, after the middle age, in the
ages of Faith muddled with reason, the Church would not
have tolerated such a use at lay hands. There is Milton un-

arguably; but I should like to submit that Milton's religious dramatisations are theological in an age of theology and that what I am anxious to discriminate in Mr. Eliot is in the dramatisation of the turbulent feelings and the voids beneath the theology. Then there is Blake, whose religion was not Christian and often not religion at all but whose religious convictions permeated his prophetic books; but Blake's religion was self-manufactured as well as self-achieved, with the consequence that it as frequently clogged as freed his insight. Here we are concerned with the operative advantage of an objective religion on the material of dramatic poetry.

That is, the great interest, here as in any domain of criticism, is in the facts that can be stated about the relation between Mr. Eliot's poetry and his religion. No fact requires so much emphasis as the fact that, just as Mr. Yeats' poetry is not magic, Mr. Eliot's poetry is not religion. Religion and magic are backgrounds, and the actual (which may include the experience of magic and religion) is so to speak the foreground for each; the poet is in the area between, and in the light of the one operates upon the other. But there is no way in which, say, the mystery and magic of the Mass can enter directly into the material of poetry; nor on the other hand can poetry alone satisfy the legitimate aspirations of religion. For all I know the Church may hold differently; these propositions are meant to apply from the point of view of poetry alone, which we may think of here as looking for light upon its subject matter. The Church, which is religion embodied, articulated, and groomed, concentrates and spurs the sensibility, directing it with an engine for the judgment of good and evil upon the real world; but it does not alter, it only shapes and guides the apprehension and feeling of the real world. The facts of religion enlighten the facts of the actual, from which they are believed to spring.[3]

The act of enlightening or of being enlightened cannot, except for the great mystic, amount to identification of the object with the light in which it was seen; and in poetry it is only the devotional order which would desire such identification. Mr. Eliot's poetry is not devotional, unless we accept the notion that the love of God is best exercised in the knowledge of his works; a notion which would include Shakespeare as above all a devotional poet since he mirrored more of the actual man than any poet we know. But that is not what we mean by devotional poetry and it is ruining the heart of a word to sustain the pretence that we do. We mean as a rule poetry that constructs, or as we say expresses, a personal emotion about God, and I think it requires something approaching a saint to be very often successful in such constructions; and a saint, as Mr. Eliot observes, would limit himself if he undertook much devotional poetry. Otherwise, whatever the sincerity, private devotions are likely to go by rote and intention rather than rise to a represented state; there enters too much the question of what ought to be felt to the denigration (and I should say to God's eye) of what is actually felt—and it is this characteristic predicament of the devout which cripples the development of poets like Hopkins and Crashaw so that we value them most in other, hindered qualities than the devout. It is perhaps indicative in this context of devotional poetry considered as poetry to remember how few from twenty Christian centuries are the great prayers.

[3] The facts of science may similarly enlighten, providing there is a medium of poetic imagination; this although Mr. Eliot finds, correctly, the falsely poetic astronomy of our day quite vitiated. It was, says Mr. Eliot, the eternal *silence* of the immense spaces that terrified Pascal.

It would seem that an earnest repetition of the General Confession is a more devout if less emotional act than the composition of a poem.

Mr. Eliot's poetry is not devotional in any sense of which we have been speaking, but, for the outsider—and we are all outsiders when we speak of poetry—it is the more religious for that. It is religious in the sense that Mr. Eliot believes the poetry of Villon and Baudelaire to be religious—only an educated Villon and a healthy Baudelaire: it is penetrated and animated and its significance is determined by Christian feeling, and especially by the Christian distinction of Good and Evil. This feeling and this distinction have in his prose reflexions led him to certain extravagances—I remember as superlative a paper contributed to a Unitarian Monthly attacking the liberal element, which ended magnificently: "They are right. They are damned."—but in his verse, where he has limited himself, if sometimes obscurely, to the actual, there is no resulting extravagance, but the liberation of increased scope and that strength of charitable understanding which is apparently most often possible through Christian judgment.[4]

That is, the Church is in Mr. Eliot's poetry his view of life; it recognises and points the issues and shapes their poetic course; it is the rationale of his drama and the witness of its fate; it is, in short, a way of handling poetic material to its best advantage. It may be much more—as there is always life itself beyond the poetry that declares it; here nothing but the poetry is in question. If we consider the series of poems united in *Ash Wednesday* apart from the influence of that view of life we shall be left in as much of a muddle as if we

[4] The least charity is moral indifference, and Mr. Eliot's attacks upon it (in *After Strange Gods*) are just, whether you share his Christianity or not; but his principles are not the only ones to secure the end in view.

consider them apart from the influence which Mr. Eliot's merely poetic habits exert upon their Christianity. We should have, in the one case, an emotional elegy without much point but human weakness; and in the other, if we recognised the Christianity and nothing else, we should have only a collection of ritual trappings and reminiscences.

I do not know if there have been efforts to appreciate the Christian tags alone; but I know that so intelligent a critic as Mr. Edmund Wilson (in *Axel's Castle*) missed the Christian *significance* in the poem and saw only a revelation of human weakness and an escapist's despair. Mr. Wilson had a non-literary axe to grind. Mr. I. A. Richards, who had, as Mr. Eliot would say, more nearly the benefits of a Christian education, saw, even if he did not share, the Christian light, although that is not what he calls it. Mr. Richards saw what the poem was about; that it was not a revelation of human weakness and an attempt at escape but a summoning of human strength and an effort to extinguish both hope and despair in the face of death. The poem is neither the devotion of a weary soul nor an emotional elegy; it is, like almost all of Mr. Eliot's poetry, a dramatised projection of experience. As it happens the experience has a religious bias; which means that it calls on specific Christian beliefs to make the projection actual.

That the poem relies on other devices of the poetic imagination is obvious, and that these in their turn make the Christian beliefs actual for the poem—as Shakespeare's devices made Othello's jealously actual—should be equally obvious. Here I want to emphasise that the abnegation in the first section of the poem is Christian abnegation (it is introduced, after all, by the governing title *Ash Wednesday,* which begins the forty days of fast and penance before the resurrection, and which also commemorates the temptation and triumph in the wilderness); and Christian abnegation is an act of strength not weakness, whereby you give up what you can of the evil of the flesh for the good of the soul. The conception is certainly not limited to Christianity; as an ethical myth it is common to most philosophies and religions; but its most dramatic because most specifically familiar form is certainly that rehearsed by the Christian Church. That Mr. Eliot should make serious use of it, aside from his private religion, is natural; and it ought to have helped rather than hindered the understanding of the fundamental human feelings his poem dramatised. Mr. Wilson should have recognised its presence, and had he done so could not have mistaken the intent of the poem, however much for other reasons he might have judged it inadequate, for many persons, to its theme.

Similarly—if there is need for a further example—in the quoted words of Arnaut Daniel in the fourth section, we should, to gain anything like their full significance, not only be aware of their literary origin in the *Purgatorio,* not only feel the weight of Dante at our backs, but also should feel the force of the Christian teaching which made the words poignant for Dante—and so for Mr. Eliot. This or its equivalent. Knowing such matters for poetry is not so hard as it seems when the process is described; perhaps in this case, if the mind strikes instinctively at all the right attitude, the context of the poem will force the right meaning into the reader's mind once the literal meaning is understood. *Sovegna vos:* Be mindful of me, remember my pain. Arnaut wishes Dante to remember him in the wilfully accepted, refining fires of purgatory. It is characteristic of the meaning and integral to the association from which it springs that the words appear in Dante's Provençal. Had Mr. Eliot translated them they would have lost their identity and their air of specific origin; their being a quotation, and the reader knowing them so, commits them to a certain life and excludes other lives; nor could they have brought with them, in bare English, the very Christian context we wish to emphasise.

A different, but associated, effect is secured by the fact that the line which, with variations, opens the first and the last of these poems, appears in Mr. Eliot's English rather than in Guido Cavalcanti's Italian: at least I assume the line would own its source. Cavalcanti's line reads: "Perch'io non spero di tornar già mai"; Mr. Eliot's first version reads: "Because I do not hope to turn again," and his second: "Although I do not hope to turn again." The difference between "Because" and "Although" is deliberate and for the attentive reader will add much to the meaning. Mr. I. A. Richards has commented on the distinction in *On Imagination*. But the point I wish to make here is not about the general influence of either form of the line; the unwary reader can determine that for himself. My point is smaller, at least initially, and consists in stating two or three facts, and the first fact is very small indeed. "Perche" may be rendered either "because" or "although," depending on the context, here supplied by Mr. Eliot. The second fact is a little larger; although Mr. Eliot may greatly admire the Ballata from which the line was taken, it was not its import in that poem which concerned him in his own, so that to have quoted it in the original would either have given a wrong impression of import or have prefaced a serious work with a meretricious literary ornament. The Italian line (with its overtones about turning and renunciation of many orders) gave him material to re-model for his own purposes in his own poem—with yet a sediment, perhaps, of objective source to act as a mooring. As it happens, which is why the line is discussed here at all, it is indissolubly associated in both its forms with the "great" lines in the poem: the prayer—

> Teach us to care and not to care
> Teach us to sit still

This is a Christian prayer (not, as I gather Mr. Wilson would have it, at all mystical) and represents in an ultimate form for poetry one of the great aspects of the Church—its humility. That it also represents, in another interpretation, a great aspect of Confucianism is immaterial; as it is immaterial that by still another interpretation it represents the heart of Roman stoicism. Mr. Eliot came to it through the Church, or his poem did, and he brought Guido's line with him; [5] and the line as used has a dominant Christian flavour which cannot be expunged. There is thus a transformation of tone in this quotation quite different but to be associated with the quotation of Arnaut's phrase. As materials in the poem, one exerted Christian feeling in its own right, and the other was made to carry Christian feeling by the context—and feeling of the deep and nameless order which is the reality of Mr. Eliot's poetry.

The reader may rightly wonder if he is expected to get at Mr. Eliot's reality so indirectly and through the coils of such close-wound ellipsis; and especially will he wonder if he has read Mr. Eliot's assertion that he would like an audience that could neither read nor write, and this because, as he says, "it is the half-educated and ill-educated, rather than the uneducated, who stand" in the poet's way. Well, the uneducated hardly exist with relation to Mr. Eliot's poetry; and very few of his audience can be said to be rightly educated for it—certainly not this writer; most of us come to his poetry very ill-educated indeed. If modern readers did not as a class have to make up for the defects of their education in the lost cause of Christianity—if we did not find Christianity fascin-

[5] It is amusing but not inconsistent to reflect that Mr. Eliot has noted that Guido was a heretic.

T. S. ELIOT

ating because strange, and dramatic because full of a hubris
we could no more emulate than that of Oedipus—there would
be neither occasion nor point for this particular essay. We
have a special work of imaginative recovery to do before we
can use Mr. Eliot's poetry to the full. However a later day
may see it in perspective, to us Mr. Eliot must be of our time
less because he seems to spring from it than because he
imposes upon us a deep reminder of a part of our heritage
which we have lost except for the stereotypes of spiritual
manners. These stereotypes form our natural nexus with the
impetus or drive of his poetry; and it is as we see them filled
out, refreshed, re-embodied, that his poems become actual
for us. Mr. Eliot is perhaps not himself in a position to
sympathise with this operation of imaginative recovery; at any
rate he rejected the to us plausible statement of Mr. Richards
that the *Wasteland* was poetry devoid of beliefs. Mr. Eliot
would prefer the advantage of a literal to that of an imaginative faith, immersion to empathy; and he has very much
doubted, in his moral judgment of Thomas Hardy, whether
what he says could "convey very much to anyone for whom
the doctrine of Original Sin is not a very real and tremendous thing." The answer to that is that we do need to know
that the doctrine of Original Sin is a reality for Mr. Eliot, and
how much so, in order to determine both what light it sheds
on Hardy and how to combine it with other insights into
Hardy; but we do not need to share Mr. Eliot's conviction of
literal application. Indeed, many of us would feel that we
had impoverished our belief by making it too easy if we did
share the conviction. Here is the crux of the whole situation
between Mr. Eliot and those outside the Faith. The literal
believer takes his myths, which he does not call myths, as
supernatural archetypes of reality; the imaginative believer,
who is not a "believer" at all, takes his myths for the mean-

ing there is in their changing application. The practical consequences may be similar, since experience and interest are limited for data to the natural world, but the labour of understanding and the value assigned will be different for each. Thus Mr. Eliot and Mr. Richards are both correct— although neither would accept my way of saying so. The *Wasteland* is full of beliefs (especially, for this essay, a belief in the myth of Gethsemane) and is not limited by them but freed once they are understood to be imaginative. Only Mr. Eliot is correct for himself alone, while Mr. Richards is correct for others as well. Our labour is to recapture the imaginative burden and to avoid the literal like death.

If Mr. Eliot could not accept this notion in the abstract, he employs something very like it in his practical view of poetry, and by doing so he suggests an admirable solution for the reader's difficulties with his own poems and especially the difficulty with their Christian elements. This is the notion of different levels of significance and response. "In a play of Shakespeare," says Mr. Eliot, "you get several levels of significance. For the simplest auditors there is the plot, for the more thoughtful the character and the conflict of character, for the more literary the words and phrasing, for the more musically sensitive the rhythm, and for auditors of greater sensitiveness and understanding a meaning which reveals itself gradually. And I do not believe that the classification of audience is so clear-cut as this; but rather that the sensitiveness of every auditor is acted upon by all these elements at once, though in different degrees of consciousness. At none of these levels is the auditor bothered by the presence of what he does not understand, or by the presence of that in which he is not interested."

I propose to apply a little later the burden of these sentences where they properly belong: to the two plays, *The Rock* and

T. S. ELIOT

Murder in the Cathedral. Meanwhile let us twist the reference slightly and apply it to our present problem: the reader's relation to the Christian element among other elements in such poems as *Ash Wednesday,* merely substituting within the quotation the word readers for audience or auditors. Clearly there are different levels of significance at which the poem can be read; there are the levels responded to by Mr. Richards and Mr. Wilson; and there is the simplest level where there is "only" the poem to consider. But if the formula is applicable with any justice it is because Mr. Eliot's contèntion is correct that "the sensitiveness of every reader is acted upon by all these elements at once," and because, further, "at none of these levels is the reader bothered by the presence of what he does not understand, or the presence of that in which he is not interested." In that case we must admit that most readers do not count for more than the simplest form of excitement and vicarious mewing; which is the truth—and it is upon that class that the existence of poetry relies. Then there is a class a little higher in the scale, the class that propagates poetry without understanding it in any conscious sense; this is the class Mr. Wilson describes, the class of young poets who, after the *Wasteland* began to sink in, "took to inhabiting exclusively barren beaches, cactus-grown deserts, and dusty attics over-run with rats." Possibly these classes are unconsciously affected by all or almost all the possible levels of significance, including those of which the author was unaware; which makes occasion both for pride and prospective humiliation in the poet. I think the notion has something Christan in it; something that smells of grace; and has very little to do with any conception of popular poetry addressed to an audience that can neither read nor write. However that may be, there remains the class that preserves and supports poetry, a class the members of which unfortunately cannot stop short on the level of their unconscious appreciation but necessarily go on, risking any sort of error and ultimate mistake, until they are satisfied as to what a poem means. This may not be the class for which Mr. Eliot or any poet writes; but it includes that very small sub-class of readers of "greater sensitiveness and understanding" for whom the meaning of a poem reveals itself gradually. It is the class for and by both the good and bad members of which honest literary criticism is written.

And it is this class which, confronted by a sensibility so powerful and so foreign as Mr. Eliot's, is determined to get at the means as well as the meaning. It is in that sense that Mr. Eliot's poetry may be a spiritual exercise of great scope. This class, then, apprehending the dominant presence of Christian doctrine and feeling in Mr. Eliot's work, must reach something like the following conclusions as representing provisional truths. The Church is the vehicle through which human purpose is to be seen and its teachings prod and vitalise the poetic sensibility engaged with the actual and with the substrata of the actual. Furthermore, and directly for poetry, the Church presents a gift of moral and philosophical form of a pre-logical character; and it is a great advantage for a poet to find his material fitting into a form whose reason is in mystery rather than logic, and no less reason for that. It is perhaps this insight into the nature of the Church's authority that brought Mr. Eliot to his most magnificent statement about poetry. "The essential advantage for a poet is not to have a beautiful world with which to deal: it is to be able to see beneath both beauty and ugliness; to see the boredom, and the horror, and the glory."

But since this class of reader is not itself Christian—any more than poetry is itself Christian—it will be to our advantage and to that of poetry to remind ourselves emphatically

of what Mr. Eliot has himself several times insisted, that the
presence of Christianity does not make a poem good. It is
the poetry that must be good. Good Christianity will be a
very watery thing adulterated with bad poetry, and good
poetry can overcome a good deal of defection in a Christian
poet's Christianity—as it does in Dante's hate. In admitting
and enforcing the advantage of the Church, we commit ourselves, and before measuring our appreciation, to define the
limits, both moral and operative, contained in our admission.
There are some orders of charity in moral judgment which
the doctrines of the Church cannot encompass; there are some
experiences, that is, that the Church cannot faithfully mirror
because it has no clues or has not the right clues to the reality
involved. Thus we find Mr. Eliot refusing to understand
Shelley and *Lady Chatterley's Lover;* and we find him also
complaining of Irving Babbitt, whom he admired, that he
made too much use of the Eastern Philosophies. I doubt, too,
if the Church would be the right docent for an inspection of
the drama of personality unfolded by Freudian psychology;
it would see a different drama. . . . And we have, too, to
decide provisionally what the Church, as a supernatural reference, makes up for, and what—whether we miss it or not—
it fails to make up for; which is not at all easy to do. Perhaps we may say that the doctrines of the Church (we are
not concerned, in poetry, with ritual worship) idealise a pretty
complete set of human aspirations, and do this by appealing
to a supernatural order. That is a great deal; but for poetry
the Church does more. As these ideals are applied for judgment and light, all human action, struggle, and conflict, and
all human feelings, too, gain a special significance. For us,
as outsiders, the significance becomes greater if we remember
that it is a special, a predicted significance, and that other
ideals, and no ideals, would give a different significance or

none at all. Taken as a whole, the Church, by insisting on being right, became one of the great heresies of the human mind.

Our final obligation with respect to the Church is our smallest but most specific: to deal with it as an element of metric, only to be understood in composition with the other elements. We shall have emphasised and exaggerated in order to accomplish a reduction. But as the Church is not itself logical neither are the other elements in the composition. We have collections of elements, of qualities, which appear side by side, engaged, or entangled, or separate, of which the product is a whole varying with each combination. And a mind, too, such as we wish to think of as whole, is subject to the "damage of a lifetime," and we must think of the pressure and stress of that damage, omnipresent, agonising, even though we cannot and would not wish to say what at the moment it is: unless we say vaguely that it is the personality.

To put together indications of the qualities of a mind and of its suffusing personality is a labour for which there are models but no principles; there is no logical structure; and the more plausible the picture made the more likely it is to be untrustworthy. Mr. Eliot's mind, let us say, is a mind of contrasts which sharpen rather than soften the longer they are weighed. It is the last mind which, in this century, one would have expected to enter the Church in a lay capacity. The worldliness of its prose weapons, its security of posture, its wit, its ability for penetrating doubt and destructive definition, its eye for startling fact and talent for nailing it down in flight, hardly go with what we think of to-day as English or American religious feeling. We are accustomed to emotionalism and fanaticism in religious thought and looseness in religious feeling; the very qualities which are the natural targets of Mr. Eliot's weapons. Possibly it may be that we are unfamiliar with good contemporary Christian writers; they could hardly infect the popular press. Possibly, or even probably, it was these very qualities which, after the demolition of the pretence of value in post-war society, drove him into the Church as the one institution unaffected by the pretence or its demolition. Perhaps the teaching of Irving Babbitt, less by its preliminary richness than by its final inadequacy, was an important influence: we see in Mr. Eliot at least one of the virtues which Babbitt inculcated—Mr. Eliot is never expansive, either in verse or in prose, and expansiveness was a bugaboo to Babbitt.

However that may be, within the Church or not, Mr. Eliot's mind has preserved its worldly qualities. His prose reflexions remain elegant, hard (and in a sense easy—as in manners), controlled, urbane (without the dissimulation associated with ecclesiastical urbanity), and fool-proof. One would say that the mind was self-assured and might pontificate; but there is a redeeming quality of reserve about the assurance of his rare dogmatic extravagances, a reserve which may be taken as the accompaniment of scrupulous emotion and humility. This is—except the reserve—the shell which a mind must needs wear in order to get along without being victimised, and in order to deal, without escape, with things as they are on the surface. It is the part of a mind which is educable from outside, without regard to its inner bias.

Beneath the shell is a body of feeling and a group of convictions. Mr. Eliot is one of the few persons to whom convictions may be ascribed without also the ascription of fanaticism. Prejudice, which he has, is only a by-product of conviction and need be raised as an issue only when the conviction goes wrong; and intolerance, which he condones, is in the intellectual field only the expected consequence of conviction. With a little skill one learns to allow for prejudice and intolerance in Mr. Eliot's mind as we do for any convicted mind. His convictions are those which stem from the Church, from the history of Christian peoples, and from the classical cultures: including the convictions which represent Sophocles, Dante, and Shakespeare, as well as those which represent Original Sin, the Resurrection, and the sin of Spiritual Pride. However complexly arrived at, and with whatever, as the outsider must think them, tactful evasions in application, his convictions are directly and nobly held. If they enhance narrowness and put some human problems on too simple a plane they yet unflaggingly enforce depth. The mind reaches down until it touches bottom. Its weakness is that it does not always take in what it passes.

But a mind furnished only with convictions would be like a room furnished only with light; the brighter the more barren. Mr. Eliot's convictions light a sensibility stocked with feelings and observations and able to go on feeling and observing, where the feelings are more important than the observations. It is this body of feelings, and not any intermediately necessary intellectualisations of them, which are his ultimate concern; and ours, when we can bear on them. We may note here the frequency in his work of physiological images to symbolise the ways of knowing and the quality of things known; the roots and tentacles and all the anatomical details. Concerned with the material of life actually lived, his convictions only confirm a form for the material, make it available, release contact with it; as I suppose, in the other direction, convictions only confirm a form for the feeling of faith. And for these operations all learning is only a waiting, a reminiscence, and a key. It is the presence of this material, living and seen, if underneath, that makes Mr. Eliot master of the big words which, when directly charged, are our only names for its manifestations as emotion. Both in his poetry when he needs to and in his prose when he cares to, Mr. Eliot is free to use all those large emotional words with absolute precision of contact which your ordinary writer has to avoid as mere omnibuses of dead emotion.

It is natural then, in connection with these remarks, that in his prose writing, whether early or late, whether in essays or controversy, appreciation or judgment, Mr. Eliot is master of the compressed insight, the sudden illumination, the felt comparison, the seminal suggestion, and a stable point of view; and it is equally in course that we should find him master of persuasive and decimating rhetoric rather than of sustained argument and exhaustive analysis. He sees and his words persuade us of the fact that he has seen and of the living aspect of what he saw; but his words hardly touch, directly, the objective validity of what he saw. This explains the scope of his influence. There is no question that he has seen what he asserts; in the field of literature his eye for facts is extraordinarily keen, though like a sharpshooter's it hits only what it is looking for. There is no question, either, if you share his point of view even provisionally, that his weapons of attack penetrate if they do not dispatch their victims. That there is more to be seen, his scruples make him admit. But as for the objects of his attack, not his scruples but his methods leave some of them alive. You cannot kill an idea unless you have first embraced it, and Mr. Eliot is chary of embraces. This explains, too, why some of his followers have turned against him and why others are content to parrot him. He has an air of authority in his prose, an air of having said or implied to the point of proof everything that could be said; when as a matter of fact he has merely said what he felt and demonstrated his own conviction. Conviction in the end is opinion and personality, which however greatly valuable cannot satisfy those who wrongly expect more. Those who parrot Mr. Eliot think they share his conviction but do not understand or possess his personality. Those who have, dissatisfied, turned against him have merely for the most part expected too much. The rest of us, if we regard his prose argument as we do his poetry—as a personal edifice—will be content with what he is.

To argue that the poetry is written by the same mind and intellectually in much the same way as the prose is to show, in this order, all we need to know. It explains what he leaves out and gives a right emphasis to what he puts in; and if we add, once again, that his mind runs almost instinctively to dramatic projections, we understand what kind of organisation his work has—and it has one, deeply innervated. And I do not mean to beg the question when I say, as Mr. Eliot said of Shakespeare, that he is himself the unity of his work; that is the only kind of unity, the only circulating energy which we call organisation, that we are ever likely to find in the mass of a man's work. We need to remember only that this unity, this effect of organisation, will appear differently in works of criticism and works of poetry, and that it will be more manifest, though less arguable, in the poetry than in the criticism. The poetry is the concrete—as concrete as the poet can make it—presentation of experience as emotion. If it is successful it is self-evident; it is subject neither to denial nor modification but only to the greater labour of recognition. To say again what we have been saying all along, that is why we can assent to matters in poetry the intellectual formulation of which would leave us cold or in opposition. Poetry can use all ideas; argument only the logically consistent. Mr. Eliot put it very well for readers of his own verse when he wrote for readers of Dante that you may distinguish understanding from belief. "I will not deny," he says, "that it may be in practice easier for a Catholic to grasp the meaning, in many places, than for the ordinary agnostic; but that is not because the Catholic believes, but because he has been instructed. It is a matter of knowledge and ignorance, not of belief or scepticism." And a little later he puts the advantage for readers of poetry "of a coherent traditional system of dogma and morals like the Catholic: it stands apart, for understanding and assent even without belief, from the single individual who propounds it." That is why in our own context we can understand Mr. Eliot and cannot understand Mr. Pound. The unity that is Mr. Eliot has an objective intellectual version in his Christianity. The unity of Mr. Pound—if there is one—is in a confusion of incoherent, if often too explicitly declared, beliefs.

Christianity, then, is the emphatic form his sensibility fills; it is an artificial question which comes first. It is what happens to the sensibility that counts; the life lived and the death seen. That is the substantial preoccupation of the poet and the reader's gain. The emotion leans for expression on anything it can. Mr. Eliot's sensibility is typical of the poet's, as that of many poets is not. There is no wastage, little thinning out, and the least possible resort to dead form, form without motion. It is a sensibility that cannot deal with the merely surface report—what we used to call naturalism—and be content, but must deal with centres, surds, insights, illuminations, witnessed in chosen, obsessive images. These, as presented, seize enough of the life lived, the death seen, to give the emotion of the actuality of the rest. These we use as poetry; some will keep and some will wear out, as they continue or fail to strike reality as we can bear to know it.[6]

---

[6] It is perhaps relevant to quote here part of Mr. Eliot's comment on Arnold's "Poetry is at bottom a criticism of life," in the essay on Arnold in *The Use of Poetry*. "At bottom: that is a great way down; the bottom is the bottom. At the bottom of the abyss is what few ever see, and what those cannot bear to look at for long; and it is not a 'criticism of life.' If we

For opposite reasons, this essay can present texts for study neither of the apposite Christian form nor of the private sensibility that fills it; it merely emphasises—with as much repetition as the reader is likely to put up with—that knowledge is better than ignorance for the one, and that the other exists to implement the first. There is the Church for inspection and there are the poems to read. There remains the common labour of literary criticism: the collection of facts about literary works, and comment on the management, the craft or technique, of those works; and this labour, in so far as it leaves the reader in the works themselves, is the only one in itself worth doing. All that has been said so far is conditional and preliminary and also a postscript to reading. The modern reader is not fitted to appreciate either a mind or its works conceived in relation to Christianity as a living discipline; and the effort to appreciate as dead manners what is live blood is as vain as it is likely to prove repulsive. If I have shown to what degree the reader must perform an imaginative resurrection, I have so far done enough.

For Mr. Eliot does spill blood for ink and his discipline does live. It is a commonplace assertion that Mr. Eliot has shaped both his Christianity and his technique to forward the expressive needs of his mind. Here let us keep to the technique; it involves the other; and say that he has deliberately shaped and annealed and alloyed and purified it: the object being a medium of language to enhold the terms of feeling and the sign of the substance felt so as to arouse, sustain, and transform interest at different levels of response; and that he

---

mean life as a whole—not that Arnold ever saw life as a whole—from top to bottom, can anything that we can say of it ultimately, of that awful mystery, be called criticism?" Here Mr. Eliot, as he commonly does at important junctures, which are never arguable, resorts to the emotional version of the actual concerned. The "abyss" is one of his obsessive images.

has done so, besides, under the severest of disciplines, adherence to the standards of the good writing that has interested him. I do not say that he has succeeded altogether. Such a technique is the greatest *practical* ambition possible to secure; it takes long to come by and is slow to direct, since if it is to be adequate it must include the craft of presenting everything that is valuable. Very young poets confuse technique either with tricks, dodges, and devices, which are only a part of it, or with doodabs.

> Ambition comes when early force is spent
> And when we find no longer all things possible.

Perhaps I twist a little Mr. Eliot's implications, but it seems to me that the great temptations to which a poet's technique are exposed are the early temptation of the adventitious—the nearest weapon and the neatest subject—, and the temptation of repetition, which comes later, and of which it is the sin that the result is bound to be meretricious. These are fundamentals for all techniques and there are modifications for each; the whole technique of any one poem can never be the whole technique of any other poem, since, such is the limitation of human experience, a new poem is more likely to represent a growth of technique than a *growth* (I do not say change) of subject matter.

Nor will such a technique, for all readers or perhaps for any, ever be completely achieved except in the sum of the greatest poets. There are too many expectations, just enough in their sincerity, that can neither be gratified nor eradicated. There are those, for an extreme example, who expect an art of happiness. But the fact is that the rest of us, whose expectations are less gross, can hardly ever at a given time get over expecting a technique to show us what is not there; nor can we invariably "let" ourselves see what is there.

Confronted by *The Rock* and *Murder in the Cathedral,*
it is at once clear, first, that it is Mr. Eliot's technique rather
than his subject matter that has grown, and, second, that this
technique, new or old, radically limits the number and kind
of our expectations. The scope of his poetry, its final magnitude, is a different matter, and the impurity or bloom of the
contemporaneous must be rubbed away before it can be
determined. What I mean here is that we get neither the
kind nor variety of emotional satisfaction from either of his
plays that we get from Noel Coward or Congreve or Shakespeare. We are not tittivated or stroked; we do not see
society brushed with the pure light of its manners; there is
no broad display of human passion and purpose; we get the
drama of the Church struggling against society towards God,
which is something new (for those who like newness) in
English drama; we get the way of the Church against the
way of the World. And we get the awful harm as well as the
good done men and women in the course of the struggle.
It is this harm and this good, this sense of irreparable damage
and intransigent glory, as it is in contact with this struggle,
that makes the drama actual. It is not spiritual drama; it is
not like Dante the drama of damnation, penance, and beatitude; it is the drama of human emotions actualised in the
light of spiritual drama. The spirit is there, and intellect,
and theology; but all these through actualised emotions of the
experience of good and evil, of fraud and ambition, self-
deceit and nobility, and the communal humility of the poor—
which is a humility beneath Christian humility. This is what
we get most in *Murder in the Cathedral,* and what we cru-
cially fail to get in *The Rock*.

It is the substance of this (the same utter view of life) that
we get in another way in "Mr. Eliot's Sunday Morning
Service" and "The Hippopotamus"—these the tough anti-cler-

ical way; and in still other ways it is the same substance in "Prufrock," "Gerontion," and the *Wasteland*. The substance is permanent; the flux representative. If we take all the poems together with this substance in mind one charge that has been made against them should disappear—that they resent the present and fly into some paradise of the past. On the contrary, they measure the present by living standards which most people relegate to the past. The distinction is sharp; it is between poetry that would have been a shell of mere disillusion and poetry that is alive, and beyond disillusion. As Mr. Eliot himself remarked, the *Wasteland* only showed certain people their own illusion of disillusionment. It is this fundamental identity of substance which marks the unity of his work; that a variety of subjects and diverse approaches conspire to complete, to develop, a single judgment.

The changes—and no one would confuse or wrongly date two of Mr. Eliot's poems—are in the changes and growth of technique. The deliberate principle of growth has been in the direction of appealing to more levels of response, of reaching, finally, the widest possible audience, by attempting to secure in the poetry a base level of significance to which any mind might be expected to respond, without loss or injury to any other level of significance. It is in the light of this re-interpretation that Mr. Eliot's desire for an illiterate audience should be considered. That it is obvious does not make it any less telling, or any less inspiring to work towards, or—remembering the tacit dogma of difficulty held by so many poets—any less refreshing for the prospective reader. That this direction is not a guess on my own part and that he meant his notion of levels of significance in Shakespeare to apply to his own poetry, Mr. Eliot provides a candid text to show. It is at the very end of *The Use of Poetry*. With the great model of Shakespeare, the modern poet would like to write plays. "He would like to be something of a popular entertainer, and be able to think his own thoughts behind a tragic or a comic mask. He would like to convey the pleasures of poetry, not only to a larger audience, but to larger groups of people collectively; and the theatre is the best place to do it. . . . Futhermore, the theatre, by the technical exactions which it makes and limitations which it imposes upon the author, by the obligation to keep for a definite length of time the sustained interest of a large and unprepared and not wholly perceptive group of people, by its problems which have constantly to be solved, has enough to keep the poet's *conscious* mind fully occupied."

The best of Mr. Eliot's paragraph I have omitted: sentences that give the emotion of being a poet. What I have quoted is that part of his prose reflexions concerned with the ideal behind the two plays. It is extraordinary how much of what we want to know these three sentences can be made to explain. The only emphasis needed is this: that the obligation to keep an audience interested is only indirectly connected with the real interest of the plays. It is primarily a technical obligation; it points to and prepares for the real interest by seeming to be connected with it; and the great liability or technical danger is that the two interests may be confused without being identified, as the great gain is when the two interests are, in crisis, actually identified.

I do not think that in his two plays Mr. Eliot has realised either the radical limitations of his substance or the insuperable limitations of the theatre. The two do not always cooperate and they sometimes overlap. Perhaps it is better so; the comparative failure which says most, like Hamlet, is better than the relative success, like *The Coward,* that says least. The elements of failure must be nevertheless pointed out both when they spread rot and when they are surpassed. *The Rock* gives us an example of failure by confusion of interest which is nearly fatal, and *Murder in the Cathedral* gives us an example of success by fusion of interests.

Contrary to custom in English drama, it is the objective, the witnessing, the only indirectly participating, passages in these plays that are the finest poetry and that do the most work. These are the Choruses, in *The Rock* the chorus that represents the voice of the Church, and, in *Murder in the Cathedral*, the chorus of the women of Canterbury. In *The Rock* there are also choruses of the unemployed, of workmen, and some songs used as ritual chorus. In *Murder in the Cathedral* there is a kind of grand chorus of Priests, Tempters, and Chorus proper, which is used once, in the crisis of the first part. Whereas the traditional uses of the chorus are to comment on and to integrate action, here they are the integrity of the action itself, its actuality. Their relation to the "ordinary" version of the action, the rest of the play, is different in the two plays; and the quality of the work they do is different. It is these differences, in the light of the notion of levels of significance and response and in connection with the effort to maintain interest of both orders, that I wish to lay down the bare bones of. They carry the flesh.

The Rock is a pageant play, superficially about the difficulties, the necessity, and the justification of building a church in modern London. The pageant is a loose form and condones the introduction of a great variety of material; and so we are shown, upon the recurring focal scene of a church foundation actually in progress, a variety of episodes in the history of London churches. The theme and much of the incident were no doubt set; it is not a promising theme in which to expand a substance as concentrated as Mr. Eliot's, it is too generous and like the form chosen too loose, and too inherently facile of execution. Where almost anything will do passably there is nothing that will do well. The resulting text is not as drama very promising either. It is the sort of thing that, as a whole, depends on lushness of production and the personality of performance. At Sadler's Wells it may have been magnificent, but not because of Mr. Eliot's poetry; and as it is now, a reader's text, what was important and the very life of the performance—the incident, the fun, the church-supper social comment, and the good-humoured satire—reduce the effect of the poetry because it points away from the poetry instead of towards it. Bad verse cannot point to good poetry, and there is here the first bad verse Mr. Eliot has allowed himself to print, as well as his first bad jokes. The whole play has an air of following the counsel of the Chorus to the worshippers.

Be not too curious of Good and Evil;
Seek not to count the future waves of Time;
But be ye satisfied that you have light
Enough to take your step and find your foothold.

It is all satisfied and nearly all spelt in capital letters. Whether the expected nature of the audience was responsible, the form chosen, or whether Mr. Eliot was mistaken about both, the fact is that the level of interest appealed to by the whole play is too low to make passage to the higher levels natural. The general level lacks emotional probability and therefore lacks actuality. It is dead level writing. The reader satisfied with the dead level can hardly be expected to perceive, even unconsciously, the higher levels; and the reader interested in the higher levels cannot but find his interest vitiated by finding it constantly let down. Take the episode of the Crusades. The conversation between the man

and his betrothed is one thing, a flat appeal to stereotyped
emotion; the taking of the Cross, with its sonorous Latin
dressing, is another, an appeal by the direct use of ritual, on
another plane, to the stereotype of the conversation; neither
is actualised. The actuality is in the Chorus; but the Chorus
is not the same thing in a different form, it is another thing
altogether. There is a gap between, which is not crossed, and
the relations between the three are disproportional. We hear
a distinct voice from another world, which is the real world,
and which is the real poem; the actuality of which the other
voices are only the substitute and the sham. And the Chorus,
in this instance, perhaps loses some of its effect because it
comes first, prefacing what it does not perform, and because
its phrasing depends on the statements it makes rather than
makes the statements.

> Not avarice, lechery, treachery,
> Envy, sloth, gluttony, jealousy, pride:
> It was not these that made the Crusades,
> But these that unmade them.
>
> . . . .
>
> Our age is an age of moderate virtue
> And of moderate vice
> When men will not lay down the Cross
> Because they will never assume it.

Mr. Eliot has not here levied enough upon that other actuality, the actuality bred in the fitting of words together; which
is not the same thing as fitting notions together. These strictures apply throughout the episodes of the play and to most
of the Choruses to the episodes. It is only rarely, in some of
the songs and parts of the general choruses, that we get lines
like these, when the poetry escapes the Oppressor.

> Our gaze is submarine, our eyes look upward
> And see the light that fractures through unquiet water.
> We see the light but see not whence it comes.

The Oppressor was the misconceived need of expressing the Church at the level of general interest, instead of intensifying the actuality envisaged by the Church in terms of a represented interest.

This last is what Mr. Eliot has done in his second play, *Murder in the Cathedral,* and I think that the play could not have been better constructed with a view to representing in a self-contained form the mutually interrelated play of different levels of significance, from the lowest to the highest. I do not expect to have exhausted anything but its general interest for a long time to come and I do expect that its actual significance—its revelation of essential human strength and weakness—to grow the whole time. Yet it deals with an emotion I can hardly expect to share, which very few can ever expect to share, except as a last possibility, and which is certainly not an emotion of general interest at all; it deals with the special emotion of Christian martyrdom. Martyrdom is as far removed from common experience as the state of beatitude to which it leads; and it is much further removed, too, from ordinary interests than is the episodic material of *The Rock.* The view of life is as seriously held in either play, and the emotion is in itself as valid in one as in the other; they are in fact substantially the same. The whole difference between the failure of the first and the success of the second play depends on the lowest level of poetic intensity employed. If anything, the lowest level of significance (that is, the broadest, appealing to more, and more varied minds) is lower in the second play than the first; and this fact is in itself an element of formal strength and a verification of Mr. Eliot's ideal theory. It almost seems as if in *The Rock* Mr. Eliot had confused conventional significance with basic significance, but in his second play had clarified the confusion.

Applying Mr. Eliot's sentences about levels of significance, we can say that there is for everyone the expectation (we can hardly call it a plot) and ominous atmosphere of murder and death; for others there are the strong rhythms, the pounding alliterations, and the emphatic rhymes; for others the conflict, not of character, but of forces characterised in individual types; for others the tragedy or triumph of faith at the hands of the world; and for others the gradually unfolding meaning in the profound and ambiguous revelation of the expense of martyrdom in good *and* evil as seen in certain speeches of Thomas and in the choruses of the old women of Canterbury. It is the *expense* of martyrdom as a supreme form of human greatness, its expense for the martyr himself and for those less great but bound with it, its expense of good and evil and suffering, rather than its mere glory or its mere tragedy, that seems to me a major part of the play's meaning. Greatness of any kind forces to a crisis the fundamental life and the fundamental death in life both for the great themselves and for those who are affected by it. Martyrdom is the Christian form of personal greatness, and as with other forms of greatness, no human judgment or representation of it can fail of a terrible humility and a terrifying ambiguity. It is the limit of actuality in what Mr. Eliot calls the abyss.

I do not expect to prove that the emotional substance of which these remarks are a reformulation may be found in *Murder in the Cathedral*. There is no proof of the actual but the experience. But if the reader will first realise that the predicament of Thomas Becket is the predicament of human greatness, and that its example affects him, the reader, by reading over the dialogue between Thomas and the Fourth Tempter and Thomas' final speech in Part One, he will at least have put himself in the frame of mind to perceive the higher levels of significance, and the identification of all levels in the six long choruses and the play as a whole. It may be impertinent to point out as a clue or indication, that the Fourth Tempter's last speech repeats, as addressed to Thomas, Thomas' speech on his first appearance in the play, where the words are applied to the Chorus:

You know and do not know, what it is to act or suffer.
You know and do not know, that acting is suffering,
And suffering action. Neither does the actor suffer
Nor the patient act. But both are fixed
In an eternal action, an eternal patience
To which all must consent that it may be willed
And which all must suffer that they may will it,
That the pattern may subsist, that the wheel may turn and still
Be forever still.

And it may be superfluous to note that in the last of Thomas' speech at the end of Part One, he addresses you, the reader, you, the audience. Impertinent or superfluous the emphasis will not be amiss.

The Choruses, which flow from the expression of the common necessities of the poor up to, and in the same language, the expression of Christian dogma, may be said to exist by themselves, but their instance is the greatness of Thomas, as the death in them is Thomas' death. Thomas exists by himself, too, and his particular struggle, but both are made actual in relation to the Choruses. They are separate but related; they combine and produce a new thing not in the elements themselves. But the Choruses themselves have interrelated parts which work together by fate because they were rightly chosen and not because, in any ordinary sense, they have natural affinity for each other. The kinds of parts and their proportional bulk are not fixed but vary with the purpose of the particular Chorus; but the predominant elements are the

concrete immanence of death and death in life, and the rudimentary, the simple, the inescapable conditions of living, and
there is besides the concrete emotion of the hell on earth
which is the absence or the losing of God. It is the death
and the coming of it, of the Archbishop which measures
and instigates all the Chorus has to say; but neither that
death, nor its coming, nor its Christian greatness creates its
words; rather what it says is the actual experience from which
the Christian greatness springs. That is why the chorus is
composed of poor women, ordinary women, with ordinary
lives and fates and desires, women with a fundamental turbu-
lence of resentment at the expense of greatness.

> What is woven on the loom of fate
> What is woven in the councils of princes
> Is woven also in our veins, our brains,
> Is woven like a pattern of living worms
> In the guts of the women of Canterbury.

It is against this, the common denominator of all experience,
that the extraordinary experience of Thomas is seen, and by
it made real.

It is shameful to quote for illustration when half the virtue
is lost without the context, but I nevertheless quote two
passages, one for concreteness of sensual image and as an
example of internal rhyme, and the other to show how actual
an emotion the expectation of death can be, and how dramatic.

> I have eaten
> Smooth creatures still living, with the strong salt taste
>   of living things under sea; I have tasted
> The living lobster, the crab, the oyster, the whelk and
>   the prawn; and they live and spawn in my bowels,
>   and my bowels dissolve in the light of dawn.

THE DOUBLE AGENT

Chorus, Priests and Tempters alternately

C. Is it the owl that calls, or a signal between the tree?

P. Is the window-bar made fast, is the door under lock and bolt?

T. Is it rain that taps at the window, is it wind that pokes at the door?

C. Does the torch flame in the hall, the candle in the room?

P. Does the watchman walk by the wall?

T. Does the mastiff prowl by the gate?

C. Death has a hundred hands and walks by a thousand ways.

P. He may come in the sight of all, he may pass unseen unheard.

T. Come whispering through the ear, or a sudden shock on the skull.

C. A man may walk with a lamp at night, and yet be drowned in a ditch.

P. A man may climb the stair in the day, and slip on a broken step.

T. A man may sit at meat, and feel the cold in his groin.

These are the easy things that come first; but without them, the other meaning that comes gradually would not come at all; they are its basis, in poetry as in life. "The world," says Mr. Eliot, "is trying the experiment of attempting to form a civilised but non-Christian mentality." He believes the experiment will fail; and I think we may be sure it will fail unless it includes in itself the insight, in Christian terms or not, of which Mr. Eliot gives an actual representation. Meanwhile he redeems the time.

1935

IX

HERESY WITHIN HERESY

B ECAUSE of the dogma that makes it so vigorous and, as I
think so wrong, this book [1] requires an equally vigorous,
and no doubt equally wrong-headed, counterstatement. Mr.
Hicks is apparently a believing communist, and like a believing Christian for him it is necessary that every interest in life
subserve the articles of his faith. He therefore attempts so to
interpret the last seventy years of American literature that its
successes and its failures may be determined by the degree in
which various authors anticipated the depression-communism
of 1933. That is, literature is being judged by its witness of
economic history and by its implicit adherence to a particular
doctrine. To an outsider this procedure is sterile and obfusca-
tory; (and it is, incidentally, largely because of the sterility
and the obfuscation that the outsider remains such); for such
a procedure seems tantamount to elevating Gascoigne's *Dulce
Bellum Inexpertis* above King Lear, or, to go a step further in
sins of omission, to convict Shakespeare of essential evasion
because he never employed, in his Histories, the tragic theme
of the Eviction of the Yeomen from the Commons, which
came to a crisis about 1515, and which was certainly a major
example of capitalistic exploitation.

In order that these remarks may not seem wholly frivolous it is necessary first to rehearse Mr. Hicks' ultimate dogma

[1] *The Great Tradition.* An interpretation of American literature since the
Civil War. By Granville Hicks. The Macmillan Company. New York.
1933. $2.50.

and then to illustrate a few of the judgments that flow from the dogmas.

The seed of dogma comes to full blossom, as it should, in the last chapter, and is to be seen most clearly in the following sentence. "The passing of the years has shown that America is no exception, and that, here as elsewhere, the only clue to the tangled web of life in the last century is the Marxian analysis." The context suggests that by Marxian analysis Mr. Hicks means not the actual economic analysis Marx made of English industrial society in the mid-nineteenth century, but rather the general view that economic life under capitalism is a class struggle, and will remain such until capital is prevented from using the machine to exploit for private profit the rest of society. In other words, Mr. Hicks believes that those convulsions of society which we call the Industrial Revolution form the most, if not the only, significant events in recent history; and he proceeds, therefore, as if by logic, to insist that the imaginative writer must "if he is accurately and intelligently to portray American life . . . ally himself with the working class." No other honest choice is possible for him once he has discovered that there is a class struggle and that he himself is taking part in it. If he does make this choice, if he does become an active revolutionary writer, and keeps both eyes and all his heart on the necessity for destroying capitalism and replacing it with communist economy, then, "as this way of looking at life becomes an integral part of his imaginative equipment, he can not only perceive the operation of underlying forces; he can also rejoice in their play because of his confidence in what they will eventually accomplish." Furthermore, to quote the final sentence of the book, "They will know they are participating in a battle, that, in the long run, is for civilisation itself, and they will have no doubt of the outcome."

This program, this creed, is elaborated with all the bigoted eloquence of a disciple, but it nowhere reaches the freed passion of the master. As special pleading it is persuasive, but as a formulation of principle it is unconvincing. It is not what Mr. Hicks has put in that is wrong, but the arrogance by which he makes what he puts in exclusive. It is "the highest hopes and deepest desires of mankind" that his program is intended to express; but we have only to stop and take thought to be reminded not only of what he has himself left out but also what the rigidity and hardihood of his scruples would prevent others from putting in.

Let us take the Marxian analysis first. A revised Marxian view—revised by a clearer dialectic manipulating enormously augmented data—is certainly a sound view to take of the economic story; but to advance by the rhetoric of desire alone and state unequivocally that the Marxian analysis is the only clue to the last century is very much like saying that the traffic in relics is the only clue to the Crusades. It represents either religious ignorance or wilful blindness—and which is the more unforgivable sin against criticism is an artificial question. Even the Marxians should remember the names of Rousseau, Malthus, Darwin, Mill, Nietzsche, and Freud. At least there is a secondary taint of all these men which the unregenerate outsider can distinguish in the most thoroughgoing Marxian. The process of becoming a communist is not the deep obliterating dye of religious conversion; it is the adoption of an additional view which modifies but which ought rather to vitalise than to destroy the existing structure of the mind.

Thus the best communists—those whose ideas have most value for society—will be those who claim least for their doctrines. Those who, like Mr. Hicks, make communism the exclusive director and interpreter of human destiny, are

[221]

simply mistaken as to what the outsider sees as the limiting character of communism, its basis in economics. Under the necessity for action, for the sake of relief, economic needs may be conceived in that exaggerated form where they master and include all other needs; but to the independent mind, whether creative or critical, such a view is impossible. To such a mind the elementary character of economics, and thus of the politics that flows from it, is ancillary. Economics is the handmaid of society, not the mistress, and in the form of the Marxian analysis she may be used to secure comforts and to exterminate pests, and those are the only secrets she knows. To assign her the duty of understanding human relations or the architecture of institutions is, in the acuity of our present plight, to overestimate her ability and to set up a society of servant-girls.

Leaving the metaphor, it is the whole of society that predicts its economics, not the economics that predicts the society. Where the communists are right is in seeing that it is necessary and possible to change our economics, but they are wrong—and are likely thereby to ruin their economics with overwork—in thinking that economic good is paramount and can subsume, except by stultifying them, the other goods of society. It is at this point that the artist, the critic, and those who meditate life from an independent attitude, must all draw back from Mr. Hicks. The economic plight, and among other analyses of it that of the Marxians, will condition their work, but not control it. Exaggeration, distortion, the assertion of supremacy—such desperations they will leave to that realm which it is their business to interpret—the realm of direct action. And this attitude applies not only to Mr. Hicks' communism; it is equally the answer to the capitalists, the agrarians, and all nihilists of whatever description.

We have been concerned so far with Mr. Hicks' major

premiss—that an economic theory can govern the subject and import of literature—and with certain *a priori* reasons for rejecting that premiss. Let us suppose the premiss were provisionally accepted, not as final, but for the sake of what could be done with it. And that is a possible assumption. Mr. Hicks is not alone as a Marxian; nor are the Marxians alone in the kind of thing they are doing. There are the psychologists, the Christians, the sectionalists, the humanists; all these, like the Marxians, attempt to subordinate literature to one or more of its conditioning aspects. An exaggeration, if not good in theory, sometimes puts normal insights in emphatic light.

What happens, then, to American literature under Mr. Hicks' dogmatic insight? It grows thin; it turns out to be full of broken hopes, defeated ambitions, dejected flight, and cowardly evasion; it is diseased. So far, Mr. Hicks differs little from many other critics—in the general indictment. But the aetiology he assigns to the disease—which is also his judgment of it—is quite different. The American literary artist since the Civil War has failed of complete success because he was unable or unwilling to seize for his subject the economic character of American life, as understood by Mr. Hicks. Let three examples—and those where the argument is plainest—suffice. Of Mark Twain: "In book after book, after the most brilliant kind of beginning, Mark Twain crawls with undisguised weariness of soul to the closing page. . . . Not one of his major fictions concerns itself with the movements and events of American life in the latter half of the nineteenth century. . . . He was, and knew he was, merely an entertainer." Of Emily Dickinson: Although "everything in her work is immediate, personal, and honest," yet it is "undeniably fragile and remote. . . . The fact that she would not publish her poems in her own lifetime . . .

indicates, among other things, that she was aware of the impossibility of coming to terms with her own age." Of Howells: Although "the economic phases of American life had become increasingly important to him . . . that interest did not lead to an understanding of economic forces. . . . That is, in short, the principal explanation of Howell's inability to make us feel that here is a master."

If you grant Mr. Hicks his bias, what he has to say has an importance beyond the bias. The fact that his contentions are arguable, or that there are other explanations, in terms of personal equipment, for the incompleteness of the three writers named, does not destroy the value of Mr. Hicks' judgments and may well sharpen them. He is dealing with influences which did actually condition the work criticised.

When he tackles the work of the last decade, where his real interests lie, the bias becomes all-important and replaces as well as instigates the terms of judgment. We hear of Thornton Wilder that his work "merely reflects the cowardice and dishonesty of his spirit," and that "the vulgarity of Wilder's way of pandering to this [leisure] class is unmistakable." The sentiment here expressed reflects back upon Mr. Hicks.

Of greater significance is his final judgment of John Dos Passos. "The concept of the class struggle and the trend toward revolution, deeply realized in the emotions and translated into action, has given Dos Passos a greater sensitiveness to the world about him. But it has done something more important: it has shown him the relations between apparently isolated events and enabled him to see the fundamental unity beneath the seemingly chaotic complexity of American life." This, I think, is as little sober criticism, and has as little place in an interpretation of literature called the Great Tradition as the remarks about Wilder. In both quotations it is the zealot speaking, the man who is guilty of the worst human heresy, the man who is the victim of one idea.

In the selected instances, because Mr. Hicks does not find in his books the politics he wants, he condemns Thornton Wilder on what seem wholly non-literary grounds; and because he does find his politics in Dos Passos he says nothing of the weakness and sentimentality with which, for example, Dos Passos' proletariat is conceived, and nothing, either, of the barbarous inadequacy of Dos Passos' general expression of the quality of life. I do not think that in either instance Mr. Hicks is dishonest. It is merely that in his mind he has subordinated literature to a single interpretation of a single one of the many interests that condition it to-day—the Marxian analysis. That is heresy within heresy; and it would be nothing but privation to follow him.

Note: The reader, not of Mr. Hicks' book, but of this review, had perhaps better now than later be informed that on page 283 these words occur: "And the criticism of such men as Yvor Winters, Dudley Fitts, and R. P. Blackmur resembles the impassioned quibbling of devotees of some game."

1933

X

SAMUEL BUTLER

Mrs. Stillman's [1] study presents, among its other recommendations, just the right amount of idolatry, the right accent of enthusiasm, to send the reader back to Butler's own books, and Mr. Bartholomew's extracts [2] from unpublished parts of the Note Books add both expected chastening and unexpected salt. Curiously, neither biographer nor editor display the qualities that marked their subject. Both are straightforward, simple, and humble. Neither is suspicious, obsessed nor eccentric. Mrs. Stillman's exposition and analysis proceed directly and unequivocally, with restraint and balance, into the heart of her subject, and she never employs the Butlerian weapon of black-handed exaggeration. Her comment is adjusting rather than sharp; her insight is cumulative and revealing, rather than instant and penetrating; she takes her author at his own valuation; altogether the reader is left admirably where he should be, with plenty of facts and plenty of reasoning, cogently displayed—and with plenty of work to do for himself. Mr. Bartholomew, with the death of Mr. Streatfield, now Butler's literary executor, is in his own field as adequate as Mrs. Stillman: he writes canonically but informatively on the characteristically unconventional bits of canon he supplies, and he understands which of his bits seem most authoritative let alone: as in the wholly delightful and

---

[1] *Samuel Butler*. A Mid-Victorian Modern. By Clara G. Stillman. New York: The Viking Press. 1932. $3.75.

[2] *Butleriana*. Edited by A. T. Bartholomew. London: The Nonesuch Press. New York: Random House. 1932. $4.00.

wholly bawdy selection of the sayings of Mrs. Boss, where he
limits himself to identification. Both books are useful. *Butleriana,* physically a lovely book, besides Mrs. Boss, gives us
sketches of Butler's relations with Pauli, one villain of his life,
with his father, the other villain, with Henry Festing Jones his
dearest friend and disciple, and with Alfred his clerk, either
more fully than, or not at all, found elsewhere. There is also
a sonnet about Miss Savage not included in the *Note Books.*
Mrs. Stillman's book ought for all but the voracious to replace
Jones' two-volume memoir, and on its merits as well as
because of its comparative brevity; lacking the true fanaticism
of the disciple, and having the advantage of perspective and
personal indifference, she takes a wider view than Jones was
able to.

There are various ways of looking at Butler—and Butler
meant them, with all the duplicity of which he was capable,
to be more various than they are; but in no aspect did he
approach perfection except in that for which he cared for
perfection least—that of the humorous essayist or lecturer.
"Quis Desiderio" is as nearly perfect as may be in its combination of wit, sense, and ridicule; it contains an analysis of
Wordsworth's Lucy poem as deft and possible as it is point-
edly preposterous. (The reader is referred to *Essays on Life,
Art, and Science,* where this piece is printed.) In this kind of
work, Butler was well rounded and sufficient to his audience
without at all depriving himself of his cherished mental
habits. Elsewhere, whether in his life or his work, he was
and meant to appear notoriously not round, but angular, off-
side, odd, and deliberately insufficient to his subject.

Another minor work, *Shakespeare's Sonnets Reconsidered,*
contains in its preface an account of how it came to be written. Not having read the Sonnets at all for a good many
years, he came on two papers in *The Fortnightly Review* by

William Archer and Sidney Lee, leaning respectively towards the Earls of Pembroke and Southampton as the real person behind the W. H. of the sonnets. Butler thought that was a good problem for him to get his own teeth into, and spent nine or ten preliminary months learning the sonnets by heart. Commentary and scholarship he let alone, requiring as always only enough knowledge to weight his argument. The book was published in 1899 and establishes W. H. as a young man of Shakespeare's own class named William Hewes or Hughes. The argument is no better than Oscar Wilde's, nor, for that matter, than those of Archer or Lee. As a literary critic, Butler was a victim of his method: the personal, intuitive, absorbed, but cranky method. It is useless to enquire how much Butler's own experience with Pauli was responsible for his seeing in W. H. a similar infatuation on the part of Shakespeare. The point is, he satisfied only himself, and thought his own satisfaction would convince others of the truth of what he felt. He was mistaken: his soberness and industry made for him here his only dull book.

The same method with a single extension made a very different book out of *The Authoress of the Odyssey*. The extension was into topography. His cogent localisation of the *Odyssey* at Trapani gives an objective persuasiveness, however illogical the connection, to his theory that the poem was written by a young woman, Nausicaa in the text, with suitable quotations where she needed them from her masculine predecessors. Mrs. Stillman quotes from W. H. Salter's *Essay on Two Moderns:* "Butler's book is typical both of his strength as a controversialist and of his shortcomings; there is a remarkably detailed knowledge of the matter in dispute with a somewhat inadequate knowledge of the surrounding facts." The surrounding facts never troubled Butler, except that he sometimes put himself out a good deal not to see them. He did not suppress or minimise; he simply did not think it worth while to see anything but the object in hand; and there is none of his books to which this stricture does not apply. He was a man of selected passions, which in separate practice came to be obsessions; so that now for us the original passion escapes in oddity.

The books on evolution, from a similar limitation, seem now to have mostly the curious, aching attractiveness of dead controversy. The biology at issue is perhaps as dead as Darwin. Butler wrote his four books partly because Darwin did not admit his debt to Erasmus Darwin and Buffon, and partly because Butler thought he was not enough in debt to them in fact. The animus, at first critical, became personal: Darwin was the intellectual villain of Butler's life for ten years and more. His last series of essays, called *The Deadlock of Darwinism,* only rephrase the argument put forth in *Life and Habit.* Butler was not a scientist—he was not a master of any of the subjects to which he addressed himself; and that fact may explain the strength and beauty of his invective, the bravura of his wit: these qualities were his real obligation. He was, however, profoundly interested in evolution, and he was by nature large enough to find, and maintain at any expense, views of his own sufficiently definite to make the controversy worth carrying on without regard to its personal inspiration. To Darwin's natural selection he opposed long-term design, to spontaneity teleology, and he set up very persuasively the view that memory is the vehicle of heredity. It was a matter of accent; and to a man of Butler's knotty independence it was always worth while pointing opposite accents to those used by the great men of the time. Had Darwin, Huxley, and Wallis been vitalists, had the scientific tone of the time been less mechanistic, Butler would doubt-less have appeared, and rightly, on the other side. As Mrs.

Stillman says, he wrote his attacks on science from the point of view of religion, and his attacks on religion from the point of view of science. He himself said he was trying to paint a picture.

This type of mind may be attacked for its apparent lapses from integrity and for its apparent inconsistency. Butler's cousin, Mrs. R. S. Garnett (in *Samuel Butler and His Family Relations*), answer charges, in *The Way of All Flesh* and elsewhere, against his parents by proving that he lacked moral robustness. She insists that Butler, if he really did so, hated his family because he had not within him that impasse of sweetness and sick strength to make him an ornament in a country parsonage. She adds, however, that he probably had the average English gentleman's physical courage and would have been reliable in such bloody emergencies as English ladies dream of. No cousin of hers could have been otherwise. For the rest, she thinks Butler was actually mistaken about his family, and that, anyway, he never meant what he said. She polishes up mother and sisters and even gives the father the dull lustre of good intentions except in the matter of money.

The accusation about the lack of moral robustness has point but pierces nothing. Whatever the lack was, it was private, and we should not have had Butler without it. Unscrupulousness and moral courage, when satire and controversy are the subjects, come very near the same thing; as Mrs. Garnett, for all her Christian virtue, should have seen for herself. That a woman like Mrs. Garnett should attack Butler is the sharpest testimony of his worth and supports the veracity of his novel. The school of criticism that judges a man by his private life is not extinct; we are still led to measure a man's intellect by the amount of blindness with which he cherished mankind; and Mrs. Stillman, when she puts Butler above

Swift because of his greater kindliness, is herself not without taint.

"We have the same respect," wrote T. S. Eliot, "for Blake's philosophy (and perhaps for that of Samuel Butler) that we have for an ingenious piece of home-made furniture: we admire the man who has put it together out of the odds and ends about the house." The difference, in this respect, between Blake and Butler is that Blake had nothing to begin with but his collected odds and ends, while Butler had resolutely to labour half his life at getting rid of advantages which had been thrust upon him at Shrewsbury and Cambridge. Butler rejected his education as far as he could, and in the process wrote the three satires, *Erewhon, The Way of All Flesh,* and *Erewhon Revisited,* to which our minds are likely to turn when we think of him. He went far enough in one direction so that Ernest Pontifex, after seeing a burlesque of *Macbeth,* says what rot Shakespeare is after that. But having so much to lose (more than Blake had, for example) he retained more than he meant to. The more thoroughly he seemed to have destroyed a thing the more tenaciously he clung to it, because in destroying he found his need for it, and had never either the courage, or the idea, of putting his soul in peril to do without.

Thus he always came back to undifferentiated common sense and gave constant counsel that men ought not be much better than their neighbours. "That vice pays homage to virtue is notorious; we call this hypocrisy; there should be a word found for the homage which virtue not infrequently pays, or at any rate would be wise in paying, to vice." Butler's own homage to vice consisted in allowing himself to smoke after four in the afternoon, and in attending, for physical relief and without sentiment, his French mistress for twenty years. He sought a kind of leaden mean, and had, not wisdom, but its dryer condiment. As witty, often as lively, and hardly more eccentric, than Laurence Sterne, he represents, with Sterne, the difference between what England could do in the eighteenth and nineteenth centuries in the way of a free spirit.

If we examine what he says about the principal object of his satire, the Church of England, it becomes difficult to see either much freedom or much spirit. We see rather a combination of false independence and moral thrift. He was exceedingly worldly about his other worldly interests. After destroying, so far as he could by exquisitely constructed satire, the miracle of Christ's resurrection in *Erewhon Revisited* (also the subject of his pamphlet *The Evidence for the Resurrection of Jesus Christ,* published thirty-one years earlier) he declares in its preface: "I have never ceased to profess myself a member of the more advanced wing of the English Broad Church." In his *Note Books* he defines the sin against the Holy Ghost. Christ, he says, "must have meant that a man may be pardoned for being unable to believe in the Christian mythology, but that if he made light of the spirit which the common conscience of all men, whatever their particular creed, recognises as divine, there was no hope for him." Again, in a lecture called "How to Make the Most of Life," he says that faith "consists in holding fast that which the healthiest and most kindly instincts of the best and most sensible men and women are intuitively possessed of, without caring to require much evidence further than the fact that such people are so convinced." Undeniably broad, such a faith is at the extreme circle of caution, and all its consolations are creature-comforts. Reduced to the bone it would not make much dust, certainly not Christian dust. It is what happens when you live in an age of progress; in a greedy age, when to save your own soul you can afford to lose nothing without pretending to keep it under another name: the name of the "healthiest and most kindly instincts."

To-day we are sharper than that and see that there is very little worth keeping between atheism and Christianity; the rest is baggage. Butler on Christianity is mainly baggage to the atheist, and to the Christian it must seem he was writing about something else—about what happens to Christianity at the hands of the great and unreligious bulk of mankind. To repeat T. S. Eliot's twisted remark, what Butler's satire really shows is that the spirit killeth and the letter giveth life. That labour is in the vineyard and valuable, and to prevent religion from becoming respectable once more it must be performed over and over again. It is perhaps a fortunate irony that Butler should have done something so ably and wittily, which himself he would have denied meaning to. The best things in *Erewhon* are the chapters on baptism, and they remind us, finally, what the Sacrament really is.

Another way of testing Butler, in his capacity of forerunner of our own times, is to put him against the Freudian notion "that to possess consciousness is to be a hypocrite" and the Freudian question, "Is not a sincere lover often reduced to making experiments and almost to tricks to auscultate his feelings and to ascertain whether they still exist?" (Quotations from Jacques Riviere: "On the Theories of Freud.") Butler would have approved the notion, but would have had nothing with which to understand the question; he did rather less than his share of living in the feelings. His prototype Sterne would have had no trouble at all, nor the Fathers of the Church.

1932

XI

THE CRITICAL PREFACES OF HENRY JAMES

THE Prefaces of Henry James were composed at the height of his age as a kind of epitaph or series of inscriptions for the major monument of his life, the sumptuous, plum-coloured, expensive New York edition of his works. The labour was a torment, a care, and a delight, as his letters and the Prefaces themselves amply show. The thinking and the writing were hard and full and critical to the point of exasperation; the purpose was high, the reference wide, and the terms of discourse had to be conceived and defined as successive need for them arose. He had to elucidate and to appropriate for the critical intellect the substance and principle of his career as an artist, and he had to do this—such was the idiosyncrasy of his mind—specifically, example following lucid example, and with a consistency of part with part that amounted almost to the consistency of a mathematical equation, so that, as in the *Poetics,* if his premises were accepted his conclusions must be taken as inevitable.

Criticism has never been more ambitious, nor more useful. There has never been a body of work so eminently suited to criticism as the fiction of Henry James, and there has certainly never been an author who saw the need and had the ability to criticise specifically and at length his own work. He was avid of his opportunity and both proud and modest as to what he did with it. "These notes," he wrote in the Preface to *Roderick Hudson,* "represent, over a considerable course, the continuity of an artist's endeavour, the growth of his whole operative consciousness and, best of all, perhaps, their own tendency to multiply, with the implication, thereby, of a memory much enriched." Thus his strict modesty; he wrote to Grace Norton (5 March 1907) in a higher tone. "The prefaces, as I say, are difficult to do—but I have found them of a jolly interest; and though I am not going to let you read one of the fictions themselves over I shall expect you to read all the said Introductions." To W. D. Howells he wrote (17 August 1908) with very near his full pride. "They are, in general, a sort of plea for Criticism, for Discrimination, for Appreciation on other than infantile lines—as against the so almost universal Anglo-Saxon absence of these things; which tends so, in our general trade, it seems to me, to break the heart. . . . They ought, collected together, none the less, to form a sort of comprehensive manual or *vademecum* for aspirants in our arduous profession. Still, it will be long before I shall want to collect them together for that purpose and furnish *them* with a final Preface."

In short, James felt that his Prefaces represented or demonstrated an artist's consciousness and the character of his work in some detail, made an essay in general criticism which had an interest and a being aside from any connection with his own work, and that finally, they added up to a fairly exhaustive reference book on the technical aspects of the art of fiction. His judgment was correct and all a commentator can do is to indicate by example and a little analysis, by a kind of provisional reasoned index, how the contents of his essay may be made more available. We have, that is, to perform an act of criticism in the sense that James himself understood it. "To criticise," he wrote in the Preface to *What Maisie Knew,* "is to appreciate, to appropriate, to take intellectual possession, to establish in fine a relation with the criticised thing and make it one's own."

What we have here to appropriate is the most sustained and

I think the most eloquent and original piece of literary criticism in existence. (The only comparable pieces, not in merit of course but in kind, are by the same author, "The Art of Fiction," written as a young man and printed in *Partial Portraits,* and "The Novel in 'The Ring and the Book.'" written in 1912 and published in *Notes on Novelists;* the first of which the reader should consult as an example of general criticism with a prevailing ironic tone, and the second as an example of what the same critical attitude as that responsible for the Prefaces could do on work not James' own.) Naturally, then, our own act of appropriation will have its difficulties, and we shall probably find as James found again and again, that the things most difficult to master will be the best. At the least we shall require the maximum of strained attention, and the faculty of retaining detail will be pushed to its limit. And these conditions will not apply from the difficulty of what James has to say—which is indeed lucid—but because of the convoluted compression of his style and because of the positive unfamiliarity of his terms as he uses them. No one else has written specifically on his subject.

Before proceeding to exhibition and analysis, however, it may be useful to point out what kind of thing, as a type by itself, a James Preface is, and what kind of exercise the reader may expect a sample to go through. The key-fact is simple. A Preface is the story of a story, or in those volumes which collect a group of shorter tales the story of a group of stories cognate in theme or treatment. The Prefaces collocate, juxtapose, and separate the different kinds of stories. They also, by cross-reference and development from one Preface to another, inform the whole series with a unity of being. By "the story of a story" James meant a narrative of the accessory facts and considerations which went with its writing; the how, the why, the what, when, and where which brought it to birth and which are not evident in the story itself, but which have a fascination and a meaning in themselves to enhance the reader's knowledge. "The private history of any sincere work," he felt, "looms large with its own completeness."

But the "story of a story" is not simple in the telling; it has many aspects that must be examined in turn, many developments that must be pursued, before its centre in life is revealed as captured. "The art of representation bristles with questions the very terms of which are difficult to apply and appreciate." Only the main features can be named simply. There is the feature of autobiography, as a rule held to a minimum: an account of the Paris hotel, the Venetian palace, the English cottage, in which the tale in question was written. Aside from that, there is often a statement of the anecdote and the circumstances in which it was told, from which James drew the germ of his story. There is the feature of the germ in incubation, and the story of how it took root and grew, invariably developing into something quite different from its immediate promise. Then there is an account—frequently the most interesting feature—of how the author built up his theme as a consistent piece of dramatisation. Usually there are two aspects to this feature, differently discussed in different Prefaces—the aspect of the theme in relation to itself as a balanced and consistent whole, the flesh upon the articulated plot; and the aspect of the theme in relation to society, which is the moral and evaluating aspect. Varying from Preface to Preface as the need commands, there is the further feature of technical exposition, in terms of which everything else is for the moment subsumed. That is, the things which a literary artist does in order to make of his material an organic whole—the devices he consciously uses to achieve a rounded form—are rendered available for discussion, and for understanding, by definition and exemplification.

These are the principle separate features which compose the face of a Preface. There are also certain emphases brought to bear throughout the Prefaces, which give them above all the savour of definite character. Again and again, for example, a novel or story will raise the problem of securing a compositional centre, a presiding intelligence, or of applying the method of indirect approach. Again and again James emphasises the necessity of being amusing, dramatic, interesting. And besides these, almost any notation, technical, thematic, or moral, brings James eloquently back to the expressive relation between art and life, raises him to an intense personal plea for the difficulty and delight of maintaining that relation, or wrings from him a declaration of the supreme labour of intelligence that art lays upon the artist. For James it is the pride of achievement, for the reader who absorbs that pride it is the enthusiasm of understanding and the proud possibility of emulation.

None of this, not the furthest eloquence nor the most detached precept, but flows from the specific observation and the particular example. When he speaks of abjuring the "platitude of statement," he is not making a phrase but summarising, for the particular occasion, the argument which runs throughout the Prefaces, that in art what is merely stated is not presented, what is not presented is not vivid, what is not vivid is not represented, and what is not represented is not art. Or when, referring to the method by which a subject most completely expresses itself, he writes the following sentence, James is not indulging in self-flattery. "The careful ascertainment of how it shall do so, and the art of guiding it with consequent authority—since this sense of 'authority' is for the master-builder the treasure of treasures, or at least the joy of joys—renews in the modern alchemist something like the old dream of the secret of life." It is not indulgence of any description; it is the recognition in moral language of the artist's privileged experience in the use of his tools—in this instance his use of them in solving the technical problems of *The Spoils of Poynton.* James unfailingly, unflaggingly reveals for his most general precept its specific living source. He knew that only by constantly retaining the specific in the field of dicussion could he ever establish or maintain the principles by which he wrote. That is his unique virtue as a critic, that the specific object is always in hand; as it was analogously his genius as a novelist that what he wrote about was always present in somebody's specific knowledge of it. In neither capacity did he ever succumb to the "platitude of statement."

It is this factor of material felt and rendered specifically that differentiates James from such writers as Joyce and Proust. All three have exerted great technical influence on succeeding writers, as masters ought. The difference is that writers who follow Joyce or Proust tend to absorb their subjects, their social attitudes, and their personal styles and accomplish competent derivative work in so doing, while the followers of James absorb something of a technical mastery good for any subject, any attitude, any style. It is the difference between absorbing the object of a sensibility and acquiring something comparable to the sensibility itself. The point may perhaps be enforced paradoxically: the mere imitators of the subject-matter of Proust are readable as documents, but the mere imitators of James are not readable at all. It is not that James is more or less great than his compeers—the question is not before us—but that he consciously and articulately exhibited a greater technical mastery of the tools of his trade. It is a matter of sacrifice. Proust made no sacrifice but wrote always as loosely as possible and triumphed in spite of himself. Joyce made only such sacrifices as suited his private need—as readers of these Prefaces will amply observe—and triumphed by a

series of extraordinary *tours de force.* James made consist-
ently every sacrifice for intelligibility and form; and, when the
fashions of interest have made their full period, it will be seen
I think that his triumph is none the less for that.

There remains—once more before proceeding with the
actual content of the Prefaces—a single observation that must
be made, and it flows from the remarks above about the character of James' influence. James had in his style and perhaps
in the life which it reflected an idiosyncrasy so powerful, so
overweening, that to many it seemed a stultifying vice, or at
least an inexcusable heresy. He is difficult to read in his later
works—among which the Prefaces are included—and his subjects, or rather the way in which he develops them, are
occasionally difficult to coördinate with the reader's own
experience. He enjoyed an excess of intelligence and he suffered, both in life and art, from an excessive effort to communicate it, to represent it in all its fullness. His style grew
elaborate in the degree that he rendered shades and refinements of meaning and feeling not usually rendered at all.
Likewise the characters which he created to dramatise his
feelings have sometimes a quality of intelligence which enables
them to experience matters which are unknown and seem
almost perverse to the average reader. James recognised his
difficulty, at least as to his characters. He defended his "supersubtle fry" in one way or another a dozen times, on the
ground that if they did not exist they ought to, because they
represented, if only by an imaginative irony, what life was
capable of at its finest. His intention and all his labour was to
represent dramatically intelligence at its most difficult, its most
lucid, its most beautiful point. This is the sum of his idiosyncrasy; and the reader had better make sure he knows what it
is before he rejects it. The act of rejection will deprive him
of all knowledge of it. And this precept applies even more

firmly to the criticisms he made of his work—to the effort he made to reappropriate it intellectually—than to the direct apprehension of the work itself.

II

Now to resume the theme of this essay, to "remount," as James says of himself many times, "the stream of composition." What is that but to make an *ex post facto* dissection, not that we may embalm the itemised mortal remains, but that we may intellectually understand the movement of parts and the relation between them in the living body we appreciate. Such dissection is imaginative, an act of the eye and mind alone, and but articulates our knowledge without once scratching the flesh of its object. Only if the life itself was a mockery, a masquerade of pasted surfaces, will we come away with our knowledge dying; if the life was honest and our attention great enough, even if we do not find the heart itself at least we shall be deeply exhilarated, having heard its slightly irregular beat.

Let us first exhibit the principal objects which an imaginative examination is able to separate, attaching to each a summary of context and definition. Thus we shall have equipped ourselves with a kind of eclectic index or provisional glossary, and so be better able to find our way about, and be better prepared to seize for closer examination a selection of those parts of some single Preface which reveal themselves as deeply animating. And none of this effort will have any object except to make the substance of all eighteen Prefaces more easily available.

There is a natural division between major subjects which are discussed at length either in individual essays or from volume to volume, and minor notes which sometimes appear

once and are done, and are sometimes recurrent, turning up
again and again in slightly different form as the specific matter in hand requires. But it is not always easy to see under
which heading an entry belongs. In the following scheme the
disposition is approximate and occasionally dual, and in any
case an immediate subject of the reader's revision.

To begin with, let us list those major themes which have no
definite locus but inhabit all the Prefaces more or less without favour. This is the shortest and for the most part the
most general of the divisions, and therefore the least easily
susceptible of definition in summary form.

*The Relation of Art and the Artist. The Relation of Art
and Life. Art, Life, and the Ideal. Art and Morals. Art as
Salvation for its Characters.* These five connected subjects,
one or more of them, are constantly arrived at, either paren-
thetically or as the definite terminus of the most diverse discussions. The sequence in which I have put them ought to
indicate something of the attitude James brings to bear on
them. Art was serious, he believed, and required of the artist
every ounce of his care. The subject of art was life, or more
particularly someone's apprehension of the experience of it,
and in striving truly to represent it art removed the waste and
muddlement and bewilderment in which it is lived and gave
it a lucid, intelligible form. By insisting on intelligence and
lucidity something like an ideal vision was secured; not an
ideal in the air but an ideal in the informed imagination, an
ideal, in fact, actually of life, limited only by the depth of the
artist's sensibility of it. Thus art was the viable representation
of moral value; in the degree that the report was intelligent
and intense the morals were sound. This attitude naturally
led him on either of two courses in his choice of central characters. He chose either someone with a spark of intelligence
in him to make him worth saving from the damnation and

waste of a disorderly life, or he chose to tell the story of some specially eminent person in whom the saving grace of full intelligence is assumed and exhibited. It is with the misfortunes and triumphs of such persons, in terms of the different kinds of experience of which he was master, that James' fiction almost exclusively deals.

It is this fact of an anterior interest that largely determines what he has to say about *The Finding of Subjects* and *The Growth of Subjects*. Subjects never came ready-made or complete, but always from hints, notes, the merest suggestion. Often a single fact reported at the dinner-table was enough for James to seize on and plant in the warm bed of his imagination. If his interlocutor, knowing him to be a novelist, insisted on continuing, James closed his ears. He never wanted all the facts, which might stupefy him, but only enough to go on with, hardly enough to seem a fact at all. If out of politeness he had to listen, he paid no recording attention; what he then heard was only "clumsy Life at her stupid work" of waste and muddlement. Taking his single precious germ he meditated upon it, let it develop, scrutinised and encouraged, compressed and pared the developments until he had found the method by which he could dramatise it, give it a central intelligence whose fortune would be his theme, and shape it in a novel or a story as a consistent and self-sufficient organism. James either gives or regrets that he cannot give both the original *donnée* and an account of how it grew to be a dramatic subject for almost every item in the New York Edition.

Art and Difficulty. Of a course, a man with such a view of his art and choosing so great a personal responsibility for his theme would push his rendering to the most difficult terms possible. So alone would he be able to represent the maximum value of his theme. Being a craftsman and delighting in his craft, he knew also both the sheer moral delight of solving a technical difficulty or securing a complicated effect, and the simple, amply attested fact that the difficulties of submitting one's material to a rigidly conceived form were often the only method of representing the material in the strength of its own light. The experience of these difficulties being constantly present to James as he went about his work, he constantly points specific instances for the readers of his Prefaces.

Looseness. Looseness of any description, whether of conception or of execution, he hated contemptuously. In both respects he found English fiction "a paradise of loose ends," but more especially in the respect of execution. His own themes, being complex in reference and development, could only reach the lucidity of the apprehensible, the intelligibility of the represented state, if they were closed in a tight form. Any looseness or laziness would defeat his purpose and let half his intention escape. A selection of the kinds of looseness against which he complains will be given among the minor notes.

The Plea for Attention and Appreciation. The one faculty James felt that the artist may require of his audience is that of close attention or deliberate appreciation; for it is by this faculty alone that the audience participates in the work of art. As he missed the signs of it so he bewailed the loss; upon its continuous exertion depended the very existence of what he wrote. One burden of the Prefaces was to prove how much the reader would see if only he paid attention and how much he missed by following the usual stupid routine of skipping and halting and letting slide. Without attention, without intense appreciation an art of the intelligent life was impossible and without intelligence, for James, art was nothing.

The Necessity for Amusement. James was willing to do his part to arouse attention, and he laboured a good deal to find out exactly what that part was. One aspect of it was to be

as amusing as possible, and this he insisted on at every opportunity. To be amusing, to be interesting; without that nothing
of his subject could possibly transpire in the reader's mind.
In some of his books half the use of certain characters was to
amuse the reader. Henrietta Stackpole, for example, in *The
Portrait of a Lady,* serves mainly to capture the readers' attention by amusing him as a "character." Thus what might
otherwise have been an example of wasteful overtreatment
actually serves the prime purpose of carrying the reader along,
distracting and freshening him from time to time.

The Indirect Approach and *The Dramatic Scene.* These
devices James used throughout his work as those most cal-
culated to command, direct, and limit or frame the reader's
attention; and they are employed in various combinations or
admixtures the nature of which almost every Preface comments on. These devices are not, as their name might suggest,
opposed; nor could their use in equal parts cancel each other.
They are, in the novel, two ends of one stick, and no one can
say where either end begins. The characterising aspect of the
Indirect Approach is this: the existence of a definite created
sensibility interposed between the reader and the felt experience which is the subject of the fiction. James never put his
reader in direct contact with his subjects; he believed it was
impossible to do so, because his subject really was not what
happened but what someone felt about what happened, and
this could be directly known only through an intermediate
intelligence. The Dramatic Scene was the principal device
James used to objectify the Indirect Approach and give it self-
limiting form. Depending on the degree of limitation necessary to make the material objective and visible all round, his
use of the Scene resembled that in the stage-play. The com-
plexities of possible choice are endless and some of them are
handled below.

The Plea for a Fine Central Intelligence. But the novel was not a play however dramatic it might be, and among the distinction between the two forms was the possibility, which belonged to the novel alone, of setting up a fine central intelligence in terms of which everything in it might be unified and upon which everything might be made to depend. No other art could do this; no other art could dramatise the individual at his finest; and James worked this possibility for all it was worth. It was the very substance upon which the directed attention, the cultivated appreciation, might be concentrated. And this central intelligence served a dual purpose, with many modifications and exchanges among the branches. It made a compositional centre for art such as life never saw. If it could be created at all, then it presided over everything else, and would compel the story to be nothing but the story of what that intelligence felt about what happened. This compositional strength, in its turn, only increased the value and meaning of the intelligence *as* intelligence, and *vice versa.* The plea for the use of such an intelligence both as an end and as a means is constant throughout the Prefaces—as the proudest end and as the most difficult means. Some of the specific problems which its use poses are discussed in the Prefaces to the novels where they apply. Here it is enough to repeat once more—and not for the last time—that the fine intelligence, either as agent or as the object of action or as both, is at the heart of James' work.

So much for the major themes which pervade and condition and unite the whole context of the Prefaces. It is the intention of this essay now to list some of the more important subjects discussed in their own right, indicating where they may be found and briefly what turn the discussions take. The Roman numerals immediately following the heading refer to the volume numbers in the New York edition.[1] The occasional small Roman numerals refer to pages within a preface.

The International Theme (XII, XIV, XVIII). The discussion of the International Theme in these three volumes has its greatest value in strict reference to James' own work; it was one of the three themes peculiarly his. It deals, however, with such specific questions as the opposition of manners as a motive in drama, the necessity of opposing positive elements of character, and the use of naïve or innocent characters as the subjects of drama; these are of perennial interest. There is also a discussion under this head of the difference between major and minor themes. In X (p. xix), speaking of "A London Life," there is a discussion of the use of this theme for secondary rather than primary purposes.

The Literary Life as a Theme (XV) and *The Artist as a Theme* (VII). The long sections of these two Prefaces dealing with these themes form a single essay. XV offers the artist enamoured of perfection, his relation to his art, to his audience, and himself. VII presents the artist in relation to society and to himself. In both sections the possibilities and the actualities are worked out with specific reference to the characters in the novels and the tales. The discussion is of practical importance to any writer. Of particular interest is the demonstration in VII that the successful artist as such cannot be a hero in fiction, because he is immersed in his work, while the amateur or the failure remains a person and may have a

[1] For possible convenience in reference I append the numbers and titles of those volumes which contain Prefaces. I Roderick Hudson; II The American; III The Portrait of a Lady; V The Princess Casamassima; VII The Tragic Muse; IX The Awkward Age; X The Spoils of Poynton; XI What Maisie Knew; XII The Aspern Papers; XIII The Reverberator; XIV Lady Barbarina; XV The Lesson of the Master; XVI The Author of Beltraffio; XVII The Altar of the Dead; XVIII Daisy Miller; XIX The Wings of the Dove; XXI The Ambassadors; XXIII The Golden Bowl.

heroic downfall. The thematic discussion in XVI properly belongs under this head, especially pp. vii-ix.

The Use of the Eminent or Great (VII, XII, XV, XVI) and *The Use of Historical Characters* (XII, XV). The separation of these two subjects is artificial, as for James they were two aspects of one problem. Being concerned with the tragedies of the high intelligence and the drama of the socially and intellectually great (much as the old tragedies dealt death to kings and heroes) he argues for using the *type* of the historical and contemporary great and against using the actual historical or contemporary figure. The type of the great gives the artist freedom; the actual condition him without advantage. If he used in one story or another Shelley, Coleridge, Browning, and (I think) Oscar Wilde, he took them only as types and so far transformed them that they appear as pure fictions. The real argument is this: the novelist is concerned with types and only with the eminent case among the types, and the great man is in a way only the most eminent case of the average type, and is certainly the type that the novelist can do most with. To the charge that his "great" people were such as could never exist, James responded that the world would be better if they did. In short, the novelist's most lucid representation may be only his most ironic gesture.

The Dead as a Theme (XVII). Five pages (v-ix) of this Preface present "the permanent appeal to the free intelligence of some image of the lost dead" and describe how this appeal may be worked out in fiction. "The sense of the state of the dead," James felt, "is but part of the sense of the state of living."

On Wonder, Ghosts, and the Supernatural (XII, XVII) and *How to Produce Evil* (XII). These again make two aspects of one theme and the rules for securing one pretty much resemble those for securing the other. They are shown best "by showing almost exclusively the way they are felt, by recognising as their main interest some impression strongly made by them and intensely received." That was why Psychical Research Society Ghosts were unreal; there was no one to apprehend them. The objectively rendered prodigy always ran thin. Thickness is in the human consciousness that records and amplifies. And there is also always necessary, for the reader to feel the ghost, the history of somebody's *normal* relation to it. Thus James felt that the climax of Poe's *Pym* was a failure because there the horrific was without connections. In both prefaces the ghost story is put as the modern equivalent of the fairy story; and the one must be as economical of its means as the other. The problem of rendering evil in "The Turn of the Screw" (XII) was slightly different; it had to be represented, like the ghosts who performed it, in the consciousness of it by normal persons, but it could not be described. The particular act when rendered always fell short of being evil, so that the problem seemed rather to make the character *capable* of anything. "Only make the reader's general vision of evil intense enough, I said to myself—and that is already a charming job—and his own experience, his own sympathy (with the children) and horror (of their false friends) will supply him quite sufficiently with all the particulars. Make him *think* the evil, make him think it for himself, and you are released from weak specifications." (XII, xxi.)

On the Use of Wonder to Animate a Theme (XI). This is the faculty of wonder on a normal plane and corresponds to freshness, intelligent innocence, and curiosity in the face of life; a faculty which when represented in a character almost of itself alone makes that character live. It is a faculty upon which every novelist depends, both in his books to make them vivid, and in his readers where it is the faculty that drives them to read. It is to be distinguished from the wonder discussed in the paragraph next above.

Romanticism and Reality (II). Seven pages in this Preface (xiv-xx) attempt to answer the question: Why is one picture of life called romantic and another real? After setting aside several answers as false or misleading, James gives his own. "The only *general* attribute of projected romance that I can see, the only one that fits all its cases, is the fact of the kind of experience with which it deals—experience liberated, so to speak; experience disengaged, disembodied, disencumbered, exempt from the conditions that we usually know to attach to it, and if we wish so to put the matter, drag upon it, and operating in a medium which relieves it, in a particular interest, of the inconvenience of a *related,* a measurable state, a state subject to all our vulgar communities." Then James applies his answer to his own novel (*The American*) "The experience here represented is the disconnected and uncontrolled experience—uncontrolled by our general sense of 'the way things happen'—which romance alone more or less successfully palms off on us." Since the reader knows "the way things happen," he must be tactfully drugged for the duration of the novel; and that is part of the art of fiction.

The Time Question (I, xii-xvi). Although the efforts dependent on the superior effect of an adequate lapse of time were consciously important to James, the lapse of time itself was only once discussed by him in the Prefaces, and there to explain or criticise the failure to secure it. Roderick Hudson, he said, falls to pieces too quickly. Even though he is special and eminent, still he must not live, change and disintegrate too rapidly; he loses verisimilitude by so doing. His great capacity for ruin is projected on too small a field. He should have had more adventures and digested more experience before we can properly believe that he has reached his end.

But James was able to put the whole matter succinctly. "To give all the sense without all the substance or all the surface, and so to summarise or foreshorten, so to make values both rich and sharp, that the mere procession of items and profiles is not only, for the occasion, superseded, but is, for essential quality, almost 'compromised'—such a case of delicacy proposes itself at every turn to the painter of life who wishes both to treat his chosen subject and to confine his necessary picture." Composition and arrangement must give the *effect* of the lapse of time. For this purpose elimination was hardly a good enough device. The construction of a dramatic centre, as a rule in someone's consciousness, was much better, for the reason that this device, being acted upon in time, gave in parallel the positive effect of action, and thus of lapsing time.

Geographical Representation (I, ix-xi). These three pages deal with the question: to what extent should a named place be rendered on its own account? In *Roderick Hudson* James named Northampton, Mass. This, he said, he ought not to have done, since all he required was a humane community which was yet incapable of providing for "art." For this purpose a mere indication would have been sufficient. His general answer to the question was that a place should be named if the novelist wanted to make it an effective part of the story, as Balzac did in his studies of the *ville de province*.

The Commanding Centre as a Principle of Composition (I, II, VII, X, XI, XIX, XXI, XXIIJ). This is allied with the discussion of the use of a Central Intelligence above and with the three notes immediately below. It is a major consideration in each of the Prefaces numbered and is to be met with *passim* elsewhere. The whole question is bound up with James' exceeding conviction that the art of fiction is an organic form, and that it can neither be looked at all round nor will it be able to move on its own account unless it has a solidly posed centre. Commanding centres are of various descriptions. In I it is in Rowland Mallet's consciousness of Roderick. In II it is in the image of Newman. In VII it is in the combination of relations between three characters. In X it is in a houseful of beautiful furniture. In XI it is the "ironic" centre of a child's consciousness against or illuminated by which the situations gather meaning. In XIX it is in the title (*The Wings of the Dove*), that is, in the influence of Milly Theale, who is seen by various people from the outside. In XXI it is wholly in Strether's consciousness. In XXIII it is, so to speak, half in the Prince, half in the Princess, and half in the motion with which the act is performed.

The Proportion of Intelligence and Bewilderment (V). Upon the correct proportion depends the verisimilitude of a given character. Omniscience would be incredible; the novelist must not make his "characters too interpretative of the muddle of fate, or in other words too divinely, too priggishly clever." Without bewilderment, as without intelligence, there would be no story to tell. "Experience, as I see it, is our apprehension and our measure of what happens to us as social creatures—any intelligent report of which has to be based on that apprehension." Bewilderment is the subject and someone's intelligent feeling of it the story. The right mixture will depend on the *quality* of the bewilderment, whether it is the vague or the critical. The vague fool is necessary, but the *leading* interest is always in the intensifying, critical consciousness.

The Necessity of Fools (V, X, XI), and *The Use of Muddlement* (XI, XIX). These subjects are evidently related to that of Intelligence and Bewilderment. In themselves nothing, fools are the very agents of action. They represent the stupid force of life and are the cause of trouble to the intelligent consciousness. The general truth for the spectator of life was

this: (X, xv)—"The fixed constituents of almost any repro-
ducible action are the fools who minister, at a particular crisis,
to the intensity of the free spirit engaged with them." Muddlement is the condition of life which fools promote. "The
effort really to see and really to represent is no idle business
in face of the *constant* force that makes for muddlement. The
great thing is indeed that the muddled state too is one of the
very sharpest of the realities, that it also has colour and form
and character, has often in fact a broad and rich comicality,
many of the signs and values of the appreciable" (XI, xiii).

Intelligence as a Receptive Lucidity (XI, XXI). The first
of this pair of Prefaces almost wholly and the second largely
deals with the methods of conditioning a sensibility so as to
make a subject. In XI James shows how the sensibility of a
child, intelligent as may be, can influence and shape and make
lucid people and situations outside as well as within its understanding. She, Maisie, is the presiding receptive intelligence,
the sole sensibility, in the book, and is furthermore the sole
agent, by her mere existence, determining and changing the
moral worth of the other characters. In XXI Strether is out-
lined as the example of the adult sensibility fulfilling similar
functions, with the additional grace of greatly extended
understanding.

The Dramatic Scene (III, VII, IX, XI, XIX, XXI, and
passim). We have already spoken under the same heading of
James' general theory of the dramatic scene. It is too much of
the whole substance of the technical discussion in many of the
Prefaces to make more than a mere outline of its terms here
possible. In III, xxii and XIX, xxiii, there is developed the
figure of windows opening on a scene. The eye is the artist,
the scene the subject, and the window the limiting form.
From each selected window the scene is differently observed.
In VII is discussed the theory of alternating scenes in terms of

a centre (p. xv). In IX which is the most purely scenic of all the books, the use of the alternating scene is developed still further. At the end of XI there is a bitter postscript declaring the scenic character of the form. In XXI there is intermittent discussion of how to use the single consciousness to promote scenes, and a comparison with the general scenic method in XIX. It is principally to IX that the reader must resort for a sustained specific discussion of the Scene in fiction and its relation to the Scene in drama, and to XIX, of which pp. xii-xxiii deal with the scenic structure of that book, where the distinction is made between Scenes and Pictures and it is shown how one partakes of the other, and where it is insisted on that the maximum value is obtained when both weights are felt. Subordinate to this there is, in the same reference, a description of the various reflectors (characters) used to illuminate the subject in terms of the scene.

On Revision (I, XXIII). The Notes on Revision in these Prefaces are mainly of interest with reference to what James actually did in revising his earlier works. He revised, as a rule, only in the sense that he re-envisaged the substance more accurately and more representatively. Revision was responsible re-seeing.

On Illustrations in Fiction (XXIII). This is perhaps the most amusing note in all the Prefaces, and it is impossible to make out whether James did or did not like the frontispieces with which his collected volumes were adorned. He was insistent that no illustration to a book of his should have any direct bearing upon it. The danger was real. "Anything that relieves responsible prose of the duty of being, while placed before us, good enough, interesting enough, and, if the question be of picture, pictorial enough, above all *in itself,* does it the worst services, and may well inspire in the lover of literature certain lively questions as to the future of that institution."

The Nouvelle as a Form (XV, XVI, XVIII). The nouvelle —the long-short story or the short novel—was perhaps James' favourite form, and the form least likely of appreciaton in the Anglo-Saxon reading world, to which it seemed neither one thing nor the other. To James it was a small reflector capable of illuminating or mirroring a great deal of material. To the artist who practised in it the difficulties of its economy were a constant seduction and an exalted delight.

On Rendering Material by its Appearances Alone (V). James had the problem of rendering a character whose whole life centred in the London underworld of socialism, anarchism, and conspiracy, matters of which he personally knew nothing. But, he decided, his wanted effect and value were "precisely those of our not knowing, of society's not knowing, but only guessing and suspecting and trying to ignore, what 'goes on' irreconcilably, subversively, beneath the vast smug surface." Hints and notes and observed appearances were always enough. The real wisdom was this:—that "if you haven't, for fiction, the root of the matter in you, haven't the sense of life and the penetrating imagination, you are a fool in the very presence of the revealed and the assured; but that if you *are* so armed you are not really helpless, not without your resource, even before mysteries abysmal."

And that is a good tone upon which to close our rehearsal of the major subjects James examines in his Prefaces. Other readers and other critics (the two need not be quite the same) might well have found other matters for emphasis; and so too they may reprehend the selection of Minor Notes which follow.

On Development and Continuity (I). Developments are the condition of interest, since the subject is always the related state of figures and things. Hence developments are ridden by the principle of continuity. Actually, relations never end, but the artist must make them appear to do so. Felicity of form and composition depend on knowing to what point a development is *indispensable*.

On Antithesis of Characters (I). The illustration is the antithesis of Mary and Christina in this book. James observes that antitheses rarely come off and that it may pass for a triumph, if taking them together, one of them is strong. (P. xix.)

On the Emergence of Characters (X, xiii). James' view may be summarised in quotation. "A character is interesting as it comes out, and by the process and duration of that emergence; just as a procession is effective by the way it unrolls, turning to a mere mob if it all passes at once."

On Misplaced Middles (VII, XIX). Misplaced Middles are the result of excessive foresight. As the art of the drama is of preparations, that of the novel is only less so. The first half of a fiction is the stage or theatre of the second half, so that too much may be expended on the first. Then the problem is consummately to mask the fault and "confer on the false quantity the brave appearance of the true." James indicates how the middles of VII and XIX were misplaced, and although he believed the fault great, thought that he had in both cases passed it off by craft and dissimulation.

On Improvisation (XII, xvi). Nothing was so easy as improvisation, and it usually ran away with the story, e.g., in *The Arabian Nights*. "The thing was to aim at absolute singleness, clearness and roundness, and yet to depend on an imagination working freely, working (call it) with extravagance; by which law it wouldn't be thinkable except as free and wouldn't be amusing except as controlled."

The Anecdote (XIII, vi). "The anecdote consists, ever, of

something that has oddly happened to some one, and the first of its duties is to point directly to the person whom it so distinguishes."

The Anecdote and the Development (XV, ix, XVI, v). In the first of these references James observes that whereas the anecdote may come from any source, specifically complicated states must come from the author's own mind. In the second he says that *The Middle Years* is an example of imposed form (he had an order for a short story) and the struggle was to keep compression rich and accretions compressed; to keep the form that of the concise anecdote, whereas the subject would seem one comparatively demanding developments. James solved the problem by working from the outward edge in rather than from the centre outward; and this was law for the small form. At the end of this Preface, there is a phrase about chemical reductions and compressions making the short story resemble a sonnet.

On Operative Irony (XV, ix). James defended his "supersubtle fry" on the ground that they were ironic, and he found the strength of applied irony "in the sincerities, the lucidities, the utilities that stand behind it." If these characters and these stories were not a campaign for something better than the world offered then they were worthless. "But this is exactly what we mean by operative irony. It implies and projects the possible other case, the case rich and edifying where the actuality is pretentious and vain."

On Foreshortening (VII, XV, XVII, XVIII). This is really a major subject, but the discussions James made of it were never extensive, seldom over two lines at a time. I append samples. In VII, xii, he speaks of foreshortening not by adding or omitting items but by figuring synthetically, by exquisite chemical adjustments. In XVII, xxv, the nouvelle *Julia Bride* is considered as a foreshortened novel to the extreme.

In XVIII, xv, after defining once again the art of representation and insisting on the excision of the irrelevant, James names Foreshortening as a deep principle and an invaluable device. It conduced, he said, "to the only compactness that has a charm, to the only spareness that has a force, to the only simplicity that has a grace—those, in each order, that produce the *rich* effect."

On Narrative in the First Person (XXI, xvii-xix). James bore a little heavily against this most familiar of all narrative methods. Whether his general charge will hold is perhaps irrelevant; it holds perfectly with reference to the kinds of fiction he himself wrote, and the injury to unity and composition which he specifies may well be observed in Proust's long novel where every dodge is unavailingly resorted to in the attempt to get round the freedom of the method. The double privilege (in the first person), said James, of being at once subject and object sweeps away difficulties at the expense of discrimination. It prevents the possibility of a centre and prevents real directness of contact. Its best effect, perhaps, is that which in another connection James called the mere "platitude of statement."

On Ficelles (XXI, xx). Taking the French theatrical term, James so labelled those characters who belong less to the subject than to the treatment of it. The invention and disposition of *ficelles* is one of the difficulties swept away by the first person narrative.

On Characters as Disponibles (III, vii-viii). Here again James adapted a French word, taking it this time from Turgenev. *Disponibles* are the active or passive persons who solicit the author's imagination, appearing as subject to the chances and complications of existence and requiring of the author that he find for them their right relations and build their right fate.

THE CRITICAL PREFACES OF HENRY JAMES

The rule of space forbids extending even so scant a selection from so rich a possible index. But let me add a round dozen with page references alone. On Dialogue (IX, xiii); Against Dialect (XVIII, xvi); On Authority (XVIII, xviii); On Confusion of Forms (IX, xvii); On Overtreatment (III, xxi; IX, xxii); On writing of the Essence and of the Form (III, xvii); On Making Compromises Conformities (XIX, xii); On the Coercive Charm of Form (IX, xvii); On Major Themes in Modern Drama (IX, xviii); On Sickness as a Theme (XIX, vi); On Reviving Characters (V, xviii); On Fiction Read Aloud (XXIII, xxiv); and so on.

The reader may possibly have observed that we have nowhere illustrated the relation which James again and again made eloquently plain between the value or morality of his art and the form in which it appears. It is not easy to select from a multiplicity of choice, and it is impossible, when the matter emerges in a style already so compact, to condense. I should like to quote four sentences from the middle and end of a paragraph in the Preface to *The Portrait of a Lady* (III, x-xi).

There is, I think, no more nutritive or suggestive truth in this connexion than that of the perfect dependence of the "moral" sense of a work of art on the amount of felt life concerned in producing it. The question comes back thus, obviously, to the kind and degree of the artist's prime sensibility, which is the soil out of which his subject springs. The quality and capacity of that soil, its capacity to "grow" with due freshness and straightness any vision of life, represents, strongly or weakly, the projected morality. . . . Here we get exactly the high price of the novel as a literary form—its power not only, while preserving that form with closeness, to range through all the differences of the individual relation to its general subject-matter, all the varieties of outlook on life, of disposition to reflect and project, created by conditions that are never the same from man to man (or, as far as that goes, from woman to woman), but positively to appear more true to its character in proportion as it strains, or tends to burst, with a latent extravagance, its mould.

These sentences represent, I think, the genius and intention of James the novelist, and ought to explain the serious and critical devotion with which he made of his Prefaces a *vade-mecum*—both for himself as the solace of achievement, and for others as a guide and exemplification. We have, by what is really no more than an arbitrary exertion of interest, exhibited a rough scheme of the principle contents; there remain the Prefaces themselves.

III

Although the Prefaces to *The Wings of the Dove* or *The Awkward Age* are more explicitly technical in reference, although that to *What Maisie Knew* more firmly develops the intricacies of a theme, and although that to *The Tragic Muse* is perhaps in every respect the most useful of all the Prefaces, I think it may be better to fasten our single attention on the Preface to *The Ambassadors*. This was the book of which James wrote most endearingly. It had in his opinion the finest and most intelligent of all his themes, and he thought it the most perfectly rendered of his books. Furthermore in its success it constituted a work thoroughly characteristic of its author and of no one else. There is a contagion and a beautiful desolation before a great triumph of the human mind—before any approach to perfection—which we had best face for what there is in them.

This preface divides itself about equally between the outline of the story as a story, how it grew in James' mind from the seed of a dropped word (pp. v-xiv), and a discussion of the form in which the book was executed with specific examination of the method of presentation through the single consciousness of its hero Lambert Strether (pp. xv-xxiii). If we can expose the substance of these two discussions we shall have been in the process as intimate as it is possible to be with the operation of an artist's mind. In imitating his thought, step by step and image by image, we shall in the end be able to appropriate in a single act of imagination all he has to say.

The situation involved in *The Ambassadors,* James tells us, "is gathered up betimes, that is in the second chapter of Book Fifth. . . . planted or 'sunk,' stiffly or saliently, in the centre of the current." Never had he written a story where the seed had grown into so large a plant and yet remained as an independent particle, that is in a single quotable passage. Its intention had been firm throughout.

This independent seed is found in Strether's outburst in Gloriani's Paris garden to little Bilham. "The idea of the tale resides indeed in the very fact that an hour of such un-precedented ease should have been felt by him *as* a crisis." Strether feels that he has missed his life, that he made in his youth a grave mistake about the possibilities of life, and he exhorts Bilham not to repeat his mistake. "Live all you can. Live, live!" And he has the terrible question within him: "*Would* there yet perhaps be time for reparation?" At any rate he sees what he had missed and knows the injury done his character. The story is the demonstration of that vision as it came about, of the vision in process.

The original germ had been the repetition by a friend of words addressed him by a man of distinction similar in burden to those addressed by Strether to little Bilham. This struck James as a theme of great possibilities. Although any theme or subject is absolute once the novelist has accepted it, there are degrees of merit among which he may first choose. "Even among the supremely good—since with such alone is it one's theory of one's honour to be concerned—there is an ideal *beauty* of goodness the invoked action of which is to raise the artistic faith to a maximum. Then, truly, one's theme may be said to shine."

And the theme of *The Ambassadors* shone so for James that it resembled "a monotony of fine weather," in this respect differing much from *The Wings of the Dove,* which gave him continual trouble. "I rejoiced," James said, "in the promise of a hero so mature, who would give me thereby the more to bite into—since it's only into thickened motive and accumulated character, I think, that the painter of life bites more than a little.' By maturity James meant character and imagination. But imagination must not be the *predominant* quality in him; for the theme in hand, the *comparatively* imaginative man would do. The predominant imagination could wait for another book, until James should be willing to pay for the privilege of presenting it. (See also on this point the discussion of Intelligence and Bewilderment above.)

There was no question, nevertheless, that *The Ambassadors* had a major theme. There was the "supplement of situation logically involved" in Strether's delivering himself to Bilham. And James proceeds to describe the novelist's thrill in finding the situation involved by a conceived character. Once the situations are rightly found the story "assumes the authenticity of concrete existence"; the labour is to find them.

"Art deals with what we see, it must first contribute fullhanded that ingredient; it plucks its material, otherwise expressed, in the garden of life—which material elsewhere grown is stale and uneatable." The subject once found, complete with its situations, must then be submitted to a process. There is the subject, which is the story of one's hero, and there is the story of the story itself which is the story of the process of telling.

Still dealing with the story of his hero, James describes how he accounted for Strether, how he found what led up to his outburst in the garden. Where has he come from and why? What is he doing in Paris? To answer these questions was to possess Strether. But the answers must follow the principle of probability. Obviously, by his outburst, he was a man in a false position. What false position? The most probable would be the right one. Granting that he was American, he would probably come from New England. If that were the case, James immediately knew a great deal about him, and had to sift and sort. He would, presumably, have come to Paris with a definite view of life which Paris at once assaulted; and the situation would arise in the interplay or conflict resulting. . . . There was also the energy of the story itself, which once under way, was irresistible, to help its author along. In the end the story seems to know of itself what it's about; and its impudence is always there—"there, so to speak, for grace, and effect, and *allure.*"

These steps taken in finding his story gave it a functional assurance. "*The* false position, for our belated man of the world—belated because he had endeavoured so long to escape being one, and now at last had really to face his doom—the false position for him, I say, was obviously to have presented himself at the gate of that boundless menagerie primed with a moral scheme which was yet framed to break down on any approach to vivid facts; that is to any at all liberal appreciation of them." His note was to be of discrimination and his drama was to "become, under stress, the drama of discrimination."

There follows the question, apparently the only one that troubled James in the whole composition of this book, of whether he should have used Paris as the scene of Strether's outburst and subsequent conversion. Paris had a trivial and vulgar association as the obvious place to be tempted in. The revolution performed by Strether was to have nothing to do with that *bêtise*. He was to be thrown forward rather "upon his lifelong trick of intense reflexion," with Paris a minor matter symbolising the world other than the town of Woolet, Mass., from which he came. Paris was merely the *likely* place for such a drama, and thus saved James much labour of preparation.

Now turning from the story of his hero to the story of his story, James begins by referring to the fact that it appeared in twelve instalments in the *North American Review,* and describes the pleasure he took in making the recurrent breaks and resumptions of serial publication a small compositional law in itself. The book as we have it is in twelve parts. He passes immediately to the considerations which led him to employ only one centre and to keep it entirely in Strether's consciousness. It was Strether's adventure and the only way to make it rigorously his was to have it seen only through his eyes. There were other characters with situations of their own and bearing on Strether. "But Strether's sense of these things, and Strether's only, should avail me for showing them; I should know them only through his more or less groping knowledge of them, since his very gropings would figure among his most interesting motions." This rigour of representation would give him both unity and intensity. The difficulties, too, which the rigour imposed, made the best, because the hardest, determinants of effects. Once he adopted his method he had to be consistent; hence arose his difficulties. For example, there was the problem of making Mrs. Newsome (whose son Strether had come to Paris to save), actually in Woolet, Mass., "no less intensely than circuitously present"; that is, to make her influence press on Strether whenever there was need for it. The advantage of presenting her through Strether was that only Strether's feeling of her counted for the story. Any other method would not only have failed but would have led to positive irrelevance. Hence, "One's work should have composition, because composition alone is positive beauty."

Next James considers what would have happened to his story had he endowed Strether with the privilege of the first person. "Variety, and many other queer matters as well, might have been smuggled in by the back door." But these could not have been intensely represented as Strether's experience, but would have been his only on his own say-so. "'Strether, on the other hand, encaged and provided for as *The Ambassadors* encages and provides, has to keep in view proprieties much stiffer and more salutary than our straight and credulous gape are likely to bring home to him, has exhibitional conditions to meet, in a word, that forbid the terrible *fluidity* of self-revelation."

Nevertheless, in order to represent Strether James had to resort to confidants for him, namely Maria Gostrey and Waymarsh, *ficelles* to aid the treatment. It is thanks to the use of these *ficelles* that James was able to construct the book in a series of alternating scenes and thus give it an objective air. Indispensable facts, both of the present and of the past, are presented dramatically—so the reader can *see* them—only through their use. But it is necessary, for the *ficelles* to succeed in their function, that their character should be artfully dissimulated. For example, Maria Gostrey's connexion with the subject is made to carry itself as a real one.

Analogous to the use of *ficelles,* James refers to the final scene in the book as an "artful expedient for mere consistency of form." It gives or adds nothing on its own account but only expresses "as vividly as possible certain things quite other than itself and that are of the already fixed and appointed measure."

Although the general structure of the book is scenic and the specific centre is in Strether's consciousness of the scenes, James was delighted to note that he had dissimulated throughout the book many exquisite treacheries to those principles. He gives as examples Strether's first encounter with Chad Newsome, and Mamie Pocock's hour of suspense in the hotel salon. These are insisted on as instances of the representational which, "for the charm of opposition and renewal," are other than scenic. In short, James mixed his effects without injuring the consistency of his form. "From the equal play of such oppositions the book gathers an intensity that fairly adds to the dramatic." James was willing to argue that this was so "for the sake of the moral involved; which is not that the particular production before us exhausts the interesting questions that it raises, but that the Novel remains still, under the right persuasion, the most independent, most elastic, most prodigious of literary forms."

It is this last sentiment that our analysis of this Preface is meant to exemplify; and it is—such is the sustained ability of James' mind to rehearse the specific in the light of the general—an exemplification which might be repeated in terms of almost any one of these Prefaces.

IV

There is, in any day of agonised doubt and exaggerated certainty as to the relation of the artist to society, an unusual attractive force in the image of a man whose doubts are conscientious and whose certainties are all serene. Henry James scrupled relentlessly as to the minor aspects of his art but of its major purpose and essential character his knowledge was calm, full, and ordered. One answer to almost every relevant question will be found, given always in specific terms and flowing from illustrative example, somewhere among his Prefaces; and if the answer he gives is not the only one, nor to some minds necessarily the right one, it has yet the paramount merit that it results from a thoroughly consistent, informed mind operating at its greatest stretch. Since what he gives is always specifically rendered he will even help you disagree with him by clarifying the subject of argument.

He wanted the truth about the important aspects of life as it was experienced, and he wanted to represent that truth with the greatest possible lucidity, beauty, and fineness, not abstractly or in mere statement, but vividly, imposing on it the form of the imagination, the acutest relevant sensibility, which felt it. Life itself—the subject of art—was formless and likely to be a waste, with its situations leading to endless bewilderment; while art, the imaginative representation of life, selected, formed, made lucid and intelligent, gave value and meaning to, the contrasts and oppositions and processions of the society that confronted the artist. The emphases were on intelligence —James was avowedly the novelist of the free spirit, the liberated intelligence—on feeling, and on form.

The subject might be what it would and the feeling of it what it could. When it was once found and known, it should be worked for all it was worth. If it was felt intensely and intelligently enough it would reach, almost of itself, towards adequate form, a prescribed shape and size and density. Then everything must be sacrificed to the exigence of that form, it must never be loose or overflowing but always tight and contained. There was the "coercive charm" of Form, so conceived, which would achieve, dramatise or enact, the moral intent of the theme by making it finely intelligible, better than anything else.

So it is that thinking of the difficulty of representing Isabelle Archer in *The Portrait of a Lady* as a "mere young thing" who was yet increasingly intelligent, James was able to write these sentences. "Now to see deep difficulty braved is at any time, for the really addicted artist, to feel almost even as a pang, the beautiful incentive, and to feel it verily in such sort as to wish the danger intensified. The difficulty most worth tackling can only be for him, in these conditions, the greatest the case permits of." It is because such sentiments rose out of him like prayers that for James art was enough.

1934

XII

A CRITIC'S JOB OF WORK

CRITICISM, I take it, is the formal discourse of an amateur. When there is enough love and enough knowledge represented in the discourse it is a self-sufficient but by no means an isolated art. It witnesses constantly in its own life its interdependence with the other arts. It lays out the terms and parallels of appreciation from the outside in order to convict itself of internal intimacy; it names and arranges what it knows and loves, and searches endlessly with every fresh impulse or impression for better names and more orderly arrangements. It is only in this sense that poetry (or some other art) is a criticism of life; poetry names and arranges, and thus arrests and transfixes its subject in a form which has a life of its own forever separate but springing from the life which confronts it. Poetry is life at the remove of form and meaning; not life lived but life framed and identified. So the criticism of poetry is bound to be occupied at once with the terms and modes by which the remove was made and with the relation between—in the ambiguous stock phrase—content and form; which is to say with the establishment and appreciation of human or moral value. It will be the underlying effort of this essay to indicate approaches to criticism wherein these two problems—of form and value—will appear inextricable but not confused—like the stones in an arch or the timbers in a building.

These approaches—these we wish to eulogise—are not the only ones, nor the only good ones, nor are they complete. No approach opens on anything except from its own point of view and in terms of its own prepossessions. Let us set against each other for a time the facts of various approaches to see whether there is a residue, not of fact but of principle.

The approaches to—or the escapes from—the central work of criticism are as various as the heresies of the Christian church, and like them testify to occasional needs, fanatic emphasis, special interest, or intellectual pride, all flowing from and even the worst of them enlightening the same body of insight. Every critic like every theologian and every philosopher is a casuist in spite of himself. To escape or surmount the discontinuity of knowledge, each resorts to a particular heresy and makes it predominant and even omnivorous.[1]

For most minds, once doctrine is sighted and is held to be the completion of insight, the doctrinal mode of thinking seems the only one possible. When doctrine totters it seems it can fall only into the gulf of bewilderment; few minds risk the fall; most seize the remnants and swear the edifice remains, when doctrine becomes intolerable dogma.[2] All fall notwithstanding; for as knowledge itself is a fall from the paradise of undifferentiated sensation, so equally every formula of knowledge must fall the moment too much weight is laid upon it—the moment it becomes omnivorous and pretends to be omnipotent—the moment, in short, it is taken literally. Literal knowledge is dead knowledge; and the worst bewilderment—which is always only comparative—is better than death. Yet no form, no formula, of knowledge ought to be surrendered merely because it runs the risk in bad or desperate hands of being used literally; and similarly, in our own thinking, whether it is carried to the point of for-

[1] The rashest heresy of our day and climate is that exemplified by T. S. Eliot when he postulates an orthodoxy which exists whether anyone knows it or not.

[2] Baudelaire's sonnet *Le Gouffre* dramatises this sentiment at once as he saw it surmounted in Pascal and as it occurred insurmountably in himself.

mal discourse or not, we cannot only afford, we ought scrupulously to risk the use of any concept that seems propitious or helpful in getting over gaps. Only the use should be consciously provisional, speculative, and dramatic. The end-virtue of humility comes only after a long train of humiliations; and the chief labour of humbling is the constant, resourceful restoration of ignorance.

The classic contemporary example of use and misuse is attached to the name of Freud. Freud himself has constantly emphasised the provisional, dramatic character of his speculations: they are employed as imaginative illumination, to be relied on no more and no less than the sailor relies upon his buoys and beacons.[3] But the impetus of Freud was so great that a school of literalists arose with all the mad consequence of schism and heresy and fundamentalism which have no more honorable place in the scientific than the artistic imagination. Elsewhere, from one point of view, Caesarism in Rome and Berlin is only the literalist conception of the need for a positive state. So, too, the economic insights of Marxism, merely by being taken literally in their own field, are held to affect the subject and value of the arts, where actually they offer only a limited field of interest and enliven an irrelevant purpose. It is an amusing exercise—as it refreshes the terms of bewilderment and provides a common clue to the secrets of all the modes of thinking—to restore the insights of Freud and Fascism and Marxism to the terms of the Church; when the sexual drama in Freud becomes the drama of original sin, and the politics of Hitler and Lenin becomes the politics of the City of God in the sense that theology provides both the sanctions

[3] Santayana's essay "A Long Way Round to Nirvana" (in *Some Turns of Thought in Modern Philosophy*) illustrates the poetic-philosophic character of Freud's insight into death by setting up its analogue in Indian philosophy; and by his comparison only adds to the stimulus of Freud.

of economics and the values of culture. Controversy is in terms absolutely held, when the problems argued are falsely conceived because necessarily abstracted from "real" experience. The vital or fatal nexus is in interest and emotion and is established when the terms can be represented dramatically, almost, as it were, for their own sakes alone and with only a pious or ritualistic regard for the doctrines in which they are clothed. The simple, and fatal, example is in the glory men attach to war; the vital, but precarious example, is in the intermittent conception of free institutions and the persistent reformulation of the myth of reason. Then the doctrines do not matter, since they are taken only for what they are worth (whatever rhetorical pretensions to the contrary) as guides and props, as aids to navigation. What does matter is the experience, the life represented and the value discovered, and both dramatised or enacted under the banner of doctrine. All banners are wrong-headed, but they make rallying points, free the impulse to cry out, and give meaning to the cry itself simply by making it seem appropriate.

It is on some analogue or parallel to these remarks alone that we understand and use the thought and art of those whose doctrines differ from our own. We either discount, absorb, or dominate the doctrine for the sake of the life that goes with it, for the sake of what is *formed* in the progressive act of thinking. When we do more—when we refine or elaborate the abstracted notion of form—we play a different game, which has merit of its own like chess, but which applied to the world we live in produces false dilemmas like solipsism and infant damnation. There is, taking solipsism for example, a fundamental distinction. Because of the logical doctrine prepared to support it, technical philosophers

employ years [4] to get around the impasse in which it leaves
them; whereas men of poetic imagination merely use it for
the dramatic insight it contains—as Eliot uses it in the last
section of the *Wasteland;* or as, say, everyone uses the residual
mythology of the Greek religion—which its priests nevertheless used as literal sanctions for blood and power.

Fortunately, there exist archetypes of unindoctrinated
thinking. Let us incline our minds like reflectors to catch the
light of the early Plato and the whole Montaigne. Is not the
inexhaustible stimulus and fertility of the Dialogues and the
Essays due as much as anything to the absence of positive
doctrine? Is it not that the early Plato always holds con-
flicting ideas in shifting balance, presenting them in contest
and evolution, with victory only the last shift? Is it not that
Montaigne is always making room for another idea, and
implying always a third for provisional, adjudicating irony?
Are not the forms of both men themselves ironic, betraying
in its most intimate recesses the duplicity of every thought,
pointing it out, so to speak, in the act of self-incrimination,
and showing it not paled on a pin but in the buff life?. . .
Such an approach, such an attempt at vivid questing, bor-
rowed and no doubt adulterated by our own needs, is the
only rational approach to the multiplication of doctrine and
arrogant technologies which fills out the body of critical thinking. Anything else is a succumbing, not an approach; and it
is surely the commonest of ironies to observe a man altogether
out of his depth do his cause fatal harm merely because,
having once succumbed to an idea, he thinks it necessary
to stick to it. Thought is a beacon not a life-raft, and to con-

---

[4] Santayana found it necessary to resort to his only sustained labour of
dialectic, *Scepticism and Animal Faith,* which, though a beautiful monument
of intellectual play, is ultimately valuable for its *incidental* moral wisdom.

fuse the functions is tragic. The tragic character of thought—as any perspective will show—is that it takes a rigid mould too soon; chooses destiny like a Calvinist, in infancy, instead of waiting slowly for old age, and hence for the most part works against the world, good sense, and its own object: as anyone may see by taking a perspective of any given idea of democracy, of justice, or the nature of the creative act.

Imaginative scepticism and dramatic irony—the modes of Montaigne and Plato—keep the mind athletic and the spirit on the stretch. Hence the juvenescence of the *Tempest,* and hence, too, perhaps, the air almost of precocity in *Back to Methuselah.* Hence, at any rate, the sustaining power of such varied works as *The Brothers Karamazoff, Cousine Bette,* and *The Magic Mountain.* Dante, whom the faithful might take to the contrary, is yet "the chief imagination of Christendom"; he took his doctrine once and for all from the Church and from St. Thomas and used it as a foil (in the painter's sense) to give recessiveness, background, and contrast. Virgil and Aristotle, Beatrice and Bertrans de Born, have in their way as much importance as St. Thomas and the Church. It was this security of reference that made Dante so much more a free spirit than were, say, Swift and Laurence Sterne. Dante had a habit (not a theory) of imagination which enabled him to dramatise with equal ardour and effect what his doctrine blessed, what it assailed, and what, at heart, it was indifferent to. Doctrine was the seed and structure of vision, and for his poems (at least to us) never more. The Divine Comedy no less than the Dialogues and the Essays is a true Speculum Mentis.

With lesser thinkers and lesser artists—and in the defective works of the greater—we have in reading, in criticising, to supply the scepticism and the irony, or, as may be, the imagination and the drama, to the degree, which cannot be complete since then we should have had no prompts, that they are lacking. We have to rub the looking-glass clear. With Hamlet, for example, we have to struggle and guess to bring the motive out of obscurity: a struggle which, aiming at the wrong end, the psychoanalysts have darkened with counsel. With Shelley we have to flesh out the Platonic Ideas, as with Blake we have to cut away, since it cannot be dramatised, all the excrescence of doctrine. With Baudelaire we have sometimes to struggle with and sometimes to suppress the problem of belief, working out the irony implicit in either attitude. Similarly, with a writer like Pascal, in order to get the most out of him, in order to compose an artistic judgment, we must consider such an idea as that of the necessity of the wager, not solemnly as Pascal took it, but as a dramatised possibility, a savage, but provisional irony; and we need to show that the scepticisms of Montaigne and Pascal are not at all the same thing—that where one produced serenity the other produced excruciation.

Again, speaking of Andre Gide, we should remind ourselves not that he has been the apologist of homosexuality, not that he has become a communist, but that he is par excellence the French puritan chastened by the wisdom of the body, and that he has thus an acutely scrupulous ethical sensibility. It is by acknowledging the sensibility that we feel the impact of the apologetics and the political conversion. Another necessity in the apprehension of Gide might be put as the recognition of similarity in difference of the precocious small boys in Dostoieffsky and Gide, e.g. Kolya in *Karamazoff* and young George in *The Counterfeiters:* they are small, cruel engines, all naked sensibility and no scruple, demoniacally possessed, and used to keep things going. And these in turn may remind us of another writer who had a predilection for presenting the *terrible* quality of the young intelligence: of Henry James, of the children in *The Turn of the Screw,* of Maisie, and all the rest, all beautifully efficient agents of dramatic judgment and action, in that they take all things seriously for themselves, with the least prejudice of preparation, candidly, with an intelligence life has not yet violated.

Such feats of agility and attention as these remarks illustrate seem facile and even commonplace, and from facile points of view there is no need to take them otherwise. Taken superficially they provide escape from the whole labour of specific understanding; or, worse, they provide an easy vault from casual interpretation to an omnivorous world-view. We might take solemnly and as of universal application the two notions of demonic possession and inviolate intelligence in the children of Gide, Dostoieffsky, and James, and on that frail nexus build an unassailable theory of the sources of art, wisdom, and value; unassailable because affording only a stereotyped vision, like that of conservative capitalism, without reference in the real world. The maturity of Shakespeare and of Gertrude Stein would then be found on the same childish level.

But we need not go so far in order to draw back. The modes of Montaigne and Plato contain their own safety. Any single insight is good only at and up to a certain point of development and not beyond, which is to say that it is a provisional and tentative and highly selective approach to its field. Furthermore, no observation, no collection of observations, ever tells the whole story; there is always room for more, and at the hypothetical limit of attention and interest there will always remain, quite untouched, the thing itself. Thus the complex character—I say nothing of the value—of the remarks above reveals itself. They flow from a dramatic combination of all the skills and conventions of the thinking mind. They are commonplace only as criticism—as an end-product or function. Like walking, criticism is a pretty nearly universal art; both require a constant intricate shifting and catching of balance; neither can be questioned much in process; and few perform either really well. For either a new terrain is fatiguing and awkward, and in our day most men prefer paved walks or some form of rapid transit—some easy theory or outmastering dogma. A good critic keeps his criticism from becoming either instinctive or vicarious, and the labour of his understanding is always specific, like the art which he examines; and he knows that the sum of his best work comes only to the pedagogy of elucidation and appreciation. He observes facts and he delights in discriminations. The object remains, and should remain, itself, only made more available and seen in a clearer light. The imagination of Dante is for us only equal to what we can know of it at a given time.

Which bring us to what, as T. S. Eliot would say,[5] I have been leading up to all the time, and what has indeed been said several times by the way. Any rational approach is valid to literature and may be properly called critical which fastens at any point upon the work itself. The utility of a given approach depends partly upon the strength of the mind making it and partly upon the recognition of the limits appropriate to it. Limits may be of scope, degree, or relevance, and may be either plainly laid out by the critic himself, or may be determined by his readers; and it is, by our argu-

---

[5] . . . that when "morals cease to be a matter of tradition and orthodoxy —that is, of the habits of the community formulated, corrected, and elevated by the continuous thought and direction of the Church—and when each man is to elaborate his own, then *personality* becomes a thing of alarming importance." (*After Strange Gods.*) Thus Mr. Eliot becomes one of those viewers-with-alarm whose next step forward is the very hysteria of disorder they wish to escape. The hysteria of institutions is more dreadful than that of individuals.

ment, the latter case that commonly falls, since an active mind tends to overestimate the scope of its tools and to take as necessary those doctrinal considerations which habit has made seem instinctive. No critic is required to limit himself to a single approach, nor is he likely to be able to do so; facts cannot be exhibited without comment, and comment involves the generality of the mind. Furthermore, a consciously complex approach like that of Kenneth Burke or T. S. Eliot, by setting up parallels of reference, affords a more flexible, more available, more stimulating standard of judgment—though of course at a greater risk of prejudice—than a single approach. What produces the evil of stultification and the malice of controversy is the confused approach, when the limits are not seen because they tend to cancel each other out, and the driving power becomes emotional.

The worse evil of fanatic falsification—of arrogant irrationality and barbarism in all its forms—arises when a body of criticism is governed by an *idée fixe,* a really exaggerated heresy, when a notion of genuine but small scope is taken literally as of universal application. This is the body of tendentious criticism where, since something is assumed proved before the evidence is in, distortion, vitiation, and absolute assertion become supreme virtues. I cannot help feeling that such writers as Maritain and Massis—no less than Nordau before them—are tendentious in this sense. But even here, in this worst order of criticism, there is a taint of legitimacy. Once we reduce, in a man like Irving Babbitt, the magnitude of application of such notions as the inner check and the higher will, which were for Babbitt paramount,—that is, when we determine the limits within which he really worked—then the massive erudition and acute observation with which his work is packed become permanently available.

And there is no good to be got in objecting to and disallowing those orders of criticism which have an ulterior purpose. Ulterior is not in itself a pejorative, but only so when applied to an enemy. Since criticism is not autonomous —not a light but a process of elucidation—it cannot avoid discovering constantly within itself a purpose or purposes ulterior in the good sense. The danger is in not knowing what is ulterior and what is not, which is much the same as the cognate danger in the arts themselves. The arts serve purposes beyond themselves; the purposes of what they dramatise or represent at that remove from the flux which gives them order and meaning and value; and to deny those purposes is like asserting that the function of a handsaw is to hang above a bench and that to cut wood is to belittle it. But the purposes are varied and so bound in his subject that the artist cannot always design for them. The critic, if that is his bent, may concern himself with those purposes or with some one among them which obsess him; but he must be certain to distinguish between what is genuinely ulterior to the works he examines and what is merely irrelevant; and he must further not assume except within the realm of his special argument that other purposes either do not exist or are negligible or that the works may not be profitably discussed apart from ulterior purposes and as examples of dramatic possibility alone.

II

Three examples of contemporary criticism primarily concerned with the ulterior purposes of literature should, set side by side, exhibit both the defects and the unchastened virtues of that approach; though they must do so only tentatively and somewhat invidiously—with an exaggeration for effect. Each work is assumed to be a representative ornament of its kind, carrying within it the seeds of its own death and multiplication. Let us take then, with an eye sharpened by the dangers involved, Santayana's essay on Lucretius (in *Three Philosophical poets*), Van Wyck Brooks' *Pilgrimage of Henry James,* and Granville Hicks' *The Great Tradition.* Though that of the third is more obvious in our predicament, the urgency in the approach is equal in all three.

Santayana's essay represents a conversion or transvaluation of an actually poetic ordering of nature to the terms of a moral philosophy which, whatever its own responsibilities, is free of the special responsibility of poetry. So ably and so persuasively is it composed, his picture seems complete and to contain so much of what was important in Lucretius that *De Rerum Natura* itself can be left behind. The philosophical nature of the insight, its moral scope and defect, the influence upon it of the Democritan atom, once grasped intellectually as Santayana shows us how to grasp them, seem a good substitute for the poem and far more available. But, what Santayana remembers but does not here emphasise since it was beyond his immediate interest, there is no vicar for poetry on earth. Poetry is idiom, a special and fresh saying, and cannot for its life be said otherwise; and there is, finally, as much difference between words used about a poem and the poem as there is between words used about a painting and the painting. The gap is absolute. Yet I do not mean to suggest that Santayana's essay—that any philosophical criticism—is beside the point. It is true that the essay may be taken as a venture in philosophy for its own sake, but it is also true that it reveals a body of facts about an ulterior purpose in Lucretius' poem—doubtless the very purpose Lucretius himself would have chosen to see enhanced. If we return to the poem it will be warmer as the facts come alive in the verse. The re-conversion comes naturally in this instance

A CRITIC'S JOB OF WORK

in that, through idioms differently construed but equally imaginative, philosophy and poetry both buttress and express moral value. The one enacts or represents in the flesh what the other reduces to principle or raises to the ideal. The only precaution the critic of poetry need take is negative: that neither poetry nor philosophy can ever fully satisfy the other's purposes, though each may seem to do so if taken in an ulterior fashion. The relationship is mutual but not equivalent.

When we turn deliberately from Santayana on Lucretius to Van Wyck Brooks on Henry James, we turn from the consideration of the rational ulterior purpose of art to the consideration of the irrational underlying predicament of the artist himself, not only as it predicts his art and is reflected in it, but also, and in effect predominantly, as it represents the conditioning of nineteenth century American culture. The consideration is sociological, the method of approach that of literary psychology, and the burden obsessive. The conversion is from literary to biographical values. Art is taken not as the objectification or mirroring of social experience but as a personal expression and escape-fantasy of the artist's personal life in dramatic extension. The point for emphasis is that the cultural situation of Henry James' America stultified the expression and made every escape ineffectual—even that of Europe. This theme—the private tragedy of the unsuccessful artist—was one of Henry James' own; but James saw it as typical or universal—as a characteristic tragedy of the human spirit—illustrated, as it happened for him, against the Anglo-American background. Brooks, taking the same theme, raises it to an obsession, an omnivorous concept, under which all other themes can be subsumed. Applied to American cultural history, such obsessive thinking is suggestive in the very exaggeration of its terms, and applied to the private

predicament of Henry James the man it dramatically emphasises—uses for all and more than it is worth—an obvious conflict that tormented him. As history or as biography the book
is a persuasive imaginative picture, although clearly not the
only one to be seen. Used as a nexus between James the man
and the novels themselves, the book has only possible relevance
and cannot be held as material. *Hamlet,* by a similar argument, could be shown to be an unsuccessful expression of
Shakespeare's personality. To remain useful in the field of
literary criticism, Brooks' notions ought to be kept parallel to
James' novels but never allowed to merge with them. The
corrective, the proof of the gap, is perhaps in the great air of
freedom and sway of mastery that pervades the Prefaces
James wrote to his collected edition. For James art was
enough because it moulded and mirrored and valued all the
life he knew. What Brooks' parallel strictures can do is to
help us decide from another point of view whether to choose
the values James dramatised. They cannot affect or elucidate
but rather—if the gap is closed by will—obfuscate the values
themselves.

In short, the order of criticism of which Brooks is a
masterly exponent, and which we may call the psycho-socio-
logical order, is primarily and in the end concerned less with
the purposes, ulterior or not, of the arts than with some of
the ulterior *uses* to which the arts can be appropriately put.
Only what is said in the meantime, by the way—and does
not depend upon the essence of argument but only accom-
panies it—can be applied to the arts themselves. There is
nothing, it should be added, in Brooks' writings to show that
he believes otherwise or would claim more; he is content with
that scope and degree of value to which his method and the
strength of his mind limit him; and his value is the greater
and more urgent for that.

Such tacit humility, such implicit admission of contingency, are not immediate characteristics of Granville Hicks' *The Great Tradition,* though they may, so serious is his purpose, be merely virtues of which he deliberately, for the time being and in order to gain his point, deprives himself of the benefit. If that is so, however expedient his tactics may seem on the short view they will defeat him on the long. But let us examine the book on the ground of our present concern alone. Like Brooks, Hicks presents an interpretation of American literature since the Civil War, dealing with the whole body rather than single figures. Like Brooks he has a touchstone in an obsessive idea, but where we may say that Brooks *uses* his idea—as we think for more than it is worth—we must say that Hicks is victimised by his idea to the point where the travail of judgment is suspended and becomes the mere reiteration of a formula. He judges literature as it expressed or failed to express the economic conflict of classes sharpened by the industrial revolution, and he judges individual writers as they used or did not use an ideology resembling the Marxist analysis as prime clue to the clear representation of social drama. Thus Howells comes off better than Henry James, and Frank Norris better than Mark Twain, and, in our own day, Dos Passos is stuck on a thin eminence that must alarm him.

Controversy is not here a profitable exercise, but it may be said for the sake of the record that although every period of history presents a class struggle, some far more acute than our own, the themes of great art have seldom lent themselves to propaganda for an economic insight, finding, as it happened, religious, moral, or psychological—that is to say, interpretative—insights more appropriate impulses. If *Piers Plowman* dealt with the class struggle, *The Canterbury Tales* did not, and Hicks would be hard put, if he looked sharp, to make out a better case of social implication in Dostoieffsky than in Henry James.

What vitiates *The Great Tradition* is its tendentiousness. Nothing could be more exciting, nothing more vital, than a book by Hicks which discovered and examined the facts of a literature whose major theme hung on an honest, dramatic view of the class struggle—and there is indeed such a literature now emerging from the depression. And on the other hand it would be worth while to have Hicks sharpen his teeth on all the fraudulent or pseudo art which actually slanders the terms of the class and every other struggle.

The book with which he presents us performs a very different operation. There is an initial hortatory assumption that American literature ought to represent the class struggle from a Marxist view point, and that it ought thus to be the spur and guide to political action. Proceeding, the point is either proved or the literature dismissed and its authors slandered. Hicks is not disengaging for emphasis and contemporary need an ulterior purpose; he is not writing criticism at all; he is writing a fanatic's history and a casuist's polemic, with the probable result—which is what was meant by suggesting above that he had misconceived his tactics—that he will convert no one who retains the least love of literature or the least knowledge of the themes which engage the most of life. It should be emphasised that there is no more quarrel with Hicks' economic insight as such than there was with the insights of Santayana and Van Wyck Brooks. The quarrel is deeper. While it is true and good that the arts may be used to illustrate social propaganda—though it is not a great use—you can no more use an economic insight as your chief critical tool than you can make much out of the Mass by submitting the doctrine of transubstantiation to chemical analysis.

A CRITIC'S JOB OF WORK

These three writers have one great formal fact in common, which they illustrate as differently as may be. They are concerned with the separable content of literature, with what may be said without consideration of its specific setting and apparition in a form; which is why, perhaps, all three leave literature so soon behind. The quantity of what can be said directly about the content alone of a given work of art is seldom great, but the least saying may be the innervation of an infinite intellectual structure, which, however valuable in itself, has for the most part only an asserted relation with the works from which it springs. The sense of continuous relationship, of sustained contact, with the works nominally in hand is rare and when found uncommonly exhilarating; it is the fine object of criticism: as it seems to put us in direct possession of the principles whereby the works move without injuring or disintegrating the body of the works themselves. This sense of intimacy by inner contact cannot arise from methods of approach which hinge on seized separable content. We have constantly—if our interest is really in literature —to prod ourselves back, to remind ourselves that there was a poem, a play, or a novel of some initial and we hope terminal concern, or we have to falsify facts and set up fictions [6] to the effect that no matter what we are saying we are really talking about art after all. The question must often be whether the prodding and reminding is worth the labour,

[6] Such a fiction, if not consciously so contrived, is the fiction of the organic continuity of all literature as expounded by T. S. Eliot in his essay, "Tradition and the Individual Talent." The locus is famous and represents that each new work of art slightly alters the relationships among the whole order of existing works. The notion has truth, but it is a mathematical truth and has little relevance to the arts. Used as Eliot uses it, it is an experimental conceit and pushes the mind forward. Taken seriously it is bad constitutional law, in the sense that it would provoke numberless artificial and insoluble problems.

whether we might not better assign the works that require it to a different category than that of criticism.

III

Similar strictures and identical precautions are necessary in thinking of other, quite different approaches to criticism, where if there are no ulterior purposes to allow for there are other no less limiting features—there are certainly such, for example, for me in thinking of my own. The ulterior motive, or the limiting feature, which ever it is, is a variable constant. One does not always know what it is, nor what nor how much work it does; but one always knows it is there—for strength or weakness. It may be only the strength of emphasis—which is necessarily distortion; or it may be the worse strength of a simplifying formula, which skeletonises and transforms what we want to recognise in the flesh. It may be only the weakness of what is unfinished, undeveloped, or unseen—the weakness that follows on emphasis; or it may be the weakness that shows when pertinent things are deliberately dismissed or ignored, which is the corresponding weakness of the mind strong in formula. No mind can avoid distortion and formula altogether, nor would wish to; but most minds rush to the defence of qualities they think cannot be avoided, and that, in itself, is an ulterior motive, a limiting feature of the mind that rushes. I say nothing of one's personal prepossessions, of the damage of one's private experience, of the malice and false tolerance they inculcate into judgment. I know that my own essays suffer variously, but I cannot bring myself to specify the indulgences I would ask; mostly, I hope, that general indulgence which consists in the task of bringing my distortions and emphases and opinions into balance with other distortions, other emphases, and better opinions.

But rather than myself, let us examine briefly, because of their differences from each other and from the three critics already handled, the modes of approach to the act of criticism and habits of critical work of I. A. Richards, Kenneth Burke, and S. Foster Damon. It is to characterise them and to judge the *character* of their work—its typical scope and value—that we want to examine them. With the objective validity of their varying theories we are not much here concerned. Objective standards of criticism, as we hope them to exist at all, must have an existence anterior and superior to the practice of particular critics. The personal element in a given critic—what he happens to know and happens to be able to understand—is strong or obstinate enough to reach into his aesthetic theories; and as most critics do not have the coherence of philosophers it seems doubtful if any outsider could ever reach the same conclusions as the critic did by adopting his aesthetics. Aesthetics sometimes seems only as implicit in the practice of criticism as the atomic physics is present in sunlight when you feel it.

But some critics deliberately expand the theoretic phase of every practical problem. There is a tendency to urge the scientific principle and the statistical method, and in doing so to bring in the whole assorted world of thought. That Mr. Richards, who is an admirable critic and whose love and knowledge of poetry are incontestable, is a victim of the expansiveness of his mind in these directions, is what characterises, and reduces, the scope of his work as literary criticism. It is possible that he ought not to be called a literary critic at all. If we list the titles of his books we are in a quandary: *The Foundations of Aesthetics, The Meaning of Meaning* (these with C. K. Ogden), *The Principles of Literary Criticism, Science and Poetry, Practical Criticism, Mencius on the Mind,* and *Coleridge on Imagination.* The apparatus is so vast, so labyrinthine, so inclusive—and the amount of actual literary criticism is so small that it seems almost a by-product instead of the central target. The slightest volume, physically, *Science and Poetry,* contains proportionally the most literary criticism, and contains, curiously, his one obvious failure in appreciation—since amply redressed—, his misjudgment of the nature of Yeats' poetry. His work is for the most part *about* a department of the mind which includes the pedagogy of sensibility and the practice of literary criticism. The matters he investigates are the problems of belief, of meaning, of communication, of the nature of controversy, and of poetic language as the supreme mode of imagination. The discussion of these problems is made to focus for the most part on poetry because poetry provides the only great monuments of imagination available to verbal imagination. His bottom contention might I think be put as this: that words have a synergical power, in the realms of feeling, emotion, and value, to create a reality, or the sense of it, not contained in the words separately; and that the power and the reality as experienced in great poetry make the chief source of meaning and value for the life we live. This contention I share; except that I should wish to put on the same level, as sources of meaning and value, modes of imagination that have no medium in words—though words may call on them—and are not susceptible of verbal reformulation: the modes of great acting, architecture, music, and painting. Thus I can assent to Mr. Richards' positive statement of the task of criticism, because I can add to it positive tasks in analogous fields: "To recall that poetry is the supreme use of language, man's chief co-ordinating instrument, in the service of the most integral purposes of life; and to explore, with thoroughness, the intricacies of the modes of language as working modes of the mind." But I want this criticism, engaged in this task, constantly to be confronted with examples of poetry, and I want it so for the very practical purpose of assisting in pretty immediate appreciation of the use, meaning, and value of the language in that particular poetry. I want it to assist in doing for me what it actually assists Mr. Richards in doing, whatever that is, when he is reading poetry for its own sake.

Mr. Richards wants it to do that, too, but he wants it to do a great deal else first. Before it gets to actual poetry (from which it is said to spring) he wants literary criticism to become something else and much more: he wants it to become, indeed, the master department of the mind. As we become aware of the scope of poetry, we see, according to Mr. Richards that "the study of the modes of language becomes, as it attempts to be thorough, the most fundamental and extensive of all inquiries. It is no preliminary or preparation for other profounder studies. . . . The very formation of the objects which these studies propose to examine takes place through the processes (of which imagination and fancy are modes) by which the words they use acquire their meanings. Criticism is the science of these meanings. . . . Critics in the future must have a theoretical equipment which has not been felt to be necessary in the past. . . . But the critical equipment will not be *primarily* philosophical. It will be rather a command *of the methods of general linguistic analysis."* [7] I think we may take it that *Mencius on the Mind* is an example of the kind of excursion on which Mr. Richards would lead us. It is an excursion into multiple definition, and it is a good one if that is where you want to go and are in no hurry to come back: you learn the enormous variety and complexity of the operations possible in the process of verbally describing and defining brief passages of imaginative language and the equal

[7] All quoted material is from the last four pages of *Coleridge on Imagination.*

variety and complexity of the result; you learn the practical impossibility of verbally ascertaining what an author means —and you hear nothing of the other ways of apprehending meaning at all. The instance is in the translation of Mencius, because Mr. Richards happens to be interested in Mencius, and because it is easy to see the difficulties of translating Chinese; but the principles and method of application would work as well on passages from Milton or Rudyard Kipling. The real point of Mr. Richards' book is the impossibility of understanding, short of a lifetime's analysis and compensation, the mechanism of meaning in even a small body of work. There is no question of the exemplary value and stimulus of Mr. Richards' work; but there is no question either that few would care to emulate him for any purpose of literary criticism. In the first place it would take too long, and in the second he does not answer the questions literary criticism would put. The literal adoption of Mr. Richards' approach to literary criticism would stultify the very power it was aimed to enhance—the power of imaginative apprehension, of imaginative coördination of varied and separate elements. Mr. Richards' work is something to be aware of, but deep awareness is the limit of use. It is notable that in his admirable incidental criticism of such poets as Eliot, Lawrence, Yeats, and Hopkins, Mr. Richards does not himself find it necessary to be more than aware of his own doctrines of linguistic analysis. As philosophy from Descartes to Bradley transformed itself into a study of the modes of knowing, Mr. Richards would transform literary criticism into the science of linguistics. Epistlemology is a great subject, and so is linguistics; but they come neither in first nor final places; the one is only a fragment of wisdom and the other only a fraction of the means of understanding. Literary criticism is not a science—though it may be the object of one; and to try to make it one is to turn it upside down. Right side up, Mr. Richards' contribution shrinks in weight and dominion but remains intact and preserves its importance. We may conclude that it was the newness of his view that led him to exaggerate it, and we ought to add the probability that had he not exaggerated it we should never have seen either that it was new or valuable at all.

From another point of view than that of literary criticism, and as a contribution to a psychological theory of knowledge, Mr. Richards' work is not heretical, but is integral and integrating, and especially when it incorporates poetry into its procedure; but from our point of view the heresy is profound —and is far more distorting than the heresies of Santayana, Brooks, and Hicks, which carry with them obviously the impetus for their correction. Because it is possible to apply scientific methods to the language of poetry, and because scientific methods engross their subject matter, Mr. Richards places the whole burden of criticism in the application of a scientific approach, and asserts it to be an implement for the judgement of poetry. Actually, it can handle only the language and its words and cannot touch—except by assertion—the imaginative product of the words which is poetry: which is the object revealed or elucidated by criticism. Criticism must be concerned, first and last—whatever comes between—with the poem as it is read and as what it represents is felt. As no amount of physics and physiology can explain the *feeling* of things seen as green or even certify their existence, so no amount of linguistic analysis can explain the *feeling* or existence of a poem. Yet the physics in the one case and the linguistics in the other may be useful both to the poet and the reader. It may be useful, for example, in extracting the facts of meaning from a poem, to show that, whether the poet was aware of it or not, the semantic history of a word was so and so; but only if the semantics can be resolved into the ambiguities and precisions created by the poem. Similarly with any branch of linguistics; and similarly with the applications of psychology—Mr. Richards' other emphasis. No statistical description can either explain or demean a poem unless the description is translated back to the imaginative apprehension or feeling which must have taken place without it. The light of science is parallel or in the background where feeling or meaning is concerned. The Oedipus complex does not explain *Oedipus Rex;* not that Mr. Richards would think it did. Otherwise he could not believe that "poetry is the supreme use of language" and more, could not convey in his comments on T. S. Eliot's *Ash Wednesday* the actuality of his belief that poetry is the supreme use.

It is the interest and fascination of Mr. Richards' work in reference to different levels of sensibility, including the poetic, that has given him both a wide and a penetrating influence. No literary critic can escape his influence; an influence that stimulates the mind as much as anything by showing the sheer excitement as well as the profundity of the problems of language—many of which he has himself made genuine problems, at least for readers of poetry: an influence, obviously, worth deliberately incorporating by reducing it to one's own size and needs. In T. S. Eliot the influence is conspicuous if slight. Mr. Kenneth Burke is considerably indebted, partly directly to Mr. Richards, partly to the influences which acted upon Mr. Richards (as Bentham's theory of Fictions) and partly to the frame of mind which helped mould them both. But Mr. Burke is clearly a different person—and different from anyone writing to-day; and the virtues, the defects, and the élan of his criticism are his own.

Some years ago, when Mr. Burke was an animating influ-

ence on the staff of *The Dial,* Miss Marianne Moore published a poem in that magazine called "Picking and Choosing" which contained the following lines.

> and Burke is a
> psychologist—of acute and raccoon-
> like curiosity. *Summa diligentia;*
> to the humbug, whose name is so amusing—very young
> and ve-
> ry rushed, Caesar crossed the Alps on the 'top of a
> *diligence.'* We are not daft about the meaning but this
> familiarity
> with wrong meanings puzzles one.

In the index of Miss Moore's *Observations,* we find under
Burke that the reference is to Edmund, but it is really to
Kenneth just the same. There is no acuter curiosity than
Mr. Burke's engaged in associating the meanings, right and
wrong, of the business of literature with the business of life
and vice versa. No one has a greater awareness—not even
Mr. Richards—of the important part wrong meanings play
in establishing the consistency of right ones. The writer of
whom he reminds us, for the buoyancy and sheer remark-
ableness of his speculations, is Charles Santiago Saunders
Peirce; one is enlivened by them without any *necessary* reference to their truth; hence they have truth for their own
purposes, that is, for their own uses. Into what these purposes
or uses are it is our present business to inquire.

As Mr. Richards in fact uses literature as a springboard or
source for a scientific method of a philosophy of value, Mr.
Burke uses literature, not only as a springboard but also as a
resort or home, for a philosophy or psychology of moral
possibility. Literature is the hold-all and the persuasive form
for the patterns of possibility. In literature we see unique
possibilities enacted, actualised, and in the moral and psycho-

logical philosophies we see the types of possibility generalised, see their abstracted, convertible forms. In some literature, and in some aspects of most literature of either great magnitude or great possibility, we see, so to speak, the enactment or dramatic representation of the type or patterns. Thus Mr. Burke can make a thrilling intellectual pursuit of the sub-intelligent writing of Erskine Caldwell: where he shows that Caldwell gains a great effect of humanity by putting in *none himself,* appealing to the reader's common stock: i.e., what is called for so desperately by the pattern of the story must needs be generously supplied. Exactly as thrilling is his demonstration of the great emotional role of the outsider as played in the supremely intelligent works of Thomas Mann and André Gide. His common illustrations of the pervasive spread of symbolic pattern are drawn from Shakespeare and from the type of the popular or pulp press. I think that on the whole his method could be applied with equal fruitfulness either to Shakespeare, Dashiell Hammet, or Marie Corelli; as indeed he does apply it with equal force both to the field of anarchic private morals and to the outline of a secular conversion to Communism—as in, respectively, *Toward a Better Life* and *Permanence and Change.*

The real harvest that we barn from Mr. Burke's writings is his presentation of the types of ways the mind works in the written word. He is more interested in the psychological means of the meaning, and how it might mean (and often really does) something else, than in the meaning itself. Like Mr. Richards, but for another purpose, he is engaged largely in the meaning of meaning, and is therefore much bound up with considerations of language, but on the plane of emotional and intellectual patterns rather than on the emotional plane; which is why his essays deal with literature (or other writings) as it dramatises or unfolds character (a character is a pattern of emotions and notions) rather than with lyric or meditative poetry which is Mr. Richards' field. So we find language containing felt character as well as felt coördination. The representation of character, and of aspiration and symbol, must always be rhetorical; and therefore we find that for Mr. Burke the rightly rhetorical is the profoundly hortatory. Thus literature may be seen as an inexhaustible reservoir of moral or character philosophies in action.

It is the technique of such philosophies that Mr. Burke explores, as he pursues it through curiosities of development and conversion and duplicity; it is the technique of the notions that may be put into or taken out of literature, but it is only a part of the technique of literature itself. The final reference is to the psychological and moral possibilities of the mind, and these certainly do not exhaust the technique or the reality of literature. The reality in literature is an object of contemplation and of feeling, like the reality of a picture or a cathedral, not a route of speculation. If we remember this and make the appropriate reductions here as elsewhere, Mr. Burke's essays become as pertinent to literary criticism as they are to the general ethical play of the mind. Otherwise they become too much a methodology for its own sake on the one hand, and too much a philosophy at one remove on the other. A man writes as he can; but those who use his writings have the further responsibility of redefining their scope, an operation (of which Mr. Burke is a master) which alone uses them to the full.

It is in relation to these examples which I have so unjustly held up of the philosophical, the sociological or historical, the tendentious, the semasiological, and the psychological approaches to criticism that I wish to examine an example of what composes, after all, the great bulk of serious writings about literature: a work of literary scholarship. Upon scholarship all other forms of literary criticism depend, so long as they are criticism, in much the same way that architecture depends on engineering. The great editors of the last century —men such as Dyce and Skeat and Gifford and Furness— performed work as valuable to the use of literature, and with far less complement of harm, as men like Hazlitt and Arnold and Pater. Scholarship, being bent on the collection, arrangement, and scrutiny of facts, has the positive advantage over other forms of criticism that it is a coöperative labour, and may be completed and corrected by subsequent scholars; and it has the negative advantage that it is not bound to investigate the mysteries of meaning or to connect literature with other departments of life—it has only to furnish the factual materials for such investigations and connexions. It is not surprising to find that the great scholars are sometimes good critics, though usually in restricted fields; and it is a fact, on the other hand, that the great critics are themselves either good scholars or know how to take great advantage of scholarship. Perhaps we may put it that for the most part dead critics remain alive in us to the extent that they form part of our scholarship. It is Dr. Johnson's statements of fact that we preserve of him as a critic; his opinions have long since become a part of that imaginative structure, his personality. A last fact about scholarship is this, that so far as its conclusions are sound they are subject to use and digestion not debate by those outside the fold. And of bad scholarship as of bad criticism we have only to find means to minimise what we cannot destroy.

It is difficult to find an example of scholarship pure and simple, of high character, which can be made to seem relevant to the discussion in hand. What I want is to bring into the discussion the omnipresence of scholarship as a background and its immediate and necessary availability to every other mode of approach. What I want is almost anonymous. Failing that, I choose S. Foster Damon's *William Blake* (as I might have taken J. L. Lowe's *Road to Xanadu*) which, because of its special subject matter, brings its scholarship a little nearer the terms of discussion than a Shakespeare commentary would have done. The scholar's major problem with Blake happened to be one which many scholars could not handle, some refused to see, and some fumbled. A great part of Blake's meaning is not open to ordinarily well-instructed readers, but must be brought out by the detailed solution of something very like an enormous and enormously complicated acrostic puzzle. Not only earnest scrutiny of the poems as printed, but also a study of Blake's reading, a reconstruction of habits of thought, and an industrious piecing together into a consistent key of thousands of clues throughout the work, were necessary before many even of the simplest appearing poems could be explained. It is one thing to explain a mystical poet, like Crashaw, who was attached to a recognised church, and difficult enough; but it is a far more difficult thing to explain a mystical poet like Blake, who was so much an eclectic in his sources that his mystery as well as his apprehension of it was practically his own. All Mr. Damon had to go on besides the texts, and the small body of previous scholarship that was pertinent, were the general outlines of insight to which all mystics apparently adhere. The only explanation would be in the facts of what Blake meant to mean when he habitually said one thing in order to hide and enhance another; and in order to be convincing—poetry being what it is—the facts adduced had to be self-evident. It is not a question here whether the mystery enlightened was worth it. The result for emphasis is that Mr. Damon made Blake exactly what he seemed least to be, perhaps the most intellectually consistent of the greater poets in English. Since the chief weapons used are the extended facts of scholarship, the picture Mr. Damon produced cannot be destroyed even though later and other scholarship modifies, re-arranges, or adds to it with different or other facts. The only suspicion that might attach is that the picture is too consistent and that the facts are made to tell too much, and direct, but instructed, apprehension not enough.

My point about Mr. Damon's work is typical and double. First, that the same sort of work, the adduction of ultimately self-evident facts, can be done and must be done in other kinds of poetry than Blake's. Blake is merely an extreme and obvious example of an unusually difficult poet who hid his facts on purpose. The work must be done to the appropriate degree of digging out the facts in all orders of poetry—and especially perhaps in contemporary poetry, where we tend to let the work go either because it seems too easy or because it seems supererogatory. Self-evident facts are paradoxically the hardest to come by; they are not evident till they are seen; yet the meaning of a poem—the part of it which is intellectually formulable—must invariably depend on this order of facts, the facts about the meanings of the elements aside from their final meaning in combination. The rest of the poem, what it is, what it shows, its final value as a created emotion, its meanings, if you like, *as* a poem, cannot in the more serious orders of poetry develop itself to the full without this factual or intellectual meaning to show the way. The other point is already made, and has been made before in this essay, but it may still be emphasised. Although the scholarly account is indispensable it does not tell the whole story. It is only the basis and perhaps ultimately the residue of all the other stories. But it must be seen to first.

My own approach, such as it is, and if it can be named,

does not tell the whole story either; the reader is conscientiously left with the poem with the real work yet to do; and I wish to advance it—as indeed I have been advancing it *seriatim*—only in connection with the reduced and compensated approaches I have laid out; and I expect, too, that if my approach is used at all it will require its own reduction as well as its compensations. Which is why this essay has taken its present form, preferring for once, in the realm of theory and apologetics, the implicit to the explicit statement. It is, I suppose, an approach to literary criticism—to the discourse of an amateur—primarily through the technique, in the widest sense of that word, of the examples handled; technique on the plane of words and even of linguistics in Mr. Richards' sense, but also technique on the plane of intellectual and emotional patterns in Mr. Burke's sense, and technique, too, in that there is a technique of securing and arranging and representing a fundamental view of life. The advantage of the technical approach is I think double. It readily admits other approaches and is anxious to be complemented by them. Furthermore, in a sense, it is able to incorporate the technical aspect, which always exists, of what is secured by other approaches—as I have argued elsewhere that so unpromising a matter as T. S. Eliot's religious convictions may be profitably considered as a dominant element in his technique of revealing the actual. The second advantage of the technical approach is a consequence of the first; it treats of nothing in literature except in its capacity of reduction to literary fact, which is where it resembles scholarship, only passing beyond it in that its facts are usually further into the heart of the literature than the facts of most scholarship. Aristotle, curiously, is here the type and master; as the *Poetics* is nothing but a collection and explanation of the facts of Greek poetry, it is the factual aspect that is invariably produced. The rest of the labour is in the effort to find understandable terms to fit the composition of the facts. After all, it is only the facts about a poem, a play, a novel, that can be reduced to tractable form, talked about, and examined; the rest is the product of the facts, from the technical point of view, and not a product but the thing itself from its own point of view. The rest, whatever it is, can only be known, not talked about.

But facts are not simple or easy to come at; not all the facts will appear to one mind, and the same facts appear differently in the light of different minds. No attention is undivided, no single approach sufficient, no predilection guaranteed, when facts or what their arrangements create are in question. In short, for the arts, *mere* technical scrutiny of any order, is not enough without the direct apprehension— which may come first or last—to which all scrutinies that show facts contribute.

It may be that there are principles that cover both the direct apprehension and the labour of providing modes for the understanding of the expressive arts. If so, they are Socratic and found within, and subject to the fundamental scepticism as in Montaigne. There must be seeds, let us say—seeds, germs, beginning forms upon which I can rely and to which I resort. When I use a word, an image, a notion, there must be in its small nodular apparent form, as in the peas I am testing on my desk, at least prophetically, the whole future growth, the whole harvested life; and not rhetorically nor in a formula, but stubbornly, pervasively, heart-hidden, materially, in both the anterior and the eventual prospect as well as in the small handled form of the nub. What is it, what are they, these seeds of understanding? And if I know, are they logical? Do they take the processional form of the words I use? Or do they take a form like that of the silver backing a glass, a dark that enholds all brightness? Is every metaphor—and the assertion of understanding is our great metaphor—mixed by the necessity of its intention? What is the mixture of a word, an image, a notion?

The mixture, if I may start a hare so late, the mixture, even in the fresh use of an old word, is made in the pre-conscious, and is by hypothesis unascertainable. But let us not use hypotheses, let us not desire to ascertain. By intuition we adventure in the pre-conscious; and there, where the adventure is, there is no need or suspicion of certainty or meaning; there is the living, expanding, *prescient* substance without the tags and handles of conscious form. Art is the looking-glass of the pre-conscious, and when it is deepest seems to participate in it sensibly. Or, better, for purposes of criticism, our sensibility resumes the division of the senses and faculties at the same time that it preens itself into conscious form. Criticism may have as an object the establishment and evaluation (comparison and analysis) of the modes of making the pre-conscious *consciously* available.

But this emphasis upon the pre-conscious need not be insisted on; once recognised it may be tacitly assumed, and the effort of the mind will be, as it were, restored to its own plane—only a little sensitive to the tap-roots below. On its own plane—that is the plane where almost everything is taken for granted in order to assume adequate implementation in handling what is taken for granted by others; where because you can list the items of your bewilderment and can move from one to another you assert that the achievement of motion is the experience of order;—where, therefore, you must adopt always an attitude of provisional scepticism; where, imperatively, you must scrutinise and scrutinise until you have revealed, if it is there, the inscrutable divination, or, if it is not, the void of personal ambition; where, finally, you must stop short only when you have, with all the facts you can muster, indicated, surrounded, detached, somehow found the way demonstrably to get at, in pretty conscious terms which others may use, the substance of your chosen case.

1935